MINDFULNESS CENTERED THERAPIES

MINDFULNESS CENTERED THERAPIES

An Integrative Approach

Including a Two-Hour DVD Demonstrating
Seven Basic Mindfulness Therapy Skills

By
J. David Cole & Carol Ladas-Gaskin, M.A.

Edited By
Lynn Morrison, M.A. & Dennis Gaither, M.D.

Including a Selected Bibliography
on Mindfulness and Psychotherapy

Compiled By
Gregory J. Johanson, Ph.D.
Hakomi Institute, Boulder, Colorado

Library of Congress Control Number: 2008903430

ISBN: 978-0-9816585-0-6

Published by Silver Birch Press, Seattle.

CONTENTS

DEDICATION

WE dedicate this book to Ron Kurtz, founder and developer of Hakomi, realizing and celebrating the enormous contribution he has made to our personal and professional lives. Through his writings and personal teaching we were introduced to a unique use of mindfulness in therapy and a deep understanding of kindness and loving presence in the process of working and being with others. His love of science fostered in us a trust in the experimental attitude that is the hallmark of Hakomi and contributes to a deeper understanding of non violence in the process of assisting others in healing. We are grateful to him as well for the delightful way he has shared relevant teachings in related fields to expand our vision of the work including introducing us to Richard Schwartz and Internal Family Systems. Through Ron's teachings we have learned to live and love on a more intimate basis and to be nourished by our work in profound ways.

ACKNOWLEDGMENTS

We want to express our deep appreciation for our teachers especially to Ron Kurtz, Richard Schwartz and Eugene Gendlin for the genius of their work and their dedication to this exploration of consciousness and their willingness to share it. We are blessed to have had the opportunity to work directly with Ron and Richard themselves as their work has evolved. We are deeply grateful to Donna Martin, our senior trainer in Hakomi who provided such a loving container for our development as therapists, teachers and trainers in Hakomi. We also want to express our gratitude for those teachers in the past, more numerous than we can mention, who have nudged us along the way in our own process.

We want to thank our dear colleagues: Lynn Morrison and Dennis Gaither who have helped us edit the book along with Peter Wright who took on the detailed editing and Dana Gaskin Wenig who did the final refinement of the text. The phrase "the soul is in the details" has become intensely apparent as we bring this work to a close. We have needed their assistance every step of the way. We also thank Debra Gronning for her suggestions and contributions to the introduction.

In producing the DVD, we appreciated the care and creativity of Theo Kappel, photographer and video editor. We were also very fortunate to meet and work with Marcella Van Oel on the design for the book cover. She carried forward our vision in a subtle and inspired fashion. We also appreciate Kestrel Wenig for her expertise in photo editing and dialogue transcription.

We experience and deeply appreciate the enormous support and existence of the Hakomi community, the Hakomi Institute, the United

States Association of Body Psychotherapy and European Association of Body Psychotherapy. Our intention and perseverance in this writing has in part been inspired by the knowledge that we are part of a greater community of individuals dedicated to mindfulness, and the wisdom inherent in the body-mind connection. The education provided by that community through conferences, workshops, publications and personal support has been invaluable in our process and our teaching. We especially want to thank Greg Johanson in that regard for all his encouragement and support in the completion of this book. We also appreciate Professional Educational Seminars Incorporated (PESI) for their willingness to market and distribute the book.

We are deeply grateful to our clients and students who have shared the raw material of their experience over the years with vulnerability, courage and dedication to the process of becoming more whole, mindful and self led.

Finally I, Carol, wish to express my gratitude to my brother Harold Ladas for introducing me to mindfulness as a young person. It has made all the difference in my life.

PREFACE

THE power of mindfulness is that it reveals the ongoing, involuntary activity of one's mind. As this book shows, its use in so many various Mindfulness Centered Therapies can be a powerful enhancement to any healing process. Mindfulness can be thought of as a unique state of consciousness, a state where the information being "broadcast to many areas of the brain" is information about what is happening to and within at each successive moment. The operational word is "about." It is noticing the spontaneous activity of consciousness itself. It is this global quality directed at present moment experience that makes mindfulness unique and so valuable.

The history described in this book offers a comprehensive look at a movement that is having profound effects on the field of psychotherapy. That history makes clear the origins of this movement and the lines of heritage within it.

More importantly, we learn about the methods themselves, and the people who brought them into being. With the common element of the use of mindfulness, a wide variety of related therapies have been developed, some of which are widely practiced. As one of those developers, I have seen my own work, Hakomi, grow year by year into an internationally accepted method.

David Cole and Carol Ladas-Gaskin are certified in Hakomi and practice it, along with other Mindfulness Centered Therapies. It is a pleasure to introduce them and their wonderful book and DVD.

Ron Kurtz

Ashland, Oregon, February, 2008

PART 1

THE METHOD

CHAPTER 1

INTRODUCTION

What on earth is going on? You might say that we are in the early stages of waking up as a culture to the potential of interiority, to the power of cultivating awareness and an intimacy with stillness and silence. We are beginning to realize the power of the present moment to bring us greater clarity and insight, greater emotional stability, and wisdom. In a word, meditation is no longer something foreign and exotic to our culture. It is now as American as anything else. It has arrived. And none too soon either, given the state of the world and the huge forces impinging on our lives.

- Jon Kabat-Zinn, *Coming to our Senses*

THIS book is a practical guide and resource for therapists to use as they explore how to integrate mindfulness into counseling and psychotherapy practices. It was written to describe and illustrate the core skills and concepts of the method we call Mindfulness Centered Therapies (MCT). Toward this end it employs a diversity of communication resources so that the reader can take away a tangible sense of the method. It includes a two-hour training DVD that describes, and then demonstrates with clips from real therapy sessions, seven key components of the Mindfulness Centered Therapies method. In addition, throughout the text there are transcripts of client/therapist dialogues that offer concrete examples of how the method works. There is also a narrative commentary that qualifies, expands, and deepens the events recorded in the DVD clips. Finally, we have added a very extensive bibliography on mindfulness in the format of the American Psychological Association.

Mindfulness Centered Therapies is the result of many years of working with our own wounds, patterns, strengths, and limitations. For each of us, our early experiences and trainings led to journeys of healing and self-discovery that acquainted us with many mindfulness based modalities. We used them as clients and then became practitioners of the methods we found useful. Our paths eventually led to our training and certification by Ron Kurtz, originator of the Hakomi method. To this we added additional training with Dick Schwartz, the author of Internal Family Systems (IFS), and the study of Focusing, created by Eugene Gendlin. These three mindfulness based systems of psychotherapy are the core components of the Mindfulness Centered Therapies method.

As this eclectic blend of methods evolved through years of clinical practice, we occasionally drew from two peripheral processes that are useful for clients who have difficulty maintaining mindfulness of their present moment experience. These practices, the Awareness Wheel/Listening Cycle® and the Progoff Intensive Journal®, are valuable tools, either as ancillary or preliminary resources. We have therefore included them in our discussion along with references to guide the reader who would like to follow up with workshops and further study.

Throughout our clinical practices, we have used Mindfulness Centered Therapies with a diverse range of clients. However, we have found that this method does not work well for everyone. We especially recommend care when using the body-centered experiential component of this method with clients who present with what is sometimes described as "underdeveloped psychological structures". The lack of normal self development is usually manifest in an inability to sustain mindfulness but it is also wise to be aware of other indicators such as underdeveloped impulse and affect regulation, ability to communicate or relate effectively with others, and response flexibility with regard to inner experience and objects. (Günther 2006)

Those that benefit the most from this approach tend to have three essential qualities that endear them to the work. First, they have a longing to heal and grow to their fullest potential. They may not be fully aware of the extent of their present suffering, or the severity of their limitations, but they have an inkling that life might be better. They want or long for what seems to lie beyond their grasp. That longing could be for peace, or relief from anxiety or depression; it could be for the company and nourishment of a secure relationship; it might be liberation from self-destructive or self-defeating patterns.

Secondly, they are able and willing to experience and explore their inner landscape with the assistance of another. This requires courage and confidence, which becomes stronger and more developed as their work progresses. It also requires at least the seeds of curiosity and the capacity for self-observation. This does not mean that the client must arrive in full possession of either capacity. But if they do not make progress in this direction after a few sessions, we often introduce the Awareness Wheel, and sometimes Intensive Journal work, and make Internal Family Systems the starting point, instead of Hakomi. If we cannot bring the client to at least brief moments of productive mindfulness, we begin to consider referral to a more structured and directive approach.

Finally, successful clients of the Mindfulness Centered Therapies method are receptive to coaching towards taking responsibility for their own experience, and for the outcomes they produce in life. If clients are unable to recognize, question, and eventually let go of blaming others for their experience and their circumstances, it is very difficult to make progress with these methods. This does not mean that we blame them for their experience, or that we do not allow them to experience their anger and hostility toward others, especially anger that has been denied and repressed. We recognize that there is a place for anger. People really do cruel and brutal things to one another. Victimhood happens. But if it persists as a system that protects one from memories and pain, then it will ultimately bring healing to a halt. It is part of the therapist's work to take people through and beyond their pain, so that they can once again assume empowerment and agency in the creation of a happier and richer life.

Those clients who have even a small measure of these three qualities (an intention to heal and grow, an ability to use mindfulness, and a willingness to assume cause and agency) have the qualities necessary to successfully learn and practice the Mindfulness Centered Therapies methods. In the early stages of the work, when these resources may be tentative and even ephemeral, it is important for the therapist to help the client feel successful in every way possible. Every small success motivates the clients toward mastery of the process. When the going gets tough, the therapist wants to stay attuned and compassionately present for the client, in order to lead the client by example back to her own innate presence.

If the therapist helps the client feel successful in learning how to stay mindfully present for herself, then the process becomes portable for the client. Success builds upon success. The client is aware and begins to operate mindfully, with a calm sense of spaciousness toward self and others, even when out and about in the world.

When the process is moving, both therapists and clients benefit. An important feature of the Mindfulness Centered Therapies method is that emotional nourishment and growth flow in both directions. The following is a list of predicted outcomes for those who participate successfully in this work:

1. Greater response flexibility: increased freedom from unnecessary suffering and self-limiting reactivity.
2. Richer, more rewarding relationships with the world and with others.
3. An increased sense of connectedness.
4. Increased acceptance and appreciation of present moment experience.
5. A more secure grounding or centeredness within one's experience of the body, and through the body with feeling and thought.
6. An expanded ability to name and talk about inner experience with others, leading to an increased capacity for intimacy.
7. Increased ability to receive and enjoy emotional nourishment from others and from oneself. This includes comfort, inspiration, recognition, encouragement, companionship, and appreciation.

8. Enlightenment—not as a sudden break with reality, or a permanent refuge from pain, but as a gradual "lightening up," so that the downswings are far briefer and less deep, and there is much more equanimity, flow, and joy.

9. Increased ability to be useful to others in listening, nourishing, understanding, and comforting.

10. More clarity, especially about inner-directed life goals and intentions, which comes when we let go of trying to please or impress others.

11. Increased compassion for self and others.

12. Ability to regulate chaotic and painful emotions through self-acceptance, self-comforting, and learning to use help from others when possible.

13. Improved health, as stress decreases and the immune system becomes better able to do its work, as well as relief from self-destructive behaviors that arise as compensations for pain and emptiness, but diminish our capacity for wellbeing.

14. Increased kindness towards others.

15. Increased empathy.

16. A more joyful and productive life.

Many forms of psychotherapy have been described as miraculous methods capable of producing breathtaking results in only a few one-hour sessions. In a sense, these claims are not completely unfounded: it is miraculous that, without medicine, using nothing more than skillfully chosen words and a compassionate and attuned presence, an individual can be relieved of a lifetime of unnecessary suffering and limitation. It is also true that all three of the core methods that we use can produce dramatic, life-altering sessions, and can even be used as brief therapy, helping clients overcome situational and lifelong conditions in anywhere from one to ten sessions. We have a library full of anecdotal evidence in the form of sessions that have produced these kinds of breakthrough results.

But from our perspective, this is not the most useful frame for the uses and benefits of a psychotherapeutic method. Of course, we all want enlightenment and ecstasy instantly (never mind the troubling question of "then what?"). A far more valuable and realistic perspective is the understanding that psychotherapy is a practice, not so different from meditation, *tai chi chuan,* or *yoga.* Its greatest benefits accrue over a period of time, through the development of a very special kind of attuned, nourishing relationship between two people who share a rewarding adventure in trust, intimacy, and growth. Sometimes there are breakthrough sessions, but if many of these occur in rapid succession, the psyche will find a way to slow the process down, or even bring it to a halt.

There is, perhaps, a limited place for showmanship in psychotherapy, in demonstrating what is possible, and in showing how to avoid what Gendlin called "dead-end" therapy. But if it leads to the false impression that this is how therapy does or should generally happen, then it can ultimately work against itself by creating false expectations for both therapist and client. Pushing against natural and necessary protections (the defenses that are frequently given the undeserved and misleading label "resistance"—as if the client were, deliberately or not, thwarting the therapist and the process) often strains the therapeutic alliance to the breaking point. This leaves therapist and client with a sense of frustration, failure, and discouragement, whereas a more gentle, patient and yielding approach brings the process to fulfillment more quickly, with less unnecessary effort and pain for both participants.

The offering at hand includes two major components: a text book on the Mindfulness Centered Therapies method and a two-hour training DVD. The DVD is self-contained, insofar as it consists of fifteen discrete chapters. The first DVD chapter is a very brief general introduction then, starting with DVD Chapter 2, the chapters work in pairs. First, there is a brief didactic description of the skill being presented (for example, "evoking mindfulness" with a client, "presenting a nourishing offering," "taking over a reaction," and so forth). The didactic chapter is followed by a demonstration chapter that presents one to three brief video clips that illustrate the skill being presented. After the first (introductory) chapter, the even-numbered chapters (2 through 14) are didactic, while the odd-numbered chapters (3 through 15) consist of demonstration clips taken from real therapy sessions.

The textbook is designed to work with the DVD. It is divided into three parts.

Part 1: The Method describes and illustrates Mindfulness Centered Therapies by summarizing the three core methods: Hakomi, Internal Family Systems, and Focusing. Each method is described separately, followed by a description of the bridging intentions and actions that move a session from one approach to another in a graceful and seamless process. We also discuss why we have found it necessary and/or useful to add each approach to Hakomi, the method that we started with many years ago. In reading this section, the reader may wish to play chapters from the video. We have made suggestions as to which chapters illustrate techniques and intentions that are especially relevant to topics covered by the text.

Part 2: Expansion and Commentary on the DVD is a series of commentaries that add to and expand on the examples in the video clips. These commentaries reference the actual sessions excerpted in the chapters, and include transcriptions of the didactic chapters that introduce each demonstration. The session commentaries illuminate the video clips, explaining why certain moves were made, and qualifying the use of some techniques and skills. Sometimes they point out mistakes or possibilities not explored by the therapist, as well as nonverbal behaviors that might not be obvious to a viewer who is new to the method.

Part 3: Bibliography lists books and articles that pertain to mindfulness, and to mindfulness as an element in psychotherapy. As a part of this process, we edited a very large (though not comprehensive) bibliography developed by Greg Johanson, and put it into acceptable American Psychological Association format. We then made this reformatted bibliography available to Greg, who has generously placed it on his website, and on the website of the Hakomi Institute. We felt that this would be useful to students of mindfulness to use as a reference tool in the book, or for documenting their own writing and research by downloading the entries from a website. It is hoped that this may become an ever-expanding resource as new entries are added to future editions of this book, and as the websites are updated.

In closing, we would like to stress that we regard Mindfulness Centered Therapies as a work in progress. While we have focused largely on experiential forms of therapy, we see that relational mindfulness has the promise of transcending the polemic that has developed between cognitive, cognitive-behavioral, and experiential approaches in psychotherapy. There may be many other avenues of expansion that we have not seen, due to our own limitations and lack of knowledge. The important constant that runs throughout this work is the concept of a psychotherapy based on principles, in contrast to methods that are based primarily on theory. These principles are guides to action that help the therapist attune to the client's present moment state, and move the process forward within the envelope of a safe and spacious therapeutic relationship. This is not to say that theory is excluded, but we emphasize that the humanistic and practical principles articulated and adopted in Hakomi by Ron Kurtz and other members of the Hakomi Institute, and by various Hakomi organizations around the world, are the basis for this method. We will require future additions to the method to be coherent and consistent with these principles. Furthermore, while these principles may be articulated in various ways, and even changed over time, the central principle is mindfulness, and that is why we have come to call this integrative method "Mindfulness Centered Therapies".

CHAPTER 2

WHAT IS MINDFULNESS?

As we use mindfulness in Hakomi, it might be called assisted meditation. In therapy, its greatest effect is simply staying with experience longer, before following immediately by "emotional reaction, discriminative thought, reflection, purposeful action." It is a matter of staying a little longer, gathering more information and allowing things to happen by themselves. Highly complex, living systems like we humans, organize our perceptions and actions around core images and beliefs. In ordinary consciousness, going about the daily business of life, these core beliefs exert control without our being conscious of their influence. They function in the background, unnoticed. One of the main goals of the therapeutic process is to bring this organizing material into consciousness, to study it and understand it. Mindfulness, as a state of consciousness, is the tool we use.

- Ron Kurtz, *Body Centered Psychotherapy*

MINDFULNESS is a way of being with our inner and outer experience. It becomes possible as we learn to relate to our present moment experience from a compassionate and unbiased state of awareness. In this state, we direct our non-judging attention to life as it unfolds; we are aware that we are thinking when we are thinking, feeling when we are feeling, and doing when we are doing. We are also aware of our attitude toward our thoughts, feelings, and behavior.

For example, we may be remembering something unpleasant, with an attitude of "I don't want to remember more of that." Another example would be, "I shouldn't feel angry (sad, frightened, bored)." We may also cling to a pleasant memory, as a new and less desirable feeling, thought, or memory unfolds. Attitudes such as these—rejecting, judging, and denying—are part of our experience, therefore, being fully aware of the present moment means that we recognize them as well. In order to do this, we set an intention to accept, even welcome, our thoughts, feelings, body sensations, memories, images, and desires. If we can do this, even for ten or twenty seconds at a time, before we lapse into distraction, we can taste mindfulness. If we practice this over a period of time, through meditation, or with a therapist who assists us in maintaining this state, it becomes easier. Through practice, we can increase our ability to live in this special state for longer and more frequent intervals.

As people practice mindfulness, they report that their lives become richer and more vivid. They also begin to have insights into patterns and systems that distract them from life, and thus from the joy, love, connectedness, aliveness, emotions, and self-expression that are possible in every consciously experienced moment. At the same time, people find that they have more choices in life, since they no longer have to unconsciously repeat their habitual actions in various situations. They become more aware of what they automatically do, and that awareness allows them to create another response, something beyond the constraints of their habitual patterns. They therefore become more free, flexible, and creative.

In order to sustain a mindful state, we develop the skill of noticing when our attention unconsciously drifts off into other, less intentional states: fantasy, dissociation, drowsiness, unconsciousness; or dwelling, without awareness, in the future or past. We also learn to recognize when we slip into an attitude that judges or holds some other prejudicial attitude toward our present experience. As we begin to develop these skills through instruction and practice, we may discover that we spend a great deal of our time not being mindful. This is evident when we observe our thoughts and feelings, and it is also manifest in our conversations with others. When, as mental health professionals, for example, we apply this perspective to examine our client-therapist or patient-doctor dialogues, we may be surprised or even shocked to discover that much of what is said in therapy involves speculating, judging, figuring out, telling stories, and explaining things that have happened in the past, or might occur in the future.

This preoccupation with the past and future distracts attention from the here and now, which is ironically where all of our feelings, body sensations, memories, images, desires, and longings exist. The irony doubles when we consider that the present moment is also the only place where we can actually experience love, the presence of others, comfort, support, and all of the other forms of emotional nourishment that are so important to maintaining balance, sustaining relationships with others, having a strong sense of self, and enjoying positive self-esteem. Indeed, the present moment is the only place where healing, growth and transformation can occur.

Simply said, *mindfulness is a special state of consciousness in which we witness and accept the experience we are having in the present moment.* In this definition, "experience" includes our perception of the outer and inner worlds: our thoughts, memories, mental images, body sensations, and feelings, including our emotions, attitudes, longings, urges, and desires. In order to engage in a mindfulness-based therapy, we need not sustain this special state of consciousness for more than ten or twenty seconds. However, with practice we can stay in mindfulness for almost an entire session, with brief lapses. Mindfulness is a learned state, one we are not born with, but one that we can acquire and cultivate through practice.

RELATIONAL MINDFULNESS

When using the word "mindfulness," we customarily think of mindfulness as it is employed in most forms of meditation, for example, in Vipassana, Transcendental Meditation, and Zazen. Within these meditation practices, mindfulness is exercised while one is being *with oneself,* even when one is sitting with others in a group setting.

In Mindfulness Centered Therapies we practice mindfulness in a different way. During a therapy session, mindfulness is exercised while being and interacting *with another or with others.* In the one-to-one therapy session, the therapist and client are doing their best to be mindful of their inner and outer experience as they relate and interact together, even though they are embodying two very different intentions. Within a session, the therapist intends to be an attuned presence, a source of emotional nourishment, and an unimposing guide. The client intends to use mindfulness to study and relate to her own inner experience. As this process continues, there is often the experience of an envelope or bubble enclosing the participants. While therapist and client may be peripherally aware of this "relational bubble," it is especially evident to observers and supervisors during training sessions. It seems to be a function of the high degree of attunement and resonance between the therapist and client. This kind of attunement feels very safe for the client, and is extremely nourishing to both client and therapist.

It is not necessary to make this into a black and white distinction. It works better to think of it as a range or spectrum, with solitary meditation on one end, and relational mindfulness at the other. In between there are activities like Progoff Journal Workshops (discussed near the end of Part 1), group meditation sessions and retreats, and practices like tai chi which are conducted in groups where there is a sense of coordinating with others while not directly interacting.

In the following pages, when we speak of mindfulness, we will be referring to "relational mindfulness" when the context is the practice of Mindfulness Centered Therapies and its component methods (IFS, Focusing, and so forth). In other contexts, "meditation," "the history of mindfulness," "research on mindfulness," and the like, we will use the word with its more conventional meaning, that is, mindfulness as a solitary practice conducted in an individual or group setting. Many forms of therapy are now emerging that employ meditation in conjunction with talk therapies of various kinds. Mindfulness Centered Therapies and its component methods are different because they use mindfulness interactively in this *relational* form.

THE HISTORY OF WESTERN MINDFULNESS

Thirty years ago it was virtually inconceivable that meditation and yoga would find any legitimate role, no less widespread acceptance, in academic medical centers and hospitals. Now it is considered normal. It is not even thought of as alternative medicine, just good medicine. Increasingly, programs in mindfulness are being offered for medical students and for hospital staff.

- Jon Kabat-Zinn, *Coming to Our Senses*

The roots of the Western mindfulness revolution arise from Eastern and Western sources, and the history of their coming together, like most root systems, is a tangle of influences and diverse connections that coalesce in the middle of the Twentieth Century in America and Europe.

On the Eastern side, there is a tradition that scholars trace back to Eighth Century B.C.E. India, where a rich tradition of inquiry and practice is clearly documented in the Upanishads. This tradition inspired Buddhism in the Sixth Century B.C.E., and Buddhism was the movement by which the mindfulness revolution moved, like a great tide across the planet's surface, from India to China and Korea, and arrived in Japan a thousand years later in 538 C.E. as Zen. Simultaneously, it spread into Southeast Asia, and reached Indonesia by 290 C.E., a few decades before the Emperor Constantine converted Rome to Christianity.

In the West, mindfulness arose independently as a grandchild of the European Enlightenment. It began as a philosophical movement that inspired Edmund Husserl (1859-1938) to inquire into the science of perception and experience. He named this inquiry "Phenomenology." It is concerned with how to witness our inner and outer experience as pure perception, bracketing out of our descriptive language elements of judgment, attitude, point of view, and other conscious and unconscious sources of distortion and bias. This work was carried forward by Martin Heidegger (1889-1976) to Jean-Paul Sartre (1905-1980), whose plays and essays made mindfulness more accessible to the European and Western public. Eventually, these philosophical wellsprings found their way into the broader cultural milieu through the work of Sartre, Albert Camus, and other Existentialist writers, and also in the form of a sensory awareness movement founded by Elsa Gindler and known as *Harmonische Gymnastik.*

Gymnastik (ordinary gymnastics) was popular in the last quarter of the Nineteenth Century. In its original form it involved the repetition of typical sets of body movements and was usually taught and practiced in groups or classes. Elsa Gindler developed a very different practice that required her students to bring consciousness into the performance of individualized movements. In Elsa Gindlers words: "We are always embarrassed when this work is called '*Gymnastik*' .... To this we can only reply that our work is not *Gymnastik* in the ordinary sense, which certainly does not bring about consciousness; what does is the mind that is present and concentrated on the situation." (Gindler, 1926 p. 49). To distinguish her work from the more common form it was eventually called *Harmonische Gymnastik* and later, during the war, "*Arbeit am Menchen*" (working with the Human Being). In this mindful adaptation created by Elsa Gindler the work might be compared to *tai chi chuan,* insofar as it involved the performance of very simple movements, including breathing, combined with the discipline of attending to the felt sense of the body while very slow individualized movements were carried out. Among Elsa Gindlers students in her Berlin classes were many psychoanalysts, as well as a pianist named Charlotte Selver, who became a devoted student and innovator of this work. Those who were able relocated to the U.S. with the diaspora of 1937, including Selver and the influential psychoanalysts Wilhelm Reich and Fritz and Laura Perls.

Charlotte Selver inspired an entire school of body-centered therapy with her popular workshops, just as Buddhism, Yoga, Vedanta, and Taoism were bringing the Asian traditions of mindfulness across the Pacific. It was the confluence of these movements, one ancient and Eastern, and one recent and Western, that brought mindfulness into Western life, and continues to influence the development of Western medicine and psychotherapy.

While this history is fascinating and informative, for our purposes it is most important to understand that all of these exciting new ideas—this mixture of Western sensory awareness and Eastern wisdom and experience from many sources—were virtually in the air during that exceptionally fertile period of the nineteen-sixties. It was during this upwelling of iconoclastic rebellion (sometimes reckless and sometimes liberating) and exceptional creativity (sometimes bizarre and sometimes brilliant) that many of the most important mindfulness-based psychotherapies were born and flourished.

Hakomi body-centered (experiential) psychotherapy is a product of this period and its influences. It was initially developed by Ron Kurtz in the early 70's as he began to use what he eventually called "little experiments in mindfulness," "probes" (renamed "offerings" in Mindfulness Centered Therapies), and "taking over reactions" in his clinical practice. The Hakomi Institute was founded in 1980 in Putman, Connecticut, and its members participated with Kurtz in further development and refinement of this first phase of the method (Weiss, Halko 2008, personal communication). Within the last five years Kurtz has continued on independently to develop a new form of Hakomi resting on the first. Kurtz calls this new form "Mindfulness Based Assisted Self Discovery" in order to more accurately distinguish it from conventional psychotherapy. While we will describe and illustrate most of the basic and some advanced Assisted Self Discovery skills in a subsequent section, it is important to mention this here because these are the historical foundation upon which Mindfulness Centered Therapies ultimately rests.

In his development of Hakomi, Ron Kurtz was deeply inspired by teachers and teachings from the East, especially the traditions of Taoism and Buddhism, and the teachings of sages like Chögyam Trungpa and Nisargardatta Maharaj. In addition, he drew upon the work of the somatics movement, especially Moshe Feldenkrais, whom he credits with the inspiration that led to Hakomi's rich repertoire of techniques for taking over reactions and management behaviors. He also drew on the character analysis work of Wilhelm Reich and other bioenergetic therapists, and was able eventually to transform it from a somewhat invasive and deterministic diagnosis and treatment process into a resource for accessing core material (Kurtz 1990). He was similarly impressed with the work of Joseph Heller, student of Ida Rolf and founder of Hellerwork (Kurtz and Prestera, 1984).

One also sees in his method many parallels to gestalt psychotherapy, although it is a gestalt that is far removed from Fritz Perls' challenging and sometimes confrontational and seemingly reckless style. Even the kind of mindfulness described by Kurtz is different, insofar as it is not described as "concentration,"[1] a word Fritz Perls (1947) used in his early work (borrowed, it would appear, from the vocabulary of Elsa Gindler), or "bare attention." These terms were sometimes misunderstood by Westerners, especially in the early days of the human potential movement, as a severe and uncompromising assault on inner experience by post-Enlightenment objectivity—a tactic guaranteed to summons a person's strongest defenses.

Ron Kurtz was able to combine and transform these very diverse influences into an extremely coherent, elegant, and effective approach to working with the whole individual (mind, body, and spirit) in an atmosphere of mindfulness and compassion, one that honors the organism's innate resources, and brings to bear technical skills in the use of mindfulness. These skills include creating safe and attuned relationships, superb listening, observing and using nonverbal communication, evoking a temporary state of mindfulness and offering gentle experiments to clients in that state, discovering the meanings of postures and gestures, and offering safe and respectful tactile and verbal emotional nourishment.

---

[1] Perls (1947) succinctly defined this attitude of "concentration" as "facing facts." Facing experience as fact seems rather impersonal or even severe when compared to the Hakomi approach of welcoming, accepting, or being friendly with one's experience.

CHAPTER 3

MINDFULNESS CENTERED THERAPIES AND HAKOMI

The helping relationship appears to be a cornerstone on which all effective helping rests.

- Gross and Capuzzi, *Counseling and Psychotherapy*

MINDFULNESS Centered Therapies is an approach to experiential, client-led psychotherapy that synthesizes three well-known methods: Hakomi body-centered psychotherapy, Internal Family Systems therapy (IFS), and Focusing. While we consider these three methods to constitute what we might call the "core resources" of Mindfulness Centered Therapy, we have found other methods that are based on mindfulness, and consistent with our principles, to be of great value. We often introduce these supplemental methods to our clients when we feel that they will advance the work.

One of these is the *Awareness Wheel* (Sherod Miller, et al., 1989) which is invaluable in teaching new clients how to be mindful and how to name their experience. Another is the *Progoff Intensive Journal* (Progoff, 1975). The Progoff Intensive Journal is taught by trained Journal Consultants in a workshop setting. Clients who have learned how to journal, and especially those who know the Progoff Intensive Journal method, have a rich resource that they can use on their own, or in conjunction with therapy sessions. Both of these methods are based on mindfulness, and both require an atmosphere of compassionate presence. They are therefore compatible with Hakomi's spacious and compassionate mindfulness and with IFS and Focusing as well.

While we will focus primarily on the three core methods in the following pages, we will give a brief introduction to the *Awareness Wheel* and the *Progoff Journal* in the closing discussion. We will also mention cognitive therapy, especially the work of David Burns (1990), and *Quantum Therapy*, developed by Steven Wolinsky (1991, 1993, 1999), who has been a pioneer and an inspiration to us in the evolution of our work.

The foundation of Mindfulness Centered Therapies: Hakomi

As we have already mentioned, Mindfulness Centered Therapies has its roots in Hakomi body-centered psychotherapy. Hakomi is an experiential psychotherapy that combines the Eastern traditions of mindfulness and nonviolence with a unique, highly effective Western methodology. It is also a body-centered, somatic psychotherapy. The body's structures and habitual patterns become a powerful doorway to unconscious core material, including the hidden core beliefs which shape our lives, relationships, and self-images. The Hakomi method quickly accesses this core material, allowing it to emerge safely into consciousness. Once conscious, it can be reevaluated, and where appropriate, powerfully transformed. New dimensions of awareness can be integrated, helping the individual to build a more satisfying and effective life. Loving presence and the healing relationship are central to Hakomi. The process creates an exquisite level of sensitivity and attunement between therapist and client, developing a deep sense of safety and connection.

During the course of Hakomi's maturation, the Hakomi Institute was founded in Boulder, Colorado, in 1981. Since then, the Institute has expanded to offer Hakomi training around the world. Workshops and training are currently held in the United States, Canada, Europe, Asia, South America, Australia, and New Zealand. The Institute also maintains a directory of certified Hakomi therapists in the U.S. and abroad. Training is also available through Ron Kurtz Trainings, which offers international opportunities to study directly with Hakomi's originator.

The Western sources of Hakomi include Carl Rogers' person-centered therapy, which emphasizes the importance of the therapeutic relationship, and Gestalt therapy, with its emphasis on experience and experimentation. It is also deeply informed by systems theory, and therefore "presumes that an underlying interconnectedness exists among people and in the natural world" (Kurtz, 1990; Roy, 2007). This recognition of interconnectedness calls for inclusion of the body, mind, and spirit as inseparable aspects of human existence. Hakomi therefore draws deeply on body-centered (somatic) traditions mentioned previously with regard to the evolution of Western mindfulness. Of the three methods used in Mindfulness Centered Therapies, Hakomi is the only one to explicitly name mindfulness as a foundational principle. It is the first Western method to realize that mindfulness is to psychotherapy what the telescope was to astronomy, and the microscope to biology. In other words, mindfulness is Hakomi's primary instrument of observation and discovery.

Hakomi is also deeply informed by Eastern traditions, especially Taoism and Buddhism. These traditions hold much in common, so it is difficult to parse and document their contributions precisely. It is probably safe to say that Hakomi's Eastern influences help to balance the propensity to idealize work and aggressive action that is found in Western medicine, and thus in many forms of Western psychotherapy, including early forms of psychoanalysis, gestalt therapy, and bioenergetics. The Western tradition strongly favors and idealizes *doing*. This *doing* includes resistance and opposition, as well as positive and constructive action and activity. In general, the Western ethos embraces an aggressive approach to life that expresses itself in technology and commerce as well as medicine and psychotherapy, and is linked to a physiological state dominated by the sympathetic nervous system.

The Eastern traditions are rooted in the parasympathetic branch of the autonomic nervous system. They emphasize and idealize qualities of contemplation, mindfulness, being, *non-doing,* accepting, and yielding. Hakomi balances Western activism with contemplative resources drawn from Eastern wisdom traditions. For example, from Taoism, Hakomi derives its fundamental disposition toward what previous therapies have called resistance. Whereas many Western therapies, especially Freudian psychoanalysis and its derivatives, have been preoccupied with the subject of resistance, and have developed a wealth of active measures designed to overcome it, Hakomi adopts a cooperative approach informed by Taoism and Buddhism, and taught in Eastern martial arts such as Aikido.

Hakomi therapists meet both active and passive protective behaviors by yielding to and even "going with" them. The Hakomi therapist is also ready to recognize his role as an active agent in the creation of "resistance." For example, it is highly probable that a client's protective behaviors indicate that things are moving too fast; or that the client feels unsafe; or that the therapist's interventions, or even her presence, or a perceived lack of safety in the therapeutic situation, has evoked an emergent experience, with a potential to disrupt the client's present equilibrium or composure. Such an experience often arouses protective responses in the client, including suppression, distraction, or some other form of control or management.

Hakomi's answer to resistance, therefore, is a readiness to 1) back off and slow down; 2) work with the client to calm fears before proceeding further; and 3) support and cooperate with protective management behaviors. The Hakomi therapist, therefore, avoids pushing back or otherwise opposing protective behaviors.

If a client reports that he cannot feel anything when talking about his loss of a job, for example, it may be that the lost job was not wanted, or was unimportant. However, it is also possible that he is managing (suppressing, denying, minimizing, distracting himself from) a painful experience of failure, shame, or rejection. The Hakomi therapist might help the client to explore this by proposing an experiment in which the client becomes mindfully aware of his internal experience, while the therapist softly repeats the phrase, "Don't feel." In this accessing intervention, the therapist is cooperatively and verbally "taking over" the client's resistance.

In doing so, the therapist is helping the client to take care of himself. He is joining with the management behavior, instead of opposing it. If the client is indeed managing an emergent experience, this "taking over" experiment is likely to access some part of his pain. As the client's ability to feel returns, the therapist is ready to provide the presence, compassion, and comfort that the client needs in order to successfully work through his experience with a minimum of unnecessary suffering. By creating an environment of presence, spaciousness, safety, and compassion, and by providing comfort (sometimes called emotional nourishment), the therapist administers to the suffering, and thereby models a healthier and more satisfying alternative to this numbing management behavior. With this cooperative approach, resistance can be used to move the process forward. It becomes an important therapeutic resource.

From Buddhism, Hakomi also adopts the values of mindfulness, compassion, and nonviolence. These values are expressed in the relationship between therapist and client, and are combined into an attitude called "loving presence." Loving presence has been previously mentioned, and will be further discussed in the next section. For now, it is sufficient to say that it is a learned attitude cultivated through practice. It is not precisely equivalent to the "loving kindness" which is the subject of meditation practiced in Buddhist traditions. It is also not simply a matter of having a loving attitude toward clients. And while it is compatible with what Carl Rogers calls "unconditional positive regard," it goes beyond it, and thereby produces some additional beneficial effects for both client and therapist.

The blending of Eastern and Western values in Hakomi gives it an originality that makes it controversial to some, and appealing to others. Nevertheless, Hakomi has gained a level of academic recognition that many other body-centered therapies have lacked. Hakomi therapy is taught as part of conventional postgraduate programs in Germany and New Zealand. It is also included in *Counseling and Psychotherapy* by Capuzzi and Gross, a standard textbook for many American postgraduate programs since its first edition in 1999.

PRINCIPLES OF HAKOMI

Hakomi is somewhat unique in the field of psychotherapy, insofar as it is not founded on a body of theory or speculation. While it includes theoretical elements, it holds them lightly. In this way it breaks from the tradition established by Freud and many derivative methods that either followed or rebelled in one way or another against Freudian psychoanalysis. Instead of basing Hakomi on a body of theory, Ron Kurtz and the Hakomi Institute founded Hakomi on a set of humanistic principles. These principles are derived from the aforementioned blending of Eastern and Western wisdom traditions. They provide the therapist with a guiding light that allows a greater tolerance for the unknown.

Even when we become lost in the process, and feel uncertain as to where a session is going, we know that there is a certain way to be in the situation, certain things to avoid, certain ways to behave that will foster the best possible outcome. If we stay within these guidelines, we will do nothing that will harm or set our client back. The principles give therapists the confidence to face the unknown, and to follow the flow of the work to its outcome without having to control the result. If the process flows like a river, and it is a river we have never navigated before, our principles serve as the riverbanks. We can work to keep the flow of the process within those banks. In this way, the principles become a container for the therapeutic process. They have served us so well in our Hakomi work that we have adopted them as guidelines for everything we do in Mindfulness Centered Therapies.

The five original Hakomi principles are set forth and described by Ron Kurtz in his basic Hakomi textbook, *Body-Centered Psychotherapy: The Hakomi Method*, published in 1990. Subsequently, two additional principles have been added, "truth" and "mutability." All seven principles are listed below, with brief explanations.

Mindfulness. In Hakomi, mindfulness is used as "assisted meditation." It is focused on present experience, and is intentionally passive and turned inward. It is always applied in the context of loving presence, which means that, like all aspects of the Hakomi method, it is consistent with the principle of nonviolence, and used with compassion.

Nonviolence. (reverence for life). While Hakomi nonviolence carries the conventional meaning of doing no physical harm to self or others, it also proscribes many kinds of mental harm that are usually not considered violent. For example, in Hakomi; criticism, diagnosis, interpretation, labeling, judging, and giving unsolicited advice are seen as potentially harmful, and therefore subtly violent. While it is recognized that these methods are often employed in other disciplines, and within families, friendships, and communities with good intentions, one need only reflect on our own response to such approaches to realize how unwelcome they usually are. And, more often than not, the shaming and damage that result from these ways of communicating tend only to impede connection with others and thwart personal growth.

Organicity. Psychotherapy is a form of healing, and healing is a universal potential that is only available to living organisms. Healing is not fixing or forcing, but an act of self-recreation. All healing is initiated and accomplished by our clients, and it occurs, so to speak, from the inside out. A therapist does not heal a client; she can only help or hinder this natural process.

Mind-body holism. This principle recognizes the inseparable union

of mind, body, and spirit. It respects the "complexity and
the unpredictability of the whole by its parts," and guides us
in avoiding faith in the arrogant application of simple linear
models to address the complexity of living systems. It means
that therapists must willingly embrace the experience of humble
"not-knowing." This embrace sustains curiosity, and nourishes the
experimental attitude that is fundamental to Hakomi.

Unity. The unity principle reminds us that we belong to nature:
an integrated event, a total ecology with social, physical,
psychological, and spiritual dimensions. The idea that mind,
body, personality, memory, feelings, and thoughts are isolated
elements within the person is absurd, and ultimately dysfunctional.
While the concept of a self as an isolated construct or object
is sometimes socially or operationally useful, belief in such a
self leads to unnecessary suffering. In the absence of language,
communication, community and connection, the self as
personality cannot arise or be sustained. In a very real sense,
therefore, this self is dependent on connection with others.
Furthermore, the larger and perhaps more essential Self, a Self we
will discuss later in relation to awareness, is also not an isolated
entity or object. In a very experiential sense, this essential Self has
qualities that are shared and universal.

Truth. This principle stresses 1) the importance of not making false
promises to clients, especially to clients who are identified with
a child state; 2) the importance of being ethical and honest in all
aspects of our lives, especially in relationships with clients; 3) the
value of the pursuit of truth for both therapist and client. This
is essentially what the helping relationship is about: not just the
intellectual truth, or facing the facts, but the whole truth, including

the heart's truth. It was proposed by Halko Weiss, a Hakomi trainer and founding member of the Hakomi Institute.

Mutability. This principle reminds us that change is inherent in life and reality. Things are in a constant state of change. This includes the idea that people can and want to change. They have a natural longing and tendency to grow toward wholeness, and it is the intention of Hakomi therapists to assist people in this change process when they are granted a contract to do so (Eisman 2000-2001).

LOVING PRESENCE

The more that the client perceives the therapist as real or genuine, as empathic, as having an unconditional regard for him, the more the client will move… in the direction of psychic health and maturity and more realistic relationships to self, others and the environment.

Carl Rogers, *On Becoming a Person*

Outside of therapy there are many sources of spiritual nourishment. But in the present moment of the therapy process, the source I use is the client. The idea is to drop the "noise of self" and see the other as spirit. With this as a base, therapy becomes a shared, deeply heartfelt journey.

- Ron Kurtz, *Getting In Touch by Christine Caldwell*

As we see in these seven Hakomi principles, mindfulness is foundational to Hakomi. In addition, Hakomi's mindfulness must be tempered by the principle of nonviolence. It therefore is not the severe objectivity of Enlightenment science that is one way of interpreting the notion of "bare attention," nor is it "concentration" or "facing facts," as originally defined by Fritz Perls. Hakomi students are taught to employ mindfulness in conjunction with the attitude of loving presence when they work with clients. This attitude is nourishing and sustaining for the therapist, and takes the severe and critical edges off of self-observation and the observation of others. It might be said that it makes the tool of mindfulness more "user-friendly."

At the heart of all these methods we are sharing with you in this book, the practice and quality of loving presence is essential for creating an atmosphere of safety, spaciousness, and trust that allows a client to move easily toward insight and healing. We call it a practice because, until we have learned it well, it requires attention and intention. Like practicing the scales in music, with time and attention it becomes easy and natural, inside and outside of our clinical practices.

Loving presence provides the essential ground of being for the healing relationship. It is a step beyond the "unconditional regard" of Carl Rogers, insofar as loving presence invites us to be willing and able to notice and appreciate specific qualities in our clients, and to allow those qualities to nourish us as we work.

The Cultivation of Loving Presence

As he spoke his sharp brown eyes met mine, widened and narrowed, flew about the room like birds. His slender hands flitted, his voice growled and then softened. And I would nod sometimes or cock my head, and my eyes would follow his, and my mouth would water; in this way I listened. How much listening is done not with the mind or the ear but the muscles of the face! And on my face he could see—I know, for it was reflected in his eyes—how much I valued his skills and his knowledge, how grateful I was for his gift.

- Sy Montgomery, *Spell of the Tiger*

WE begin our practice of loving presence by noticing and appreciating something simple: our client's face, the colors in her hair, the sparkle in her eyes, the way he smiles. We move on to noticing more universal qualities like her courage, his vulnerability, or her energetic presence, her determination or dedication to the work. We allow these qualities to nourish us, to fill us up. When we take this nourishment in, not only are we refreshed and renewed, but also a natural human exchange arises. This exchange facilitates a state of exquisite attunement, and stabilizes an optimal healing relationship.

In order to be in loving presence, it is vital for us to be able to be present and engaged with our clients. We must listen to and see them with a warmhearted attention that is authentically present in our eyes and in our facial expression. We are not trying to fix them, or figure them out, but simply to see them as another human being who deserves our respect and caring. This presence and attitude optimizes the healing relationship, and it is good for the therapist as well. It prevents what some therapists call burnout or compassion fatigue, since we do not become burdened with the impossible task of solving our clients' problems, or carrying their pain.

In our view, Carl Rogers set us on the right track in the nineteen-sixties when he emphasized the importance of "unconditional regard" in psychotherapy. Although his work focused primarily on the verbal content of the therapeutic encounter, he understood quite deeply the importance of seeing the beauty of "the other." Ron Kurtz echoes Rogers when he states, in *Getting in Touch* by Christine Caldwell (1997), "Not only did I learn that I needed the cooperation of the unconscious, I also learned that I had to be worthy of it. I needed to earn it." In exercising loving presence, we earn our client's trust by maintaining an appreciative attitude that fosters an exquisite attunement and resonance. This practice also nourishes and sustains us as we work.

Loving presence allows us, at the end of the day, to feel nourished, inspired, and uplifted by our work with clients. When the Indian spiritual teacher Ammachi was asked how she could receive so many people without burning out, she said, "When a bee hovers over a garden of varied flowers, what it beholds is not the difference between the flowers but the honey within them."[2] Practicing loving presence means learning how to nourish ourselves with the beauty and strength of another being sitting right there

---

[2] Mata Amritanandamayi Devi (www.Amma.org/amma, accessed 12/15/07).

before us. To the degree that we are successful, we are renewed and refreshed by what happens in each therapy session.

THE BODY IN HAKOMI
BODY-CENTERED PSYCHOTHERAPY

The body is not an enclosure, but actually a passageway, like an entrance into a cave or a cathedral.

Stephen Schwartz, *Prayer of The Body*

The first foundation of mindfulness is awareness of the body. Awareness of the body is in the body, not observing the body from some distant place—actually feeling all the aspects of the body whether it is an ouch of the body, the pleasure of the body or the way the body is always changing.

Attributed to the Buddha
by Chögyam Trungpa Rinpoche

In her landmark contribution to Counseling and Psychotherapy by Capuzzi and Gross (1995-2007), Donna M. Roy writes: "Central to the concept of the mind-body interface is a belief in the profound effect of the body's early experience (prenatal and perinatal) on psychological and social development"[3] (p. 361). We hasten to add that this somatic record of experience extends beyond infancy into childhood, adolescence, and adulthood. The truth of this assertion is well-known to therapists who work with victims of trauma and posttraumatic stress, where the correlations between the precipitating injury and the psychosomatic consequences are subject to recent memory and documentation. This somatic record of experience manifests in a multitude of subjective sensations and objectively observable expressions, such as:

---

[3] Roy cites Caldwell (1997); Kleman (1985), Kurtz (1990); Peso (1997) as sources for this statement, and it would not be difficult to add many more.

- Tics
- Restrictions of mobility
- Postural misalignments
- Repetitious gestures
- Facial expressions
- Alterations in natural breathing patterns
- Constriction of breath
- Holding of breath
- Pace of breath
- Pace of speech
- Verbal tics, like the repetitious use of phrases like "you know" and "anyway"
- Muscular twitches
- Many expressive hand movements
- Trembling, as in traumatic trembling and quaking
- Freezing
- Variations in gaze, from avoidance patterns to seductive or clinging gazes
- Angles and alignments of the head
- Affectations of stride and gait

This list is far from exhaustive, and could easily be extended to a number of pages. Almost every human being has acquired a number of these "indicators"[4] and carries them unconsciously, until and unless they are brought to their attention and worked through. Learning to observe these indicators, in order to access what we might call their "back-story"; the memories, affects, and cognitive decisions, beliefs, and convictions associated with their adoption, is an important intention in Hakomi body-centered psychotherapy. It does not take long for students of Hakomi to

---

[4] "Indicators" is a term used by Ron Kurtz. It refers to any physical trait or behavior that is repetitious, unconscious, and potentially meaningful with regard to a client's back-story or psychological history.

discover that these somatic indicators are, in fact, an extremely direct road to the unconscious.

In order to read the body's subtext, Hakomi therapists are especially attentive to nonverbal communications. This does not mean that we ignore our clients' words. We hear them automatically, as context, while we foreground nonverbal expressions, so that words—the narratives, descriptions, complaints, explanations, and so forth—are not the primary focus of our attention. By placing our primary attention on our clients' nonverbal communication, we are able to observe and respond to the rich stream of information about their physical, mental, and emotional states.

All of this information pertains specifically to the present, since, unlike the references of words, the body's expressions never leave the present moment. In focusing mainly on nonverbal expressions, the Hakomi therapist notices the client's posture, gestures, facial movements, tone of voice, energetic state, and a wealth of repetitive, usually unconscious, tics and movements. By inviting clients to attend to nonverbal indicators, and helping them to explore their bodily experience in the present moment, we assist them in turning inward toward their unconscious back-stories in a respectful and spacious way.

Reading our clients' nonverbal communication is far more possible when we are clearly centered in our own body experience. This requires that Hakomi therapists do their own work, and do it in a way that includes being in the body. Body-centered therapy involves awareness of how the body is related to cognition, emotional wellbeing, and learning. It is by being in our bodies that we find ourselves and transform our own limitations and core organizing structures. By doing our own healing work with our bodies and our back-stories, we acquire the ability to stabilize in the present moment, and sustain an attitude of loving presence, while working with our clients' emotionally charged experience. This allows us to provide a comforting and reassuring presence for our clients—exactly what was missing during their most traumatic and overwhelming moments. In doing this, we model the influence of comfort, and help clients internalize our model as self-comfort, so that it becomes their own resource. With repetition, they learn to use this resource to anchor their present moment experience in the body, and to attend to their feelings with their own compassionate presence.

Hakomi processes

The process of Hakomi unfolds within the context of a therapy session, as a collaborative exercise of assisted self-discovery, in which the therapist serves as an attuned presence, witness, and guide. While the content of the session is largely client-led, the therapist facilitates movement by drawing on a repertoire of specific sub-processes: tracking, evoking mindfulness, conducting experiments, taking over responses, deepening, nourishing, discovering meaning, and integration. While these sub-processes can, and often do occur in a variety of sequences, there is a certain sequence that most therapists hold as a model. We might think of this model as a map of a typical Hakomi session. In the absence of a client-initiated departure, this model is used as a guide. It could also be described as an ordered set of lightly-held anticipations that help to order the therapist's intentions. A Hakomi therapist will do this only if not otherwise influenced by the client, or by the process as it unfolds organically. For purposes of description, in the following pages we have parsed, labeled, and ordered these sub-processes according to this ideal model.[5] They are described below, with example dialogues, under the headings of:

1. Tracking
2. Testing and accessing
3. Deepening and nourishing
4. Going for meaning
5. Integration

---

[5] We have taken some liberties in naming and summarizing the phases described by Ron Kurtz in his trainings and texts (1990) to simplify the description.

The reader will note that two of these steps or phases of the work have dual intentions. This is because, as processes, they have two closely related intentions and outcomes. In the case of testing and accessing, identical activities—experiments conducted in mindfulness—often accomplish two things at once. On the one hand, they confirm a hypothesis derived from tracking; on the other, they evoke an experiential response in the client. Often this response, a feeling, thought, body sensation, or physical gesture, pertains to something that was previously unconscious. Thus, the same intervention simultaneously tests a hypothesis and accesses unconscious experience. Similarly, an intervention intended to deepen a faintly experienced emotional state—for example, an acknowledgment like "I see how sad you are right now." may simultaneously provide comfort and emotional nourishment to an emergent feeling. These dual intentions are made increasingly clear in the following examples, and in the DVD that accompanies this book.

Tracking

We usually begin a session with a process called "tracking"[6], in which the therapist listens to and observes the nonverbal and verbal communications of a client, while maintaining a state of loving presence, and making occasional contact statements and acknowledgments. This phase has a number of important intentions. It quickly establishes relationship, trust, safety, and attunement between therapist and client. Also, by naming and validating the client's state, the therapist reinforces the client's awareness of the present moment. Simultaneously, as the client's feelings are acknowledged, his attention and disclosures move to a deeper level.

In addition, while tracking, the therapist sometimes maintains a parallel process as he or she looks for indicators and listens for key words pertaining to the back-story, the historic circumstances behind what is unfolding. The

---

[6] Tracking is a term invented by Ron Kurtz. It involves using nonverbal skills to track a client's changing present moment state and sometimes using contact statements to deepen this process.

therapist will test intuitions and ideas about this back-story in the next phase of the process. We think of this parallel activity as perceiving deeply in order to read the unconscious "core beliefs" (also called "core convictions," "decisions," or "anticipatory structures") that lie below the surface of the client's words and present moment psychobiological state. The following are some common examples of unconscious organizing convictions:

- I'm not loveable.
- The world is not safe.
- People are dangerous.
- I'm not enough.
- I'm too much.
- People cannot be trusted.
- I can't trust myself.
- Those I love will abandon me.
- Letting people get close to me is dangerous.
- I don't belong here (in the world, with others, on the planet).
- I'm not welcome.
- I'm a bad person.
- My inner feelings are bad or dangerous.
- It's not okay to need other people.
- I must work very hard to be loved.

These are a few examples of core convictions that Hakomi therapists recognize as attractors that determine how people organize their experience and behavior. Almost everyone has a few of these kinds of organizing factors, unless they have done a lot of work in an effective therapy. They are derived from experience, usually during early childhood. The circumstances and events they are derived from are usually painful and sometimes life-threatening, or were believed to be life-threatening when they occurred. They may exist as verbal structures, but they are more commonly recognized as schemata, images, actions, attitudes, and dispositions.

Clues or "trailheads" to these core beliefs are found by exploring nonverbal indicators. It is important to distinguish tracking present moment states from noticing nonverbal indicators. They are different processes, with different intentions, but they are sometimes done in a parallel, multitasking mode. This might seem like a lot to ask of a therapist, but with practice it is not much harder than driving a car while talking on a cell phone, or playing a piano where the right and left hands are producing entirely different melodies.

Tracking while looking for indicators and key words requires the development of five skills that were either created or adapted by Ron Kurtz. These skills are taught to students training in Hakomi, and they are practiced over a period of years as the student moves toward certification.

1. **Attending to nonverbal communication**. Backgrounding the content of the client's speech, and foregrounding (placing primary attention on) the client's nonverbal behavior, with the intention of noticing the client's present moment psychobiological state.

2. **Listening for key words**. As clients speak, they often return to words that stand out as clues to the importance of certain themes. For example, in the dialogue below, the word *look* in phrases like, "Jim *looks* at me," "That *look* he has," and "How sad and hurt he *looks*," suggests the importance of visual information, which is verified in the client's response to the therapist's observation, "It looked like you might be seeing an image of that face in your mind's eye as you spoke."

3. **Making contact statements**. Contact statements are very brief, and they are slipped into a client's monologue, or spoken during pauses when she is silent. The intention is not to disrupt the client's process and, at the same time, to name the client's present moment-state. An example would be "sad, huh." There

is the slightest hint of a question in the word "huh," which can also be heard as an affirmation. This keeps it from being a pronouncement. It makes it tentative. If the contact statement is wrong, or not precise enough, the client will usually correct it, for example, "more like hopeless." The therapist immediately adapts to this, and is grateful for the new information. The therapist pauses after making a contact statement, and just watches what happens. If the statement "lands," the client usually shifts to a new level. For example, the sadness deepens, or what is underneath it emerges.

4. **Making acknowledgments**. Acknowledgments are simple statements that acknowledge or validate a client's psychobiological state, or the situation as the client perceives it in the present moment. For example:

    "I see how painful this is for you."
    "I know how hard you work to make things better."
    "I sense how important this is for you."

Acknowledgments validate the client, as they reflect back important information about the therapist's recognition. They tell the client that the therapist has really listened. They often have the effect of deepening a client's experience of a feeling or state, and they also convey emotional nourishment, insofar as they tell someone directly that they are not alone in their recognition of something—and therefore, not alone.

Answers to questions about when to perform tracking, and how much tracking to do with a certain client in a specific session, depend on many variables, including the therapist's style, the client's skill in doing their own work, and the client's preferred mode of information processing (analytic, expressive, and so on). With a new client, a therapist may spend most of the session tracking. This is a good way to create relationship while the client discovers what it's like to be listened and attuned to. It might be a new client's first experience of attunement with another human being since infancy.

On the other hand, there are times when a new client walks into the office and the therapist will notice something about the client's present state within the first few seconds that will prompt her to move on with the work to testing and accessing or nourishing. In addition, tracking does not just happen at the beginning of a session. It can be called for at any time. For example, as a therapist proposes an experiment, she tracks the client's nonverbal communication to see how he responds to the idea. Also, after an experiment has been conducted, a therapist not only receives the client's verbal report, but she watches for nonverbal state-changes as well. Again, as the therapist provides emotional nourishment, she tracks closely to see if the client is able to take it in. Sometimes a client makes what seems to be an "appropriate response" while nonverbal indicators tell a very different story. Shaking one's head from side to side while saying "yes" would be a simple example drawn from a Western context. (In some cultures, side-to-side head movement is consistent with "yes.")

In order to illustrate how tracking is used, we will provide a brief vignette that closely follows an actual Hakomi session. Names and a few superfluous details are altered to maintain the client's anonymity.

An example of tracking

Background: Susan, the client, has recently decided to leave her marriage of fifteen years. In previous sessions it has come to light that the marriage no longer meets her needs for intimacy, companionship, and growth. She has felt stifled and trapped for the last five years. She does not blame her husband for this. In fact, she still loves and respects her husband, and wants to remain his friend. She feels their marriage was not a failure. It's just time to move on, and she has made her mind up about it. She has also had a recent affair that her husband knows about, and while he feels some anger and disappointment, especially about being deceived, he still wants the marriage, and is very upset about what has happened. He does not understand why she wants to leave, or why she would even think of it, since, from his perspective, it has been a happy marriage.

Start of third session: Susan eases into her chair and the therapist takes his seat in front of her. They are facing each other in identical swiveling office chairs, with nothing but a few feet of space between them. The therapist is sitting straight on, relaxed, not leaning forward. He is appreciating her warm smile, while also noticing Susan's nonverbal indicators as he greets her.

> **Therapist:** Good morning.
> **Client:** Morning. How are you today?
> **Therapist:** Good... I like the warm weather.
> **Client:** Yeah, isn't it great?

Nonverbal indicators: The therapist has noted that Susan is sitting in a posture that suggests a kind of shrinking back, with her head lowered and her shoulders drawn forward. Also, her left leg crosses her right, and her hands are making wringing gestures that suggest both self-comforting and worry. This gesture is all but hidden in the left side of her lap behind her knee, and it appears that she is unconsciously hiding it from the therapist's view. Her upper body leans toward the right, and the chair is slightly swiveled to the right, so the effect, while subtle, suggests a turning down and away, and seems to say something about self-esteem. Her face is tense, and the skin appears tight. There is a slight appearance of sadness and strain in her eyes as they try to smile. Her eye contact, however, is good, and there is an apparent dissonance between her solid gaze and her posture that makes the insecurity and hiding posture even more evident.

[The therapist already knows that she participated in est during the seventies, and also that she works with the public, and has been successful in sales. This may explain the eye contact and her ability to be mindful, which was present right from the start of her Hakomi work.]

She could be anxious as well as sad, and the anxiety might be somewhere in the neighborhood of shame, guilt, humiliation, and embarrassment. Many of these indicators point in the direction of self-esteem, and the therapist is already thinking about a verbal offering like "You are a good person" as a good way to test this idea. We are less than a minute into the session.

> **Therapist:** Little sad this morning maybe. [*A contact statement, wordy, but okay.*]
> **Pause.**
> **Client:** Yeah, sad…and something else. I don't know what, but there's something else. [*She looks and sounds as if she is curious about it.*]
> **Therapist:** Curious, huh? [*Contact statement.*]
> **Client:** Yeah, I am. It's been bugging me for days. It gets stronger every time Jim **looks** at me with this **look** he has…this really hurt **look**… and I see how much pain I'm making him… ah… making him feel. It makes me sad.
>> [*The contact statement dropped her to a deeper level. Also, notice the key word "**look**." As she says "ah" and hesitates, she drops her head a bit lower, her shoulder raise slightly and she looks up at the therapist, leaning her head down and forward.*]
> **Therapist:** It looked like you might be seeing an image of Jim's face in your mind's eye as you spoke. [*This was a guess, based on the key word "**look**"*]
> **Client:** [*Surprised*] You're right. It's right here. Every time I think about the divorce, I see his face… with that expression… that hurt *look*. It's like he's *blaming* me.
>> [*"**Blaming**" might be another key word here, even though it's used only once. As she says this she drops her head again.*]

Therapist: I wonder if you noticed that when you said that, you dropped your head and leaned forward and looked up at me. You have done that a few times as you talked about Jim's face. Are you aware of doing that? *[Drawing client's attention to an indicator.]*

Client: *[She repeats the gesture without prompting, and says, almost immediately]* I'm bowing to him.

[There is a pause while the therapist lets this sink in. The client appears a little surprised and embarrassed, and then she seems to go inside for a moment.]

Therapist: A little surprised, huh.

Client: Yeah. I guess I'm really feeling guilty. *[Pauses again.]* Yeah, that's it... guilty. *[Another example of dropping to a new level after a contact statement.]*

Pause.

Therapist: I wonder if you could repeat that gesture slowly, as you go inside to find out what that gesture wants to say. *[Proposing a little experiment in mindfulness.]*

Client: Close my eyes?

Therapist: If that helps. You know. You can just be mindful, like we did last week. And slowly do the head thing eh, the... the bow.

Client: *[Repeating the gesture a few times.]* It says, "I'm sorry, please forgive me."

[The sadness now deepens, her eyes water, and a tear starts to roll down her cheek.]

Therapist: More sadness... tears.

Client: Yeah. I can cry, but it isn't easy for me.

Comment: Now the therapist will work to help Susan be with and acknowledge the sadness. As the sadness is comforted, the feeling of guilt emerges more clearly. It is felt in the body as a hot feeling that extends from the lower abdomen to her chest. At this point the therapist is thinking that Susan is not only feeling bad about herself, but that she seems to be going beyond compassion for

Jim. She seems to be over-caring for his feelings. She feels guilty and "to blame" for how Jim feels. It seems that his feelings are more important than hers. This suggests a back-story in Susan's life that Jim's face is evoking, probably a time, now forgotten, when she had to caretake someone's feelings. A time when she felt like she was in trouble, or had done something she thought was bad. This idea is only an intuition, and in the next phase, the therapist will attempt to test it out. If it is accurate, or even close, the test will probably access something that is now unconscious, and that is where the transformation will begin.

TESTING/ACCESSING PHASE

There comes a time in most sessions when the tracking phase yields to the "testing" or "accessing" phase. At this point, the Hakomi therapist gently intervenes in the client's verbal and nonverbal monologue in order to test an intuition that has arisen about what the client has presented in the "tracking" process. While this subsequent phase has the intention of testing, it is also designed to access unconscious experience. The emergence of unconscious reactions or experiences in response to taking in offerings of emotional nourishment serves to validate the intuitions being tested. In this phase, therefore, two different but inseparable intentions are exercised simultaneously.

There are many kinds of accessing/testing processes. Here are a few examples (many more are demonstrated on the DVD):

1. The therapist, wanting to test an idea that the client has derived an organizing belief that the world is not a safe place, helps the client to assume a mindful state, and then makes a verbal offering such as, "You are safe here." The client may respond by sighing and feeling relief, or he may hear a voice in his head that says, "Don't

believe that!" Either reaction indicates that safety is an important issue. A neutral response—nothing happens—would indicate that the idea is not important at the moment. The evoked experience might be relief, or a thought that may be accompanied by anxiety or anger.

2.   The therapist, testing the idea that belonging is an issue, might use an offering like "You're welcome here," "You belong here," or "I'm glad to see you." The evoked experience might be relief, or perhaps grief, and a memory of rejection.

3.   A client who talks very fast might be asked to slow down to an extremely slow pace, and continue talking for a minute or so, while being mindful of how it feels to do that. This could be a way of testing possibilities: that talking fast is a result of growing up with many siblings, or in a competitive environment, perhaps, or was developed as a way to avoid difficult feelings. The evoked experience might be impatience or frustration, or it could be a strong feeling of sadness or fear.

The unconscious material that is evoked by testing processes might be a sensation, like tightness in the chest; an affect, like a feeling of panic, or panic mixed with sadness; a memory; or a gesture, or postural shift. Often, it is a combination of these kinds of responses. It is something that was not in consciousness prior to the testing/accessing experiment.

At this point, the testing/accessing phase ends, and a new phase begins. We have named this third phase the "affect-deepening and nourishing phase." In some sessions, this next phase unfolds without any action other than the client talking and the therapist tracking. Unconscious material simply emerges as a consequence of the trusting relationship, enhanced, perhaps, with the judicious use of occasional acknowledgments and contact statements.

Example with Susan continues

Context: By now, the therapist has comforted Susan's sadness, and allowed her to comfort it, and it has calmed down. The burning feeling she described as guilt has intensified, and the therapist has helped her to calm it down by assuring her that he is not judging her. He has also helped her to distance from a "self-critical part," and this has helped her to calm down enough to where the guilt feeling is less intense, but still present. (As Ron Kurtz would say, "We only need a teaspoon of it to work with.")

Therapist's impression: The therapist speculates that the session is largely about a sense of "being in trouble," and there seems to be a secondary theme about caring for other people's feelings. Habits of taking care of other people's feelings usually begin early in life. From earlier sessions, the therapist knows that the client was adopted into a second family at an early age, and that strong bonding did not occur in her adoptive family. This lack of bonding is especially painful with regard to her mother. He therefore suspects that the issue of belonging is crucial for the client, but within this, that caretaking might be an important factor. Insecure children often become hypervigilant toward their parents, and work hard at making them happy, avoiding behavior that might upset them, taking it very hard when they are upset or disappointed.

Next step: At this point, the therapist holds these thoughts lightly, as speculation about the session's back-story. It would be useful to have a memory to work with, if there is one, so he decides to offer an experiment in mindfulness designed to evoke memories that reference the present moment somatic feeling of guilt.

> **Therapist:** Seems calmer now. *[Contact statement.]*
> **Client:** Yeah, better. It's still there, but it's not as strong.
> **Therapist:** Would it be okay to explore it? Maybe we could find out more about what it means. *[Asking permission.]*
> **Client:** Sure. I'm curious. It's a little scary, but I'm okay with it.

Therapist: It would be nice to have a memory. That would help us to understand it. But it doesn't work to go looking for one. That's a lot of work. It usually doesn't help much. But there is a way, if you would like to try it. *[This introduction employs the power of suggestion.]*

Client: Sure. I'm really okay now.

Therapist: Well, here's how it works. You just go inside. You know, that mindful state where you're just being with the hot sensation. Just allowing it to be the way it is. Not too close. Standing back from it. And I will ask it about a memory. See, we want the hot part to give it to us. All you have to do is sit back and observe, just watch. Passive. It's okay if nothing happens. You needn't go looking for one.

Client: Okay. Should I close my eyes now?

Therapist: Good. Yeah. Just turning inward, being with that burning feeling.

Client: *[Follows the instructions. She looks calm and inwardly focused. Her eyelids flutter, indicating a relaxing of the muscles that usually focus the eyes.]*

Therapist: Just give me a nod when you're ready.

[Some time passes, then Susan nods.]

Therapist: *[Delivered very slowly, and with compassion.]* Just notice what shows up when I ask that hot, guilty-feeling part *[Pause]:* "What do you remember about this hot feeling you have?" *[This is said in a very evocative, soft voice.]*

Pause.

Therapist: No need to go looking. It's okay if nothing shows up.

Pause. *[Client seems to be studying something internally.]*

Therapist: You don't have to tell me about the content of the memory, if you don't want to. Just remember it of yourself if you like. *[Sometimes memories are very private.]*

Client: *[Silent, but obviously studying something. Holds her breath for twenty seconds or so, then a long sigh.]*

Therapist: Memory, huh.

Client: Yeah. It's my mother again. I did something bad. She is disappointed in me. I feel bad, really bad.

Therapist: Would it help to have my hand? *[She reaches out. Therapist gently takes her hand.]* Does that feel good? *[It's good to check.]* *[Client nods. A minute of silence transpires. The client is obviously attending to internal events. She seems fairly calm, transfixed.]*

Client: She feels pretty bad.

Therapist: Maybe you could just be with her, and I'll just say something. Is that okay? *[Permission is important: this could be delicate.]*

Client: Okay.

Therapist: Just notice what she feels, when she hears me say: "I see how bad this made you feel." *[This is addressed to the inner child in the memory. It is delivered in a sympathetic, soft voice, as an acknowledgment.]*

Long pause.

Therapist: What happened, when she heard that?

Client: *[Silent tears are flowing now.]* I think it's relief. She was so alone. There was just her mother… how could she be like that?

Deepening/nourishing phase

In this phase, the therapist intends to help the client *be with*, explore, and process the emerging unconscious experience that arises from testing and accessing. In the course of this process, the client will be supported in naming, learning about, regulating the affect of, bringing mindfulness to, and accepting nourishment for the emerging unconscious experience.

In doing this, the conventional Hakomi method is to address the experience directly. For example, if the experience is one of sadness, the therapist may use an acknowledgment which provides recognition, connection, compassion, naming, and nourishment in a single speech act.

This might take the form of the therapist saying, in a very compassionate voice, "I see how sad you are." The Hakomi therapist may do this in a nonverbal way as well, by gently taking the client's hand, if there is explicit or implicit permission to touch. There are many kinds of direct moves that the therapist can make to support and deepen the unfolding of the experience in its richness and fullness, while comforting and nourishing the client so that she is able to stay present and mindful as the experience unfolds. One of the most effective measures in many cases is to do nothing, except perhaps offer a gentle hand, or otherwise be silently present, so long as the client is doing (his) own work (Kurtz, 2007).

At this point in the Hakomi session, the client will often began to convey, through appearance or voice, the impression that she has become identified with a "child part." Hakomi therapists are trained to work with the emergence of these parts (Kurtz, 1990). In Hakomi, we handle them by altering our voice to the kind of voice that would be both appropriate and comforting to a child of the age and gender that the child part appears to be.

Here again, the Hakomi method is to work with this part directly. The therapist addresses the client as if speaking directly to the child, using acknowledgments; contact statements; nourishing phrases; giving permission to the needs and feelings that the child part conveys through words, affects, and actions; and using words that a child would use and understand.

Throughout this part of the session, the client is encouraged to maintain mindfulness as an observer of the interaction between the therapist and the child part. If the unconscious material is simply a feeling, and does not manifest itself in a personified form, the interaction is much the same: the therapist offers comfort directly, while the client mindfully observes and explores the unconscious material. If the client is overwhelmed with affect, the therapist provides nourishment and supports spontaneous behavior. This allows the client to return to a calmer state, and restores the client to observant mindfulness.

Example with Susan Continues

In the testing/accessing phase above, Susan retrieved a memory in response to the experiment. She remembers a moment in the distant past, when she was a child. In the memory, she is sad and distressed in the presence of her mother's expressions of being "disappointed in her." The therapist now moves to deepen Susan's experience and her connection with the memory, especially with the little girl who appears as a figure in this memory fragment.

> **Therapist:** Can you connect with the little girl part, the one in the memory?
>
> **Client:** Yeah, she's right there. *[Client's eyes water.]*
>
> **Therapist:** Sad huh.
>
> **Client:** I think it's regret... and grief.
>
> **Therapist:** I wonder if it would be okay if I said something to her. It would be something kind. Would it help if I held your hand, just to comfort her?
>
> **Client:** I think she might like that.
>
> > *[Therapist extends his hand, and Susan takes hold of it. Susan and therapist just sit. Tears flow; there is some deep crying. Susan bends over with some deep spasms of grief.]*
>
> **Therapist:** *[Almost whispering]* I'll stay right here with you while you feel this.
>
> > *[More grief, then the wave passes. Client lifts her head.]*
>
> **Therapist:** *[Uses a tissue in his left hand to gently dry her tears, holding her in a caring, soft gaze, while also holding her hand.]*
>
> **Therapist:** Calmer now. *[Contact statement, more tracking.]*
>
> **Client:** Yeah, whew... took me by surprise.
>
> **Therapist:** Is the little girl still there? Can you stay with her?
>
> **Client:** *[Closing her eyes.]* She's still there.

Therapist: I wonder if you can just be with her, while I tell her something. Would that be all right with you?

Client: Sure.

Therapist: Maybe you could go inside and check with her *[the girl in the memory]* to see if it's okay with her. Let her know that it is something she might like to hear, not something mean or hurtful.

Client: *[Closes her eyes. Then, after a few moments…]* She's okay with that.

Therapist: Fine, then you just stay with her. Maybe you could hold her hand, just like I held yours. And you just notice how she feels when I say it, okay?

Client: Okay.

Pause.

Therapist: Just notice how she feels, when she hears me say: I won't leave you, or push you away, even if I'm disappointed.

> *[Client pauses. Deep sigh. Her body lets go. There is an obvious release of deeply held tension.]*

Pauses.

Therapist: Can you tell me what happened?

Client: Oh, something just let go. *[Tears now, but obviously tears of relief.]*

Therapist: Relief, maybe.

Client: Yeah. Big relief.

GOING FOR MEANING

In Hakomi, we presume that painful experiences are often exiled to the unconscious, along with memories of the situation that caused them. They include implicit memories of body sensations, feelings, body gestures and postures, habitual management behaviors, and images of events that were especially significant moments in the formation of our personalities. In the process of surviving painful and traumatic moments, we make decisions about ourselves, other people, and the world. These decisions are in the form of thoughts that we identify with and come to adopt as anticipatory structures, or what Ron Kurtz has called "core beliefs" or "core convictions" (1990). Together, they form something like an unconscious worldview or model. When we uncover these structures, they are articulated in words and phrases appropriate to the age of the individual when these thoughts were adopted into the client's unconscious model, for example: "Don't trust anyone," "It's not safe," "Nobody loves me," "People who love me always leave."

Exploring present moment experience and accessing the unconscious through little experiments in mindfulness offers relatively easy access to these traumatic memories. Once a client has brought them into consciousness, Hakomi therapists provide missing comfort and support, and model how the client can provide that soothing nourishment to himself through mindfulness and self-compassion. Once the overwhelming aspects of a painful, overwhelming, or seemingly life-threatening experience are comforted, we can help the client to explore and become aware of the meanings associated with these life-altering circumstances and events.

As Jung once said, "That which remains unconscious becomes our destiny." Making anticipatory structures or "core beliefs" conscious allows the possibility of revising our model of the world. Generally this happens automatically once these structures are known. The idea "Don't trust anyone." becomes "Some people can be trusted, and some cannot." "Life is not safe." becomes "Sometimes it's not safe." "Nobody loves me." becomes "Some people do not like me."

It is the nature of young brains to think in generalities, to frame reality in terms of black and white, to take things personally, to minimize and exaggerate, and so forth. All of the cognitive distortions cataloged by Burns (1980) are the products of young brains, or adult brains that are suffering from arrested development. We all had young brains in our early life, and it was during that phase that we acquired our predictive models of the world. Going for meaning is a Hakomi process by which these distorted models can be updated and made more precise. This updating is an important part of the healing process.

Example with Susan continues

Now that Susan is calmer and less blended with the experience, the therapist can help her to witness what happened. The therapist lets Susan explore this on her own as much as possible, intervening gently to guide her when necessary. He will help her to find out what happened, what she felt, what she needed in those moments, what she might have decided, or what she did to keep her spirit alive. This part of the session represents about half of its total length. The following is a brief but poignant excerpt.

> **Therapist:** Seem calmer now. *[Contact statement, tracking.]*
>
> **Client:** Yeah. *[Reflecting, after pause]* I never knew how insecure I was with her *[client's mother]*. I was on edge a lot.
>
> **Therapist:** You see that more clearly now. *[Contact statement, also could be considered an acknowledgment.]*
>
> **Client:** Really. It's still like that with her... even now... when I see her, and my father, too. She *[the little girl in her memory]* was terrified when she thought they disapproved. She didn't bond with them. But she was afraid they were going to leave her, or disappear somehow.
>
> **Therapist:** *[Silent.] [Letting Susan study this for herself, as long as the insights continue to unfold.]*
>
> **Client:** Whew. Just like it is with Jim. I don't feel close to him, but I'm afraid he will leave me if I disappoint him. It's just the same. I don't want him to be mad at me. You know, I knew my birth mother didn't want me. She *[the little girl in the memory]* feels guilty about that. She thinks it was her fault.

This realization comes with more tears and grief, that the therapist helps her comfort by offering her a hand again, and, as she calms down, by having her listen to the offering, "It's not your fault." and other forms of comfort that she takes in. Eventually, he instructs her to say this to the child part, helping her to use this modeling to comfort herself.

INTEGRATION

Core beliefs are foundational anticipatory structures formulated upon early experiences. They are considered by various authors to be beliefs, decisions, convictions, response patterns, neural networks, and so forth. We prefer to think of them as "anticipatory structures," since they form the unconscious basis upon which we automatically and unconsciously anticipate the world, the actions of others, and how the world and others will interact with us. They also determine how we react to the world and others as we perceive them through these structures of anticipation, which tend to be self-reinforcing. These structures are the low-level "machine code" that determines self-regulation and survival behaviors. They also filter our perceptions, and provide us with self-reinforcing interpretations of sense data. *Their most salient feature, and the one that makes them important to therapists, is that we remain unconscious of them.* Core anticipatory structures are unconscious. It is our unconsciousness that gives them the power that Jung spoke of, the power to "…become our destiny."

In Hakomi, we discover the current limiting core structures that have created and continue to create limitations on freedom, and to perpetuate unnecessary suffering. We do this by inviting and encouraging clients to experience a deeper relationship with their present moment experience. When the past emerges, we are attentive to it. We practice this in many ways: by observing, by helping the client slow down, by directing attention, by doing experiments, taking over voices, and speaking to and engaging with child parts, and by providing comfort and emotional nourishment. In doing so, we assist our clients in accessing psychological realities previously walled off from consciousness as part of early survival and self-regulatory strategies.

We consider the process of bringing these fragmented realities into awareness "integration." This integration contributes to and is supported by the creation of a coherent life narrative. This integrative process encompasses a number of self states which we will later discuss as "parts" within the framework of Internal Family Systems. These self states are what Hakomi therapists track, contact, and help clients bring to consciousness and then comfort, nourish, and update. Ultimately, Hakomi is an integrative process. By making the unconscious more conscious, and helping clients discover and revise their often contradictory models of the world, and their associated conflicting self states, Hakomi constantly moves with them in the direction of healing, which literally means "to make whole again."

INTEGRATION IN SUSAN'S SESSION

During this Hakomi session, Susan has discovered that her experience with her husband is a repetition of earlier experiences with her adoptive mother, and her interpretation of the circumstances of her adoption. Underlying her grief about disappointing both her husband and her mother is the fear of being rejected and abandoned. As a child, she believed that she had to constantly keep her mother from being disappointed with her, in order to insure that she would not be rejected and abandoned. Now, even though she would like to leave her marriage, she continues to be hypervigilant to avoid disappointing her husband.

> **Therapist:** I wonder if you can return to that image of Jim's face, and see it again in your mind's eye.
> **Client:** *[Closes her eyes.]* Yeah. I can see it. Still looks the same.
> **Therapist:** Good. Let's just check and see how you feel as you

hold it here. Do you still feel the same way? The burning? The guilt?

Client: No, the feeling is gone now. I feel okay.

Therapist: Surprised. *[Contact statement.]*

Client: I am. *[She smiles broadly. Her posture is now more open, and she is sitting erect, with her head level.]*

Therapist: I wonder if you could just notice your body, your posture right now. How does your body feel?

Client: Strong. Much stronger.

Therapist: I wonder if you could say something to that image right now. What does your body want to say?

Long pause.

Client: I'm still sorry that he feels so hurt and disappointed. You know. Like, sympathetic. But you know, I now see that it's okay. That's just how he feels. I can't change that, and really, I didn't make him feel that way.

Therapist: What could you say to him about that?

Pause.

Client: I'm sorry you feel hurt.

Therapist: Anything else?

Client: It's not my fault that you feel that way. *[This is delivered in a very straight and matter-of-fact manner, without anger or bitterness.]*

Therapist: Can you put that together; maybe say it all at once? Right from how your body feels. Mindfully… just see how it feels to say that to that image of Jim's face.

Client: I'm sorry you feel so bad about this. *[Pause.]* But now I know, in my gut…in my heart…it's not my fault.

Therapist: How did that feel to say that?

Client: Good. Solid. Really good. My chest feels free.

Therapist's comment: This session is rendered as an example taken from a real session, and captures the essential unfolding of the work. In recalling the session, I cannot recapture the exact words. However, it is as close to what happened as I can remember, and it will serve as an example of the kind of work that takes place in a typical or ideal Hakomi session.

Ron Kurtz has produced a rich library of video tapes documenting the breadth of his imagination in using humor, games, and enactments to ground clients in the insights that emerge during sessions. The embodiment of a healthy feeling state, and encouraging clients to take a first step, even if it is only in their imagination, are two of many options that help them move forward in expressing their transformation in their daily lives.

Daniel J. Siegel has written extensively about integration from an interpersonal-neurobiological point of view that follows closely the work of Allan Schore. In The *Developing Mind,* Siegel writes:

> Integration can (also) help us understand the notion of "selves" within a given individual.
>
> (1999, p. 309)

> The integrating mind attempts to create a sense of coherence among multiple selves across time and across contexts. Just as the body is made up of its component parts, the mind as a whole system is made up of the activity of these multiple self states. Self states have a repeating pattern of cohesive activity which lends a sense of historical continuity to their existence. At the transition between self states, there may be a temporary disorganization or incohesion and discontinuity in the activity of the brain; however once a new state of mind is instantiated, cohesion is reestablished.
>
> (1999, p. 315)

> Self organization at the level of the mind must involve the integrative processing of these self states across time and context. It is at the moments of transition that new self-organizational forms can be constructed. Indeed, integrating coherence of the mind is about state shifts. Congruity

and unity emerge at the interface of how information and energy—the defining elements of the mind—flow across states. Integration is about how the mind creates a coherent self-assembly of information and energy flow across time and context. Integration creates the subjective experience of self.

(1999, p. 316)

The excerpts from this session with Susan illustrate this process, insofar as they demonstrate the various phases of an idealized Hakomi session.

CHAPTER 4

EXTENSIONS OF
CONVENTIONAL HAKOMI

In a discussion or conversation, we talk about rather than study our internal experience. In ordinary consciousness we tell the story; in mindful awareness, we watch the experience of the story unfold in the present moment, through changes in body sensation, movement, sensory perception, emotion and thought.

Pat Ogden, et al., *Trauma and the Body*

GIVEN the long history of Hakomi, it is not surprising that extensions other than Mindfulness Centered Therapies have been developed. Three of these that bear mentioning are described very briefly below.

SENSORIMOTOR **Sensorimotor** **Processing:** One very important extension of Hakomi is an approach to the treatment of trauma developed by Pat Ogden, a Hakomi therapist and trainer who has founded a bottom-up, sensorimotor approach to working with shock, trauma, and post-traumatic stress (Ogden, Minton, and Pain, 2006). In an introduction to her recent book *Trauma and the Body*, neurophysiologist and trauma specialist Bessel A. Van der Kolk, M.D. writes:

During the past few decades, several body-oriented practitioners specifically have addressed the somatosensory impact of trauma. To my mind, the three outstanding teachers in this area – those who have had the most profound influence on myself and many clinicians I work with—have been Pat

Ogden, the author of this book, Peter Levine, and Al Pesso. After decades of training in Rolfing, Hakomi and other body oriented techniques, Pat Ogden integrated the psychological and neurobiological effects of trauma with body work and has founded a new school of therapy that incorporates work with sensorimotor processes firmly anchored in attachment theory, neuroscience, and traditional psychotherapeutic practice.

(Ogden, Minton, Pain, 2006, p. xxiii.)

Working with couples: Hakomi's bottom-up approach has also been found to be extremely useful in working with couples. Rob Fisher is a pioneer in this application of Hakomi. In his book, *Experiential Psychotherapy with Couples*, Fisher, a Hakomi therapist and trainer, describes how body-centered interventions derived from Hakomi can be added to couples counseling, with profound results. His book describes a wealth of provocative experiments that can be conducted in mindfulness to elicit insights and changes in behavior. Couples who engage in this form of assisted self study "discover a tremendous amount about who they are and how they are unconsciously affecting their relationships." (Introduction by Kurtz, in Fisher, 2002.)

The R-CS method: Jon Eisman, senior Hakomi trainer, and one of the founding members of the Hakomi Institute, has created an extension of conventional Hakomi called the Re-Creation of the Self (R-CS) method, that both complements Hakomi and departs in an alternate direction. Beginning in 1984, R-CS has evolved a theoretical model of the Self that closely resembles the Internal Family Systems model of Richard Schwartz (described in the next section). The R-CS model is based on Eisman's formulation of the process, in which each of us emerges from our origins with a sense of intrinsic wholeness (called "organicity" in Hakomi). This emergent Self utilizes and develops innate resources and pursues ongoing personal wishes towards further experience and ever-expanding self-expression. When opposed in this pursuit of Selfhood, this Self simultaneously accommodates the various obstacles and hurts it endures, and protects its ultimate integrity, by fragmenting consciousness into various trance-like self states, thereby creating a fragmented perception of Self.

Unlike the Internal Family Systems models, the R-CS model does not attribute distinct personalities to each of these fragments, but employs a neurobiological perspective in which personality fragments are compared to trance states (apparently following Wolinsky) produced by semi-isolated neural networks that link specific cognitive, affective, and sensorimotor elements, including implicit (and sometimes explicit) memory patterns.[7]

In addition, Eisman describes the R-CS model as not being process-oriented in the same sense as Hakomi and IFS, insofar as the method of working with parts and child states is very different. R-CS employs Hakomi principles and techniques, but unlike Hakomi and other process-oriented therapies, it asserts that it is not necessary to access the history and content of wounds, since a parallel and positive state can be found and reinforced. This reinforcement entails deliberately shifting consciousness from painful and dysfunctional states toward an embodied experience of the preexisting and preferred parallel state.

The Hakomi Institute also publishes a professional journal entitled *Hakomi Forum*. This excellent resource includes articles which update, qualify, and extend our knowledge about Hakomi and how Hakomi can be used with other methods. The Institute makes all back issues from 1984 to the end of the previous year available for downloading from its website at www.HakomiInstitute.com.

HAKOMI AS A SOURCE OF ALIGNMENT, ATTUNEMENT, AND RESONANCE

In... "Healers on Healing", dozens of renowned therapists, doctors, spiritual teachers, healers of all types are asked to summarize what heals. The most often repeated word,

---

[7] Eisman has not explained this exclusion of sensorimotor behaviors related to personality attributes from other behaviors controlled by underlying neural networks. Were he to include these behaviors, his model of the person, with its Aware Self, its Fragmentary Parts, and even the various kinds of parts identified in his R-CS model, it would conform very closely to the Internal Family Systems formulation developed by Schwartz and used in Mindfulness Centered Therapies.

and perhaps the theme of the book, is "resonance." If there is a magic ingredient, it is the resonance created in the healing relationship: one human being meeting another in a space of safety, mutual acceptance, respect and—dare I say it?—love! Ron Kurtz, the developer of Hakomi therapy, calls this work, "developing loving presence," after the quality most desirable, most efficacious in the being of the therapist.

- Deepesh Faucheaux and Halko Weiss.
Training psychotherapists in the almost impossible task of just paying attention.

Hakomi therapists cultivate a combination of mindfulness, loving presence, and attention to the body, producing the necessary conditions for a state that attachment researchers call *alignment*. Alignment is a relational state in which interacting participants experience presence, connectedness, and safety, while being responded to in a timely and appropriate manner. More precisely, it is a quality of interpersonal interaction in which the state of one individual (or group) is continuously altered to sympathetically simulate the psychobiological state of another (Siegel, 1999, Siegel and Hartzell, 2003). In an aligned interaction between a parent and infant, the parent sympathetically meets the quality (not necessarily the intensity and degree of identification) of an infant's present moment state as it moves through various kinds and degrees of affect and expression.

For example, an infant may move from sadness and tears, through successively calmer states, to peaceful, playful, excited, and joyful. As the infant cries, the parent adopts an *as-if-sad* expression of sadness. From this aligned state, the parent takes leadership by gently coaxing and modeling an affective gradient. This is accomplished through interactions that provide mirroring, and add comforting and cajoling, while modeling transitioning gestures. If successful, the parent leads the infant to a peaceful, more regulated state. Repetition leads to internalization of the parent's modeling, allowing the developing child to develop social skills and an increased ability to self-regulate overwhelming and chaotic emotional states. In contrast, non-alignment occurs when the parent becomes frustrated and angry, and reacts to the upset child's state with unsympathetic scolding, shaming, punishing, or abandoning behavior.

The process of alignment is what Allan Schore describes in the following excerpt. In this passage, Schore uses the word attune instead of align, but he is referring to the same process.

> The mother's role in this face to face dialectic is thus to grossly [align] and then by monitoring her infant's response to fine-tune her inputs to the particular baby's level of communicative capacity. In other words, she initially attempts to attune to, that is, to match and synchronize to the infant's inner state, but as his state is dynamically activated (or hyperactivated) and expressed in an alternation of gaze and behavior, she fine-tunes, that is, adjusts and corrects the intensity and duration of her stimulation in order to maintain a positive affect state in the child. In this way she provides optimal "chunking" of bits of socioaffective stimulation that the child's developing right hemispheric socioaffective information processing system can efficiently process.
>
> (Schore, 1994, p. 87).

The psychobiological result of nonalignment is shame (Schore 1994; Siegel 1999; Siegel and Hartzell, 2003). The degree of shame that results from nonalignment depends upon the abruptness, severity, violence, and the degree of shock. Some instances of moderate shame are unavoidable, and considered to be a natural and, with repair, a useful part of the development process. More intense shame is generally dysfunctional, damaging, and traumatizing. It endangers a child's ability to regulate affect and interact socially (Siegel, 1999; Siegel and Hartzell, 2003).

Attunement is another key word in the current vocabulary of attachment. Attunement includes alignment, and requires a broader perspective and a more encompassing intention. Studies of parenting reveal that a continuous, unbroken state of alignment is both impossible to maintain and suboptimal for the infant's development. Whereas the ground of being of attunement *is* alignment, attunement also includes episodes of nonalignment within the attuned interaction. However, when episodes of nonalignment occur, or are intentionally initiated, the break is not unduly abrupt or shaming. It does not completely rupture the envelope in which alignment is possible. If a rupture accidentally or incidentally occurs, the attuned other provides repair and comfort in order to restore the envelope of trust and safety.

In a typical Hakomi session, the therapist creates trust, safety, and presence by aligning with a client's flow of psychobiological states. This alignment, which is produced by the activity called "tracking" (described above), is the ground state of a Hakomi session. Performed with skill, tracking creates an exquisite alignment, an adult version of the parent-child alignment described by Siegel. During tracking, the therapist contacts both higher and lower states without bias (sadness, joy, fear, anger, hopelessness, hope) to avoid leading the session through what Stern has described as selective attunement (Stern, 1985, p. 207-211).

While alignment is the ground state, the therapist frequently departs from tracking in order to further the session's movement. The therapist might bring the client back to the present moment when the client is drawn into telling a long story; or gently interrupt him to draw attention to a significant gesture; or introduce an experiment; or otherwise address a pattern that impedes or forestalls the session's unfolding. In this way, the therapist goes beyond alignment, and attunes to something larger than the client's psychobiological state. One might say the therapist is aligning with the client's larger intention to heal and grow beyond constraining and stultifying behavioral and affective patterns. She is undertaking leadership in promoting movement out of a nonproductive pattern, or initiating a further step in what the client, at a deeper level, wants to happen.

The experience of attunement between two individuals, or between an individual and a group, often lingers long after an attuned encounter, in much the same way that a bell continues to reverberate long after it is initially sounded. In the language of attachment research, this lingering of attunement is called *resonance* (Siegel, 1999). Attunement and resonance combine to produce the state that children experience in infancy when they are being attended to by a good parent or caregiver. There is an accumulating body of research indicating that attunement and resonance in a therapeutic relationship provide an ideal state for promoting healing and growth. This evidence also suggests that deficits in parenting that result in various kinds of insecure attachment can be addressed in adulthood by participating in attuned relationships with a well-matched partner, a twelve-step group, an intentional community, or a therapeutic relationship, in which a high degree of attunement is present. Attachment researchers call the healing that results from attunement that occurs after childhood "earned attachment" (Flores, 2004).

Over the past half century, attachment research has validated clinical practices that have been part of Hakomi for decades. On the one hand, attachment research has demonstrated that early insufficient or chaotic attachment during parenting and in the family of origin is potentially damaging to the limbic and cognitive brain of the infant. On the other hand, it has also shown that repair (healing) of attachment-related suffering and disconnection is possible. This is because, as recent fMRI research has shown us, the brain is more plastic, more malleable, than was previously imagined.

Fortunately, as therapists, we can create an environment where implicit memories and unworkable convictions formed in early years can come to the surface and be available for insight and revision by the client. That revision of neural patterns is optimal in the presence of an attuned emotional connection formed later in life. This kind of nurturing connection provides a strong possibility of resonance: a positive mutual state that persists in the minds of participants even when the interaction is no longer occurring. This resonance is a crucial resource for the client in the therapist's necessary absence between sessions, and for the addict between twelve-step meetings, just as an attuned parent's presence is internalized as resonance by the child until it becomes the child's own resource for comfort and affect regulation.

What Happens When Awareness
is Overwhelmed

I was seized by fear. I had visions of furious buffaloes charging at us from every direction. My heart was pounding, every particle of my body was begging me to run for shelter. Feeling exposed and useless, I sat obediently next to Adam while he kept his eyes fixed on the thick forest and listened. We sat like that for a long time and after a while my breathing subsided, my heartbeat adjusted to his. It was as if his calm had slowly poured into me like a blood transfusion. Our silence gave way to sounds. I had not been aware of the wind through the foliage, the chirping of distant birds and crickets. All the screaming particles of my body calmed down and sank like sand in the river. Now everything inside me was quiet, I could feel the forest come alive and give out its fragrant breath of moss and fresh soil.

- Francesca Marciano, *Rules of the Wild*

There are times in therapy when the client enters a strong emotional state. *Riding the rapids* is a phrase used by Ron Kurtz to describe these occasions. While it is not the intention of this form of work, it happens quite often. When it does, it is important for the therapist to remain calm. We have already pointed out that this is a good reason for therapists to do their own inner work. By remaining calm and compassionately connected, the therapist's mere presence is a source of comfort for an emotionally overwhelmed client.

In addition, in Hakomi we support whatever spontaneous behavior occurs in the client. If he curls up into a ball, we may gently help him to do that (assuming that we have permission for this kind of touch, and always watching for any sign that it is not helpful). If we cannot touch them in this way, we simply remain present with our gaze, and sometimes a few words of comfort, touching them, so to speak, with our tone of voice. By providing nourishing presence and reliable support in that moment, we are often providing what was missing in the original painful experience.

After the rapids are navigated, we offer nourishment in a form that the client can take in. If the client expresses willingness, we might offer comfort in the form of words, a gentle touch, holding a hand, providing a pillow to hold, a blanket, a cup of tea. In general, we are intent on expanding our client's ability to receive nourishment from others. This emotional nourishment is always offered in a way that respects the client's boundaries, and is within the personal ethical guidelines for the therapist.

Hakomi is extremely effective in accessing unconscious experience. Practicing the Hakomi method therefore requires that the therapist and client slow down. Both participants in the work must cultivate patience and gentleness—conditions that are often not present in our fast-paced world. In recognition of this ever-present cultural conditioning, we begin with new clients by helping them to shift their normal pattern of sharing, and invite them to slow down, so that they are better able to be with their present moment experience. As they become quieter, the unconscious material becomes more available. We also assure them that that there is no reason to hurry; we need not push, or try to go too fast. When we perceive signs that things are moving too quickly—fear, panic, nausea, dizziness, distraction, resistance—we slow down again, and look for what will help the client to regain mindfulness and distance from an unfolding experience.

CHAPTER 5

THE EVOLUTION OF MINDFULNESS CENTERED THERAPIES

Empirical research during the past quarter-century disproves the idea that there is any single method that will work for everybody… There are always some clients for which the approach under review simply won't work, though some other modality might well succeed. The finding that there's no perfect, single method and probably will never be has led therapists to expand upon the strategies and interventions of their favorite modalities in an effort to improve outcomes… Surveys show that most therapists now label themselves integrative or eclectic. "Pragmatic" might be a better description. Clinicians today tend to be far more focused on doing what works than on sticking rigidly to a sacrosanct model.

- Jay Efran, Michael Lukens,
Mitchell Greene, *Defining Psychotherapy*

OUR personal work with Mindfulness Centered Therapies began with Hakomi. It was our original training, and we absorbed it from Ron Kurtz for six years, attending two years of supervision, and eventually teaching it to others as certified Hakomi teachers and trainers. To this foundation of Hakomi, we have added two other mindfulness-based methods, Internal Family Systems (IFS) and Focusing, to produce an eclectic approach unified by a solid grounding in Hakomi principles: loving presence, mindfulness, nonviolence, organicity, mind-body holism, unity, truth, and mutability (Kurtz, 1990, 23-33; Eisman, 2000-2001).

The expansion of Hakomi to include Internal Family Systems and Focusing was possible because mindfulness, though called by different names, is methodologically central to all three methods. Like Hakomi, IFS and Focusing are also experiential and client-led. They are also easily adapted to the Hakomi principles. While these three methods are very similar in spirit, however, they are quite different in practice.

For example, Hakomi, from the beginning, and especially in its latest form, is an extremely subtle and implicit method. It proceeds by means of quiet, empathic listening, artful tracking of changing emotional states and nonverbal indicators, sharing lightly-held intuitions, using evocative language, and providing emotional nourishment directly to control the depth and distance of experience. In many parts of the process, the less said by the therapist the better. Questions are kept to a minimum.

Internal Family Systems, on the other hand, typically proceeds by asking a succession of questions, for example: "How are you feeling now? Where do you feel it? How close are you to that part? How do you feel about that part?" Compared to Hakomi, it is much more verbal and explicit. The synthesis of these two methods into a seamless process in Mindfulness Centered Therapies took considerable trial-and-error practice, and one of the intentions of this book is to make that process much easier by providing sample dialogues that illustrate how easy and seamless transitions can be negotiated.

Focusing, in contrast, is a technique that can be easily incorporated into many different methods, and Eugene Gendlin has provided excellent examples of this in *Focusing-Oriented Psychotherapy* (1996). There are, however, some aspects of Focusing that make it especially useful as a supplement to IFS and Hakomi, and in integrating Focusing with the Mindfulness Centered Therapies synthesis, we have added elements that are drawn from his work, but not fully developed in his book.

CLIENTS WHO "CANNOT BE MINDFUL"

Our motives for adding Internal Family Systems to Hakomi arose in the course of our clinical practices. They evolved as a result of working with clients who were unable to exercise sufficient mindfulness to profit from work in Hakomi. Ron Kurtz has been the first to point out that Hakomi, as it is taught in its purest and most refined form, which he now calls *Assisted Self Discovery* (ASD), requires mindfulness. This is made clear in the following passage:

> ...assisted self discovery [using the Hakomi Method] requires a commitment on the part of the person being assisted (still called the client), that he or she be capable of entering into a present-centered, self-focused and vulnerable state of mind. The client must understand the process as experiments done in mindfulness. He or she must be willing to enter that process even though painful emotions may arise. This commitment is also required of people doing an ASD [Assisted Self Discovery] training [8](Kurtz, 2007).

This requirement on the part of clients—that they must be able and willing to be mindful—is one of the first difficulties we encountered in using Hakomi exclusively in clinical practice. Many, if not most, clients who find their way to psychotherapy come without this ability. Fortunately, Hakomi does not require a high degree of mindfulness, and many of our clients can learn it quite quickly, using conventional Hakomi methods. However, there are also many clients who find even minimal self-awareness of present moment experience quite challenging. Included in this group are a surprising number of mental health professionals, including practicing psychotherapists, social workers, substance abuse counselors, psychiatrists, and psychologists.

---

[8] ASD or Assisted Self Discovery is a name applied by Ron Kurtz as a synonym for psychotherapy as it is performed in Hakomi. The use of this term has become increasingly preferable to Kurtz in recent years as he has continued to refine and perfect Hakomi practice.

In working with these clients, we have employed every means at our disposal to assist them in learning how to be sufficiently mindful for Hakomi Assisted Self Discovery. We simply could not find it in ourselves to say, "I'm sorry, you're just not ready for this." We know that, chances are, they will never be ready if someone doesn't help them now! Their chances of trying therapy again are diminished if they learn from their first therapist that they are inadequate or incompetent as a client. This is not to say that Hakomi does nothing to teach, evoke, and sustain mindfulness in new clients. On the contrary, Hakomi therapists are constantly looking for new ways to help clients learn how to recognize and name their inner experience. But what does one do when the known Hakomi methods are exhausted?

Grappling with this problem has taught us that some beginning clients have difficulty with identifying emotions, while others have difficulty recognizing and naming body sensations. A few clients still have trouble naming and describing their feelings and/or sensations after ten or twenty sessions. Some may be able to sense their feelings, and even express them powerfully, but find it difficult to step back from them in order to observe them mindfully. Others find it very hard to stay in present time. Many are simply out of touch with their own bodies. Often these are people who "live in their heads." They are full of thoughts, ideas, stories, plans, self-analysis, generalizations, and explanations. This is especially true of highly trained academic professionals. This propensity is often accompanied by an aversion to introspection. Sometimes there is dissociation caused by trauma. It can also be due to a childhood environment that discouraged introspection, or a family of origin that dismissed or denied feelings. (One wonders what kind of a Hakomi client Julius Caesar would have made. Here was a man who could order the decimation of a legion, or watch 40,000 men die on a bloody field of battle, and apparently still sleep soundly afterwards!)

For very cerebral clients, we have often found that Internal Family Systems provides a better pathway into mindfulness. They may not be able to describe feelings of guilt or shame, but with a little help, they can readily hear the voices of their internal subpersonalities: their self-critics, the internal ranting of their angry parts, and the parts who tempt them toward binges of various kinds. From these beginnings, we can move on to identify parts that "figure out," skeptical parts, parts who like to argue, and those who want to look good, or seek approval from others. Before long, they have developed very competent "parts detectors," and we can start to talk about angry, sad, and frustrated parts. It is as if we are approaching feelings from the direction of thoughts, where these cerebrally-oriented clients feel more competent and less afraid. Once they have had a few successes, and see that the inner life is not threatening or alien, we can begin to do more work with their emotions and sensations. At this point, we can often introduce Hakomi.

Similarly, some people respond very well to Focusing. It is a simple process. While it is true that it takes from three to twelve hours to learn it well, we have occasionally taught basic Focusing skills to a client in a single one-hour session. Focusing is introduced as a teaching/learning process. The client may come into the therapist's office, terrified that they are putting themselves into the hands of a powerful, all-knowing therapist, and then become relieved to discover that they are there to be students. Their therapist is basically a "teacher," or "tutor," who is going to help them learn a skill involving a few simple steps. Many people love to be students. They have been successful at it, and are adapted to it. They are terrified by the psychotherapy situation, even when it is called Assisted Self Discovery. On the other hand, they trust the learning situation, especially when the learning is described as a simple four- or six-step process that can be written on a note card. One can say, "Let's start by thinking about some person or situation that you really like or enjoy. Now see if you can notice how you feel when you think about that."

Once they have come to trust their teacher, it is possible to make the transition to Hakomi, which Kurtz has also reframed as a learning process. IFS can also be initiated as a kind of learning, in which the client is taught to recognize and interact with parts. This commonality, along with those already mentioned, affords a seamless transition back and forth between these three methods. In fact, unless the client is told by the therapist, he does not know, and has no reason to suspect, that we are using more than one method.

In addition, conventional Hakomi methods do not always work well with clients who frequently dissociate due to severe trauma (Ogden, 1997; Roy, 2007), are troubled by psychotic states that overwhelm identity and prevent distancing, or for clients who are inadequately identified with an aware self (individuals who are often labeled as narcissists, or borderline). In training situations, Kurtz has also declined to work with clients suffering from severe depression, and people who are unable to sufficiently sustain a state of mindfulness for other reasons.

Getting Around the Use of Touch In One-On-One Therapy

A second difficulty in using Hakomi, especially Kurtz' newer form of Hakomi, is related to the use of touch. Touch is an important part of comforting and providing nourishment. As Ron Kurtz explains:

> If the reaction is an emotional one I do two things that I didn't do in previous versions of the method: one, I touch the client (or I have an assistant touch the client), gently, on the arm or shoulder or leg. It is a sympathetic touch. (It is a very natural thing to do; chimpanzees do it, ordinary humans, even children, do it. Since touching clients is against the law in some states, like California, you must be careful if you do this in one-on-one sessions. Still, I would argue, in Shakespeare's words, "It is a custom more honored in the breach than the observance" (2006).

Like many body-centered therapies, Hakomi makes considerable use of touch. It is worth noting, in this regard, that a great deal of Hakomi training is conducted in a workshop environment where trainees interact alternately as clients and therapists. There are many assistants available, and the group situation provides safety for the use of nourishing touch. However, in one-on-one situations, touch can be very difficult to do safely, especially in the first few months of therapy. It is also very difficult to use touch in agency situations, and in states where touch is against the law.

It is usually more difficult for a male client to accept it from a male therapist than from a female. For this reason, it has been sometimes useful to bring a female trainee into private sessions to work with male clients where physical touch is an important issue for the client, and we find that learning to accept this form of comfort from someone, anyone, can be quite important for the client's growth and healing. Even so, great care must be taken, and sometimes it is simply not possible to use touch as a therapeutic tool.

Since, outside of training situations and workshops, we do one-on-one therapy most of the time, we have had to find other ways to provide the nourishment that many clients obviously need. It was this situation, more than anything else that led us to integrate Hakomi with IFS in the way that we have. It provides a way for clients to interact with their inner parts as a Hakomi therapist would do in a group situation, so that they can provide nourishment for their own inner parts, including what might be called "virtual touch." Using this approach, the therapist can coach clients so that they provide nourishment for themselves in a safe and spacious manner.

While the requirement of mindfulness and the issue of touch were major motivations for going outside of Hakomi, there are many other good reasons for adopting an eclectic approach. It is probably most accurate to say that Mindfulness Centered Therapies evolved in response to the needs that arose in our daily practices, as we worked with people from many walks of life and socioeconomic classes. For our purposes, it seems that the eclectic toolbox is richer and more resourceful.

Sometimes we need parts language. It helps us to keep some clients separate from experiences that would otherwise be overwhelming. Some clients resonate very easily with the idea of parts. The Internal

Family Systems model (Schwartz, 1995) also offers a very concise way to conceptualize the Self, a key element that is not included as an essential part of conventional Hakomi or Focusing. Richard Schwartz has spent much of his clinical practice with clients who have been severely abused (Goulding and Schwartz, 1995). We find that abuse survivors, and many other clients, naturally gravitate toward construing their inner experience in terms of parts. They also find something very grounding about thinking of the Self as an invisible essence that is known to them by virtue of awareness, its single sensible property (Deikman, 1982).

In addition, Focusing is a method that is very well adapted to working with the future. The client who is anticipating surgery, or speaking in public, or avoiding something (like filing taxes, or living alone after a divorce), can get something very precious from a Focusing session (see the Focusing demonstration in DVD Chapter 15). Sometimes emotional states are not primarily retriggered memories of past situations and events. Sometimes no clear categorical experience like anger, sadness, grief, or anxiety arises. There is only a vague uneasiness, the kind of experience that Gendlin has aptly named a *felt sense*. In these situations, we find Focusing an excellent place to start, or to transition to, as the need arises. We have even produced very satisfying results by supporting clients who have previous experience with Gendlin's work in using Focusing as they work with parts.

Limitations of Client-Led Mindfulness Based Therapies

This discussion leads to a question with regard to the limits of mindfulness therapies within a client-led context. Generally speaking, we have found that while Mindfulness Centered Therapies produces satisfying movement and outcomes with a broad spectrum of presenting issues for individuals and couples, there are clients for whom this method may not be well adapted. We are speaking here of clients who systematically blame other people or outside causes, and are unable or unwilling to own or take responsibility for their own mental and emotional states, or for their part in interpersonal, social, and economic situations in which they have become involved. In this regard, we find ourselves in agreement with Greg Johanson, when he writes:

> At present, it is fair to say that mindfulness has a wide applicability with presenting issues considered in the neurotic range, defined as patients who have a sense of their own involvement in their issues, and a willingness to be introspective. Dealing with personality disorders, defined as those who place responsibility for their conditions on a variety of external sources, requires a regimen of counseling in ordinary consciousness before they are willing to engage in therapy that requires them to look inside themselves. Those on the edges of psychosis do not have sufficient psychic structures in place to allow them to study themselves mindfully. However, mindfulness of the concrete, historical world can help build structure. For instance, "Can you hear (feel, touch) me? How do you know you are hearing (feeling, touching) me? Can you sense your feet against the floor, your back against the chair?" etc.
>
> (Johanson, 2006).

This is not to say that other approaches (psychodynamic, cognitive, or more highly structured or directive) may not be effective in meeting the needs of these clients. At the present time, Dialectical Behavioral Therapy is one example of a more structured and directive approach that employs mindfulness, especially with clients diagnosed with disorders pertaining to the self, such as narcissism and borderline personality disorder.

In addition, we cannot claim great experience in applying mindfulness based methods with clients with severe personality disorders. Because of the nature of our practices and the channels through which our clients find us, our experience with extremely disturbed clients is limited. Richard Schwartz, on the other hand, has worked with a much wider range of clients, and has reported considerable success using Internal Family Systems therapy, unquestionably a mindfulness based method. In order to provide balance, and in the interest of keeping our minds open, we include a quotation from an excellent article on this subject:

> [In working with people whose behavior fits the diagnostic label of Borderline Personality Disorder, BPD] ...if the therapist cannot maintain Self-leadership [mindfulness] and, instead, reacts protectively to the client's parts, the client is unlikely to ever expose his or her Self. Therefore, the success of therapy with such clients depends entirely on the therapist's knowledge of and ability to work with his or her protective parts. It requires a commitment to personal exploration and healing that can be exceedingly challenging and painful but ultimately is highly rewarding. Further, the therapist may not always be aware when his or her parts are interfering so it requires a commitment to soliciting frequent consultation with a colleague or supervisor who is able to facilitate inner exploration. If these requirements are met, therapy with clients labeled BPD can be extremely growthful for client and therapist alike. If they are not met, the therapy is likely to be nightmarish for both, only perpetuating the dreadful reputation that "borderlines" already carry
>
> (Norman and Schwartz, 2003).

In summarizing this topic, we feel that keeping an open mind about the limitations of mindfulness as an approach to psychotherapy is essential. While the use of mindfulness in this context is in its infancy, and Mindfulness Centered Therapies is even younger, many therapists have studied and used Hakomi and Internal Family Systems together without naming or articulating their methods of integrating these skill sets in articles or monographs. We feel that, as investigation of these methods advances, questions regarding the limitations of either client-led experiential therapies or therapies based on mindfulness will be more profitably approached from a relativistic perspective with clinical research data to guide us in matching different therapeutic traditions with specific varieties of unnecessary suffering and dysfunctional limitation.

MINDFULNESS CENTERED THERAPIES: AN EXPERIENTIAL METHOD

Having developed Mindfulness Centered Therapies as an eclectic approach, the question arises regarding how to place it among the existing schools and methods that make up the field of psychotherapy. In this regard, Mindfulness Centered Therapy is first and foremost an experiential method, since its primary emphasis is "the client's experiencing in therapy." This is the criterion set forth by Watson, Greenberg, and Lietaer in the introductory chapter of their *Handbook of Experiential Psychotherapy* (1998, pp. 24-25). It is also aligned with Eugene Gendlin's perspective in placing primary value on asking clients to name or otherwise represent their experience, and holding this awareness and articulation of experience as a major therapeutic value or condition to be encouraged and supported during the counseling session. In addition, it emphasizes helping clients study and understand how their experience is organized (Kurtz, 1990). This orientation and valuation is unequivocal, and all of the methods employed in Mindfulness Centered Therapies (Hakomi, Internal Family Systems, and Focusing) support these objectives.

Mindfulness Centered Therapies goes beyond many experiential therapies in attending to the intra-psychic relationship, that is, the relationship between the client's awareness and his experience. Since this emphasis distinguishes Mindfulness Centered Therapy from many other experiential therapies, we will articulate it here in more detail. The ideal or optimal relationship between a client's awareness and experience is clearly specified in the definition of mindfulness used in Mindfulness Centered Therapies. This definition states that "mindfulness is a state of nonjudgmental and compassionate awareness of present moment internal and external experience." Through its articulation of this definition, it stipulates that clients are not fully and completely aware of their experience unless they are experiencing it from the point of view of an awareness that is nonjudgmental and compassionate. The word compassionate can be construed to mean "experience-friendly" or "experience-welcoming/ accepting"—the precise wording is not important, it is the intention that counts.

In practice, this definition does not mean that the client must always be in a mindful state. Indeed, as we have already mentioned, many clients do not know what mindfulness is, and are almost incapable of attaining or maintaining it for more than a few seconds when they begin this kind of work. It is essential, however, for the therapist to be able to track the client's ever-changing relationship to experience, and to discern whether the client is being mindful or not, and what degree of mindfulness is present at a given moment.

This discernment depends upon three things: Is the client experiencing his experience? Is the client "in" or attending to the present moment? Is the client's attitude friendly, compassionate, accepting and/or welcoming toward her experience? Once mindfulness is thoroughly understood by the therapist, it is very possible to track these elements. With practice, this kind of tracking becomes second nature. If therapists are familiar with mindfulness, and can sustain a state of mindfulness over a significant period of time, then they can be trained to recognize and track it in others with roughly two to eight hours of training. Additional practice will be required to perfect this ability, and there are a number of helpful signs of mindfulness that can be useful in the learning process. For example, Richard Schwartz recommends a list of "c" words: conscious, calm, curious, compassionate, clear, courageous, confident, creative. All of these are signs of a mindful state (called a *Self* or *Self-led* state in Internal Family Systems).

Similar criteria of mindfulness are used in Hakomi, which also encourages therapists to pay attention to precise nonverbal indicators. If the eyes are closed as the client turns his senses inward, we look for a fluttering movement of the eyes behind the lids. We track facial expressions, gestures, and body posture, along with inflection and tone of voice. While Hakomi avoids the excessive use of questions, which can break the client's process, in

Mindfulness Centered Therapy we sometimes ask questions such as, "What is your attitude (or feeling) toward that experience (sadness, anxiety, anger, tightness, critical voice, and so forth) right now?" If the attitude is reported as sympathetic (without smothering), curious, neutral, or compassionate, and if this verbal assessment is congruent with nonverbal signals, we might conclude that the client is indeed being mindful. However, an experienced therapist can usually tell from the client's response to questions. It becomes very obvious with practice.

Another aspect of the client's relationship to experience that is important to track is the distance the client is holding from his experience at a given point in time. The metaphor of distance is used to refer to the degree of identification. If the client is overwhelmed or flooded by a strong feeling or a compelling thought, we say that he is very identified (or "blended") with it. In this state, it is impossible to be mindful. If the client is cold and totally disconnected from his experience, as in dissociation, or withdrawn from his feelings, we consider the client to be filtering the experience through an attitude, another part, or another feeling state. The ideal state of distance or identification between awareness and experience is one in which there is connection, but also a measure of distance.

Using IFS language, we say the client is "unblended," "in Self," or "Self-led," with regard to the experience. In Hakomi, it is simply a matter of seeing whether the client is being mindful, or if they are overwhelmed, or "in the rapids," in which case we use comfort, nourishment, and other methods to help the client regain some distance, while staying in touch with the feeling or child state that has emerged. In Hakomi, we also use the metaphor of *deepening*. To deepen an experience is to bring the client closer to it, to make it more evident, to connect the client with it more closely. Deepening too far can result in *flooding*, or overwhelming. We try to avoid that. In Focusing, Gendlin uses the idea of stepping back from the experience, not getting pulled into it. Each of these experiential therapies has the same idea about how the client should *be* in relationship to their experience. This is why they work so well together and why we can subsume everything about them as a part of a single approach.

Therapists who are aware of the importance of mindfulness as it is described here work differently, depending upon the individual client's degree and state of mindfulness. For example, with this distinction in mind, a therapist would not encourage, say, a two-chair dialogue between polarized, hostile, or unfriendly "parts" (distinct feeling-states or aspects within the client). They would handle this situation by having the client relate to each part mindfully, from a state of experience-friendly, accepting awareness. They would fully recognize and acknowledge each part's experience, including its point of view, purpose, feelings, memories, and what it construes or imagines to be true about the world. Each part would receive the client's compassion and respect.

Even an internal critic who uses shaming thoughts in an attempt to control behavior is doing so to protect the client, either from being shamed by others, or from making, or repeating, a mistake that will, from its point of view, harm or bring shame onto the client. The wise therapist will acknowledge and respect its protective agenda or purpose (Cornell and McGavin, 2005). When such a critic's voice and anger are understood with compassion by the client in a state of mindful attention, the critical part is much more likely to participate in reevaluations and updating that will allow it to soften its message and delivery. Similarly, the offending part, the part that feels bad when the critic shames it, can be contacted and acknowledged by the client in a similar compassionate state, and from this mindful state, the client can soothe and nourish this part with his presence. The aware Self thus acts directly with experience in all cases. Its agency lies in its presence, compassion, and intention to mediate and harmonize. In Mindfulness Centered Therapy, it is considered an act of violence to set one part or state against the other, or to facilitate an unfriendly dialogue between them. Doing so increases their polarization.

In facilitating this relationship between the client's aware self and his experience, the therapist models the optimal or ideal by maintaining a nonjudgmental, experience-friendly attitude toward the client and the client's experience. What we say about safety between therapists and clients, therefore, also extends to the intra-psychic relationship between clients and the elements of their experience, whether these are construed as feelings, body sensations, thoughts, emotions, semiautonomous parts, or felt sense experience.

THREE KINDS OF EXPERIENCE

In order to illustrate the next point, we propose a thought experiment, and invite the reader to join us on an imaginary expedition. On this journey we will encounter a territory that is diverse, and relatively unexplored. This adventure is modeled after the great voyages of discovery into the Pacific and the New World. In keeping with this tradition, we will be taking some experts along with us. They will help us collect specimens and document what we encounter. For this purpose, we have invited a naturalist, a geologist, and an anthropologist. On our first night out, we sit around a campfire and listen to these experts describing the day's discoveries. (You and I are not specialists on this occasion.) We begin by chatting about the hot weather, the friendly people in one village, the rather unwelcoming folks in another, things like that. We are just ordinary people who have not been trained in mindfulness. It is okay for us to be judgmental and critical. After we have exhausted ourselves with our complaints, criticisms, comparisons, assessments, and evaluations, the experts have their say.

The geologist speaks up first. He names the various types of rock that are exposed in outcrops. He names the volcanic beds that are relatively unweathered; the basalt, obsidian, and opalized wood fragments found in beds overlying much older sedimentary layers, containing sandstones and silicon deposits, the remnants of ancient lakebeds. From his survey, he has pieced together something of the history of the landscape over the past ten million years.

The geologist is followed by the naturalist, whose plant presses are bulging with specimens. She talks about the ecology of the area, how the slash-and-burn agriculturalists have converted the semitropical high-altitude oak rainforest into grasslands in the central valleys, and how exhausted the lateritic clays become after only a few harvests of *Ipomea batata* (sweet potato). She suspects that she has discovered a few previously unknown *Ipomea* cultivars.

The anthropologist has recorded some wonderful creation myths, and describes the people of this region as being patrilineal. He says that their lineages, clans, and phratries are organized on the basis of descent from males through their sons. Wives are drawn from other clans to form alliances, and provide connections for trade.

You and I blink and struggle to keep up with the jargon. We are slightly embarrassed by how little we actually saw on our first day, and also surprised by how differently each specialist experienced the landscape and its inhabitants.

This example is designed to illustrate something about experiential psychotherapy. When we, and our clients, turn our attention inward with an observant attitude, we become explorers of an inner landscape that is inhabited by a plentitude of unique and unnamed experiences. What we recognize there, and how we interpret it, depends largely on how we are trained. If we are trained to see the "categorical emotions and feelings," we will find anger, sadness, grief, anxiety, boredom, joy, enthusiasm, hope, hopelessness, disappointment, despair, confusion, and so on. These are interpretations of body sensations, associated with certain preparations for action and dispositions toward the world that are commonly acknowledged within Western culture.

There are other emotions, feelings, and feeling states that are combinations of these categorical emotions. For example, disappointment is a mixture of anger and sadness; despair is a mixture of sadness and hopelessness; impatience is a certain kind of restlessness, mixed with anxiety. Boredom is a lack of stimulation, with an edge of anger or irritation. These categorical emotions, and their derivatives, are relatively easy to name. We have nouns, readymade and right at hand, to name them with. They are the bedrock of experience in Western culture. There is plenty of agreement for their existence and for their properties: the sensations, dispositions, facial expressions, tones of voice, and so forth by which we identify them, providing we have an education in how to talk about the inner life. Unfortunately, in current Western culture we do not study our experience in much detail. Most individuals, including a surprising number of licensed therapists, psychiatrists, and psychologists, have not been trained to observe present moment inner experience.

Even fewer individuals come to us with knowledge of how to experience and name somatic sensations. Of these, there are also many that can be described as "categorical," including pain, tension, congestion, headache, pressure, nausea, and many others. These are body sensations—fairly common ones, that are also relatively easy to name.

We also have thoughts. The trick with thoughts is to stop identifying with them, so that we can begin to observe them. Most Westerners *live* in their thought worlds: their stories, interpretations, judgments, assessments, complaints, worries, obsessions, and so forth. They do not observe them— they believe and identify with them. For inner explorers, however, thoughts are like quicksand. The therapist must often throw clients a rope to help them out of their thoughts, so they can unblend from them, and describe them as worry, figuring out, fantasy, imagery, story, explanation, speculation, interpretation, and so forth.

Another kind of inner experience that we are relatively familiar with consists of memories. Memories occur to us in present moment experience. If they are explicit memories, they come with information about when they were acquired. There are other kinds of memories that we experience as emotional states, fragmentary images, and body sensations that we experience without that identifying information. They don't seem to be memories at all. They seem to be experience that is arising in present time, just like other real-time experiences.

The kinds of experiences we have discussed so far are recognized broadly by Western culture, and Western languages have names for them. Our culture also classifies them. They are classified as emotions (also called affects or feelings), body sensations, thoughts, images, and memories. For many experiential therapists, categorical experiences like these exhaust the entire domain of inner experience. And it is indeed possible to conduct therapy using the language of categorical experiences alone. It is no small accomplishment to become facile in using categorical language to describe one's inner life.

Returning to our expedition analogy, however, when we are limited to using nothing more than categorical language, it is as if we are taking only the geologist along on our expedition. We can find out a great deal about the landscape and its history by studying the rock and rock formations, but without the additional help of the biologist and the anthropologist, our account of the journey will certainly be limited, and will lack the richness made possible by having an interdisciplinary team. Furthermore, we know that there are other ways to observe our experience. Psychotherapists have been using other languages of description for many decades.

In his excellent book *The Mosaic Mind* (1995, p. 7) Schwartz cites Jung, Assagioli, Beahrs, Hillman, Johnson, Putman, Redfearn, Stone and Winkelman, and Watkins and Watkins as theorists and therapists who have recognized the multiplicity of the mind.[9] This list is by no means exhaustive. All of these authors described a more anthropomorphic way to experience the inner world. Who cannot identify the inner critic, who seems to have an autonomous existence in the psyche; the shaming voice, who tells us what fools we are when we embarrass ourselves, make silly mistakes, or eat things that are bad for us?

We have asked this question to thousands of people in workshops across the country, and have yet to find anyone who cannot identify a familiar inner critic who shows up like a personality in their psyche. Similarly, we can distinguish semiautonomous subpersonalities who are compulsive worriers;

---

[9] See Goulding and Schwartz, 1995, for bibliographic citations to the works alluded to here.

parts who show us worst-case scenarios that scare us half to death; caretaker parts who look after others; compulsive shopper parts; parts who like to do bad things; angry parts who go berserk when we are behind the wheel of a car; young and tender parts who carry the burden of unresolved and overwhelming pain, parts whom we would rather not attend to, because we are afraid that they will overwhelm us with their feelings; manager parts who steer our lives around surreptitiously to avoid our triggering those younger parts who live in the shadows of our awareness; and distracting parts who can create catastrophes to take our attention away from those young parts, when all else fails.

These anthropomorphic elements are there, if we look for them. They are conglomerates that include the categorical experiences, but they seem to be organized as subpersonalities, and they seem to have agendas, mainly intending to protect and sustain us, even though they are often acting on outdated knowledge. Schwartz calls them parts (1987, 1995); Ron Kurtz refers to them occasionally as "maids and butlers," and also writes and teaches techniques for "working with the child" (1990). They are also known as ego states (Watkins, 1978; Emmerson, 2003), subpersonalities (Rowan, 1990; Schwartz, 1987, 1995), and trance states (Wolinsky, 1991).

If we choose to experience our inner landscape as one that is inhabited, we can take along this "anthropological" (anthropomorphic) point of view. We will find that this approach has many uses, and we can keep our categorical experiences at the same time. The inclusion of this dimension of experience does not force us to abandon anything. It simply enriches the inner environment, and gives us an additional perspective on almost everything we encounter.

We can also include felt sense as another kind of experience that we may encounter on any inner journey. Unlike categorical experience, felt sense experience evades simple description and classification. Once we are trained to recognize it, however, we discover that it is present much of the time. Each of these ways of exploring inner experience gives us a different handle on the therapy process. While there are many other ways to experience and talk about the inner life, these perspectives have been found to be especially useful. One need not think of them as being opposed to or in conflict with each other. Surely, the contributions of the geologist, in our imaginary example, need not detract from those of the botanist or the anthropologist. Their different points of view and vocabularies are additive and complementary. They make for a richer, more informed perspective.

Merging Internal Family Systems with Hakomi

Mindfulness Centered Therapies began to depart from Hakomi as it is conventionally practiced when we started to integrate it with the work of Richard Schwartz, especially as we discovered the value of using "parts language," and seeing and helping our clients to see their inner experience as the interaction of a family of anthropomorphic "parts" (Cole, 2006). This is the perspective of the therapeutic method known as Internal Family Systems (IFS). In IFS therapy, "parts" are defined as internal experience construed as autonomous subpersonalities (Schwartz, 1997). Since we have trained with Schwartz, the founder of Internal Family Systems, we found it natural to use the language of parts (also sometimes called "parts language") with our Hakomi clients.

However, it is not necessary to use parts language with the adaptation presented here. In most of the client-therapist dialogues offered below, therapists can substitute phrases like, "Go inside and say to that *sadness*..." for "Go inside and say to that *sad part*..." In the former, we are addressing a feeling as if it were a part; in the latter, we are addressing a part to which we are attributing a feeling, and possibly other properties like body sensations, thoughts, and motivations. We favor the use of "parts language" because we think the use of the word and concept "parts" adds an increased capacity for separation between the client's awareness and his present moment experience. It is also more accurate with regard to how feelings and other internal experiences actually behave.

In addition, it is not necessary to think of this adaptation as a new kind of therapeutic alliance, from direct to indirect, or as a role shift, from therapist to coach. Rather, one can think of it simply as a different way to use language. In this regard, Ann Weiser Cornell (2005) has described a "presencing language" which has evolved out of her work with Focusing. This "presencing language" accomplishes much of what we are describing here, and does not depend on introducing the notion of parts or parts language. However, in her examples and her discussion she also uses the language of parts. Perhaps this reinforces our conclusion that, while it is not necessary to use the concept and language of parts, it is natural and almost unavoidable to do so when using experiential therapies that employ mindfulness.

CHAPTER 6

INTERNAL FAMILY
SYSTEMS (IFS)

The essential thing is to differentiate oneself from these unconscious contents by personifying them, and at the same time to bring them into relationship with consciousness. That is the technique for stripping them of their power. It is not too difficult to personify them, as they always possess a certain degree of autonomy, a separate identity of their own. Their autonomy is a most uncomfortable thing to reconcile oneself to, and yet the very fact that the unconscious presents itself in that way gives us the best means of handling it.

- Carl Jung, *Memories, Dreams and Reflections*

IN order to fully understand this merger of methods, it will be helpful to have some background information about Internal Family Systems. Internal Family Systems (IFS) is a psychotherapeutic model of the human psyche and a therapeutic method. It was developed by Richard C. Schwartz Ph.D. in the early nineteen-eighties. It recognizes the natural and healthy multiplicity of the personality and, like Hakomi; it brings to bear the tool of mindfulness as its primary instrument of discovery and healing. In our estimation, therefore, it stands with Hakomi as one of the truly significant innovations in experiential and mindfulness based psychotherapy, comparable to and in many ways, with all due respect, going beyond the humanistic, client-led foundations provided by Carl Rogers. Also, like Hakomi, it conforms well to the experiential traditions described by Greenberg, Watson, and Lietaer in their recent *Handbook of Experiential Psychotherapy* (1998).

One of the salient features of this method is its development history, insofar as it evolved out of its originator's clinical practice that includes decades of experience with "difficult to treat" conditions, such as bulimia in its many forms. This is the context in which Schwartz began to develop the IFS method. (Schwartz 1987, 1988, 1992). He took his lead from the language used by many of his clients to describe their inner experience (Schwartz, 1995). From this beginning, as a family therapist working primarily with eating disorders, he went on to work for additional years with survivors of extreme sexual abuse (Schwartz, 1993; Goulding and Schwartz, 1995). Schwartz has also applied the IFS method successfully to severe depression, anxiety disorders, disorders that bear the diagnostic labels of narcissism and borderline and other conditions that challenge to the utmost an individual's ability to be mindful. These behaviors also challenge therapists to remain mindful or "in Self" with regard to counter-transference. In the IFS model, counter-transference is described as a consequence of the client's protective parts inadvertently triggering the therapist's inner parts. This places a responsibility on therapists to do their own inner work. It also explicitly reframes difficult therapy to include the therapist, and it encourages us to perceive our work with challenging clients as an opportunity for further growth.

In other words, Schwartz created and refined the IFS method through working with clients whose conditions tend to make normal multiplicity more apparent and mindful awareness more difficult. The universal tendency to identify intensely with highly aroused internal parts as they struggle to manage extreme situations, emotions, conflicts, and memories becomes experientially obvious to anyone who can remember facing a life-threatening or otherwise urgent situation. It is almost impossible for an individual who is not disciplined by many years of meditative practice to keep calm or safely "distant" in an extreme emergency. Yet, keeping calm, or remaining somewhat distant (while not dissociating entirely), is essential to maintaining an observant self (Deikman, 1982).

This "back-story" of the development of Internal Family Systems accounts for its extraordinary repertoire of communication skills. These skills allow trained IFS therapists to help clients separate from and compassionately observe their inner experience in order to relieve unnecessary suffering, increase mindfulness or Self-leadership, and provide more response flexibility, and therefore more freedom. While Hakomi also includes methods for evoking mindfulness, we have found that the IFS approach can be very useful with clients who are extremely challenged either because they have very limited access to Self, are highly identified with extremely conflicted or emotionally flooded "parts," or both.

While Internal Family Systems Therapy is primarily a way to work with people, it is also a way of thinking about who we are. It posits a very specific model of the human being. This model represents the human personality—the ego, or self, with a small "s"—as an inner family of semi-autonomous subpersonalities. These subpersonalities are called "parts." Like individuals, these parts possess feelings, motivations, memories, and creative abilities. Also like individuals, much and sometimes all of their properties and activities exist outside of consciousness.

In addition to parts, the IFS model posits another essential aspect of the individual called the Self (Schwartz, 1990). According to the model, the Self is not a part and, unlike parts, it does not possess feelings or an agenda. This Self is recognizable in experience as that aspect of experience that seems to witness or observe experience. While it is not possible to directly experience the Self, it can be said that we are "in Self" or "identified with Self" or, as we say in IFS, "Self-led," when we are being mindful. In other words, the Self is the observer or witness aspect of conscious awareness. It is the perennial subject that makes an object of everything it observes. Some IFS practitioners compare it to the Atman; some call it the little Buddha that resides in each of us; others think of it in more secular terms, as conscious awareness, or the pure executive oversight of the orbito-frontal cortex.

It is not hard for Hakomi practitioners to understand this Self; since it can be equated with the state we call mindfulness. In Hakomi we talk about mindfulness as a "state of consciousness" (Kurtz, 1990, p. 27); in IFS we talk about being "in Self." We address something very much like this Self when we ask our client, "What does that feeling remember?" or, "What does that child need right now?" These questions are asking for information about a feeling or a part, but they are addressed to something other than that feeling or part. They are directed to a consciousness that can observe and report about the feeling or part. One can think of this Self that is addressed as being the client's "adult self," the "executive of pure consciousness," or simply as the Self. In Hakomi we recognize this Self in practice and do not explicitly define it, whereas in IFS it is explicitly defined and named with the word Self.

Regardless of how we name it, the experience of being in Self, or being mindful, has certain properties. Basically, to the degree that one is in Self, one is calm, clear, curious, compassionate, creative, courageous, and confident. Keeping these qualities in mind (the "c"-words are helpful), the IFS therapist can learn to judge when a client is identified with Self, just as a Hakomi therapist knows when a client is being mindful from observing nonverbal indicators. An IFS therapist can also often help a client to attain and sustain a Self-led state, just as a Hakomi therapist can often help a client to achieve and sustain mindfulness.

COMBINING HAKOMI AND IFS
AS AN ALTERNATIVE TECHNIQUE

When working in conventional Hakomi, we tend to work directly in relationship to the client's experience. For example, if the client is sad, we typically address that sadness directly, perhaps by naming it ("sad, huh") or with an acknowledgment ("I see how sad you are"). Or we might evoke a memory by asking, "What does that sadness remember?" Even when working with a part, such as a "child part," in Hakomi, the child is addressed directly, spoken to by the therapist, and comforted directly by the therapist or an assistant in a group or workshop (Kurtz, 1990).

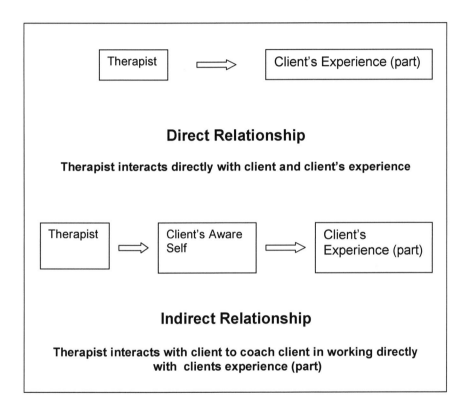

Figure 1. Direct and Indirect Relationship between Therapist and Client's Experience (part).

In conventional IFS therapy, on the other hand, the therapist usually assumes an indirect relationship toward the client's experience, where the experience is always considered to be the experience of a part (child, critic, approval-seeking part, and so on). Working from this indirect, coaching relationship, the therapist helps the client who is in a mindful (Self-led) state to interact directly with one of these internal parts. This is usually accomplished through a series of questions that guide the process and encourage the client to consult their experience.

The therapist might ask, "Can you get in touch with that sad part?" (thus setting up a relationship or connection between client and part); then, "How do you feel toward that part?" (thereby checking to see if the client is in Self, and therefore not identified with another, possibly polarized, critical, or hostile part); proceeding to, for example, "How is that part feeling right now?" or, "What does that part want to tell you about that?" (Note how these questions require that the client consult present moment experience.)

There is a very large repertoire of these coaching questions, along with some suggestions that the therapist uses to guide the client through the process, and help the client connect with and work with her internal parts. This method of coaching through asking questions is very explicit, and quite different from how a Hakomi therapist works. Hakomi therapists minimize the use of questions. Instead, they have a large repertoire of very evocative phrases that are extremely effective in creating an exquisite attunement between the therapist and client, while deepening, nourishing, and going for meaning with the client.

The essence of the fusion between Hakomi and IFS amounts to taking the idea of parts and the indirect coaching role from Internal Family Systems, and combining it with the evocative and implicit style of Hakomi. This fusion amounts to teaching the Self-led client to be a Hakomi therapist to his or her own internal parts. We call this fusion of methods *the alternative approach*, because it is an alternative way to use Hakomi, and it is also an alternative way to apply IFS. It is the Alpha and Omega, so to speak, of Mindfulness Centered Therapies, since it was our discovery of this possibility that led organically, through time and experimentation, to what is unique and most valuable about our method. It also opened the door to the addition of other mindfulness based methods, such as Focusing. We have even had sessions in which we have helped clients teach their internal parts to Focus, and we have also learned ways to transition between these different options without confusing our clients. Before discussing this, however, let us explore the alternative method as it is used in some typical therapy situations.

How we Introduce the Alternative Approach in a Hakomi Session

In our earlier outline of a typical Hakomi session (*Processes of Hakomi*, above), we described the form of a typical session as a sequence of sub-processes: tracking, testing/accessing, deepening/nourishing, going for meaning, integration. When we begin a session with Hakomi, we most often introduce the alternative technique in the deepening/nourishing phase of the session. We will therefore review and summarize this portion of a Hakomi session, and explain how this transition to the alternative is accomplished. We will then provide an idealized annotated transcript to illustrate the generalized explanation. For purposes of this demonstration, we will assume that the client has been introduced to the idea of parts and Self in a previous session. He knows what the therapist means by the term "parts," and has already had some experience working with a part in the past.

The main departure from conventional Hakomi is as follows: as the unconscious material emerges, instead of moving to work with it by directly acknowledging the experience, the therapist moves to have the client's adult consciousness, or Self, connect with the experience. The intention is to set up a relationship between the client's Self and the part. So long as the client is identified with her aware Self, the therapist supports the client in providing presence, acknowledgment, comfort, naming, and nourishment to the emergent part. If at any time this arrangement breaks down, the therapist shifts from indirect to direct relationship with the client. Once a stable Self-led state is reestablished, the therapist will step out of direct relationship to turn the direct connection over to the client. The intention is to maintain the client in the driver's seat, and to have the client engage directly with the part as much as possible. In order to do this, the therapist calls upon that powerful effect of language that allows us to connect ourselves to an event or experience, while distancing ourselves at the same time. This is illustrated further in the following example.

Setting Up the Indirect Relationship: An Ideal Annotated Transcript

The following idealized scenario illustrates how a therapist sets up this indirect relationship between therapist, client, and client's part. We start by working directly with the client. The steps in the example lead to a new relationship, in which the therapist is acting as a coach or trainer, while the client assumes the role of a Hakomi therapist to an internal part.

We enter this hypothetical session with a testing/accessing move. This is a conventional Hakomi technique, demonstrated in the DVD *Chapter 4 Nourishing Offerings*. In this move, the therapist first assists the client in becoming mindful, and then speaks a simple, nourishing phrase or statement. The therapist usually prefaces the statement by saying something like, "Just notice what happens when I say… [the nourishing phrase or statement]." These offerings often either evoke a reactive response, or they are "taken in" (the client experiences a pleasant or warm feeling of relief or wellbeing), or nothing happens. If nothing is evoked, we take it that the nourishment offered is not particularly relevant at that time, and move on.

In the example, the therapist offers the nourishing phrase, "You are safe here." and it evokes a reactive feeling of anxiety, accompanied by a tight feeling in the client's chest. Here is the transcript:

Therapist: *[Making a trial offering of nourishment to the client in mindfulness.]* Just notice what happens when I say, "*You are safe here.*" **Pause.** *[Therapist is attentive to nonverbal indicators as she waits and sees the client's chest compress.]*

Therapist: Something seems to change when you hear those words. *[Therapist notes the client's response.]*

Client: My chest got tight, and I felt afraid. *[This is where we shift away from Hakomi as usual, and introduce the alternative move.]*

Therapist: I wonder if you can think of the tightness in your chest and the feeling of fear as a part, a part of yourself that feels afraid, and feels its chest getting tight. *[This distances and unblends the client from the part, while affirming the connection between the client and the part.]*

Client: Yes, a part. Okay. *[The client knows what we mean, because of previous work.]*

Therapist: Now see if you can go inside; see if you can just be with that part, with its tight chest and its fear. Can you do that? **Pause.**

Therapist: It looks like you're being with that part now.

Client: Yes.

> *[Therapist uses nonverbal indications, empathy, intuition, client's tone of voice, and client's timing, checking to see if the connection is really there, and what kind of a connection it is. We especially want to be sure that it is mindful and nonjudgmental—in other words, compassionate.]*

Therapist: Good! Now, see if you can say to that part, silently, from your heart, in a sincere way... just say to it, "I see how scared you are."

> *[This is a Hakomi acknowledgment, and the therapist models the compassionate, empathetic connection through tone of voice and through facial expression, even if the client's eyes are closed. Similar acknowledgments are used in many other methods, including IFS and*

Focusing. Sometimes I completely avoid reference to words by saying,
"Send a silent message from your heart…"]

Pause.

Therapist: What happens for that part, when it feels your
presence and it hears you say that? [*Here the therapist is coaching the*
client on observing and reporting results.]

DISCUSSION OF INDIRECT INTERVENTION

This is the essence of the alternative intervention. It illustrates what a
therapist needs to do in order to reposition the client with regard to emerging
experience, so that the therapist is no longer interacting directly with the
(formerly) unconscious material or the "part," but instead supports the
client in making a "Hakomi-like" direct connection. While the move itself
is a simple one, there are important things happening in this interaction that
may escape notice.

First, when the therapist speaks the acknowledgment, in this case, "I
see how scared you are," there is the possibility of its having a powerful
direct effect, even though it sounds as if the therapist is merely giving
the client a suggestion. To fully realize this possibility, the therapist must
intend the nourishing phrase toward the subject's part. In the example,
while it seems as if the therapist is talking to the client's Self, the phrase is
actually intended toward the frightened part. The intonation of the phrase
is therefore very important. As we speak, we are also providing a model
for the client. Generally, the client will tend to imitate our delivery in every
respect. He will imitate what we say, how we say it, and where we are when
we offer it the first time. We are therefore not only modeling the intonation
and intention; we are demonstrating where the client should be when the
acknowledgment is offered. In other words, to imitate what we do, the
client must move into a mindful, compassionate, Self-led state, since it is

only from such a state that this kind of calm and attentive compassion can be mustered.

Secondly, it is important that the therapist pay attention to nonverbal signals during this process. With practice, a therapist can tell whether a client is in a mindful state or not, as the subject part emerges. We are trained to do this in Hakomi. If the part emerges with overwhelming emotions, the therapist must first calm the emerging part down before proceeding. This can be done in the usual direct manner, or the therapist can ask the client if he or she would like help in having the part pull its feelings back. I usually do this by asking, "Would you like some help in having that part pull its feelings back?"

If they say yes, I say, "Just ask that part to pull its feelings back, so that you can be with it and not be overwhelmed. Tell it that you can't be with it when its feelings are too strong." If the feelings are too strong for this, you may have to shift to direct Hakomi mode, supporting the client's spontaneous behavior and providing comforting emotional nourishment until the feeling calms down (Kurtz, 1990).

Third, it is good to fully appreciate the power of language when using this option. Any sentence used in direct address that contains a subject, verb, and object, has the rhetorical power to objectify a feeling, thought, sensation, or part. For example, if fear arises in the experience of a client, when the client names it as fear, that naming makes separation possible. Furthermore, when a client attributes the status of "part" to that fear, this act of attribution increases the sense of distance. It also reduces identification and promotes unblending. When we teach the client to say, "I see how scared you are..." this sentence automatically and powerfully creates the following conditions with regard to the frightened part: (1) "I am not you," (2) "I am witnessing (experiencing) you and your fear," (3) "I am connected (in relationship) with you."

In addition, by using a compassionate voice, the client also says "Through my empathy and compassion, I want to accept and support you." Seen from this perspective, a simple acknowledging sentence carries a very powerful rhetorical effect, and the more we appreciate this, and experience it, the better we can use it. When we teach this to clients, we are giving them "more than a fish"—we are truly "teaching them how to fish for themselves." We begin to do this by modeling it repeatedly in sessions with them. When they are ready, we can tell them what we are doing, and teach them refinements, so that they eventually can do this for themselves, without our presence.

Finally, the last question or request in this little sequence is deceptively important. In this move, the therapist asks the client, "What happens (what does this part do, what do you notice) when this part hears you say that?" Without this move, the repositioning is likely to fail. Anyone who has done supervision sessions with Ron Kurtz in the past few years will be familiar with his phrase, "Get the data!" In Hakomi, when we work directly with a client, we are trained to find out what happened after we have performed a testing or accessing move (Kurtz, 1990). In working indirectly, it is equally important that we train the client to do the same thing. "Getting the data" has a number of important benefits. It returns the client's attention back to the part after nourishment has been offered. If it is done with good timing, the client will return to the part in time to see the effect of contact and compassion. They will actually feel the part calming down, or they may feel the emotion shift to something else—for example, from anger to sadness or from sadness to grief, or from bitter to sweet sadness—when it is given recognition and comfort.

Furthermore, when they report their observations, they are restoring or reaffirming the Self's connection with the therapist. This move on their part affirms the full set of roles in play in this situation, and provides an opening for the therapist to suggest the next move. Last, but not least, it gives the therapist feedback that she can use to confirm or revise interpretations of nonverbal signals. If nothing has happened, then usually something has been left out: the connection is not solid, the client has been hijacked by an unfriendly or critical part, or the part that has been addressed does not trust the client's Self yet. This last possibility is fairly common, and will be discussed later in more detail.

If the client reports a shift in the part—even if that shift is simply from fear to mistrust—a great deal has been accomplished. If the part takes in the nourishment, then the emotion will usually calm down. In this case, I usually encourage the client to "Just stay with the part." I might say something like, "Just see if you can stay with that part, and experience what happens next." If mistrust is shown, I help the client work with the part's mistrust. For example, I might suggest, "Why don't you go back to that part, and reassure it. Just say, 'I can see that you don't trust me yet'... notice what happens when the part knows that it's okay to not fully trust you." If the mistrust does not move, I might have the client reassure the part with: "It's okay... I know it takes time to trust." This is a very potent intention, and often shifts a part's reluctance to trust within a few seconds.

Training the Client To Work With a Part: A New Skill Set

Once the indirect relationship has been established and can be sustained, a large repertoire of moves becomes both possible and profitable. One way to catalog the moves is by intention.

Being with experience, nonjudgmental witnessing, self study. This intention involves having the client witness a part's experience, or its memories of a specific incident or event. This includes feeling the feelings that come up during the process. Instead of telling the client about its feelings, a part will have the client feel them. As each feeling comes up, we help the client to acknowledge it, and see and report what happens. Occasionally I remind the client: "Oh, so now (he/she/name of part) is letting you know how it is feeling. It can't actually tell you how it feels with words, but it lets you know by letting you feel its feeling. See if you can just stay with its feelings. If they get too intense, you can let me know. I'll help you". "Just say, 'I see how scared you are.'".

Typical coaching:
"Say, 'I feel your sadness.'"
"Tell it to pull its feelings back a little, so you can be with them."
"Thank (him/her/the part) for showing you that.
"Find out if (he/she/the part) has anything more to show you."
"Ask that part, 'What else do you want me to feel or know right now? '"

Nourishment or affect regulation. This intention pertains to soothing the part's unregulated or painful feelings. Sometimes this means taking the part out of a very traumatic situation, having the client hold the part on their lap, speak to it, and so forth. Sometimes a pillow helps to give the client the felt sense of holding the part. Tiny baby parts can be held against the chest until they calm down. Parts with vacuous or empty feelings can be given a sip of warm milk (I keep a microwave handy). Child parts who have experienced colic often need lots of this kind of quiet comforting.

Typical coaching:
Have the client nourish the part physically, as described above.
Have the client acknowledge the feeling, in a compassionate voice and from a compassionate place:
"Say, 'I see how upset you are.'"
"Say, 'I know it hurts.'"
"Say, 'I won't leave you. I'll stay with you.'"
"Tell (the part), 'I understand you,' or 'I want to understand you.'"

Discovering core beliefs and decisions, insight, cognitive therapy. In Hakomi, we often focus on discovering what decisions were made as a part of surviving the crisis. Often the child decides, "I'll never trust like that again," or, "No one loves me," or, "There is something wrong with me." The client can work with this by (1) acknowledging the decision and validating it for the time it was made, (2) providing nourishment: "There's nothing wrong with you," or "You are okay just the way you are," (3) helping the part to understand what happened, (4) updating the part.

We do all of these things in Hakomi, and they have equivalents in IFS. We do them here as well, but instead of doing them directly; we model them and have the client do them with their part, just as if the part is their Hakomi client.

Typical coaching:
"Ask the part what it learned from all of that."
"Find out what decisions this part made."
"Maybe this part can tell you what it decided."
"Let's just stay in this calmness now, and see if someone shows up."
"Maybe some wisdom or truth, maybe some insight, will come to you out of this peace and silence."

Letting pain go (unburdening). Unburdening is a technical term from IFS Therapy. Once the witnessing is accomplished, we can suggest that the client ask the part if it is ready to let go of its pain. Often this will stimulate a whole new phase of working with the part at some earlier or later age, or working with some other emotion, or another aspect of the remembered situation. Eventually, the part will have nothing more to reveal, and it will be time to help it let go of the pain.

Typical coaching:
"Ask the part, 'Is there anything else to know before we move on?'"
"Ask the part if it's ready to let go of that now."
"Find out how the part would like to release that pain."

Working with the future. One of the nice IFS moves, after the pain is released, is to find out what qualities the part would like to have to replace the pain. It might be playfulness, or creativity, or more love or nourishment (more touch, more comfort, more sleep). Once the desired replacement is named, the therapist can help the client, while still in the indirect relationship, to create a little guided imagery ritual to implant the idea of that quality flowing into the part, into the space that is left when it gives up the pain.

Typical coaching:
"Now that its pain is gone, what would the part wish to have instead?"
"See if this part would like to have something to carry in place of the pain."

Trying new behaviors (response flexibility). Sometimes interaction with the part is around some new skill, such as asking for what you want, or saying no. I usually leave this to the end, and do some work on it directly with the client. This is a Hakomi move, and it is one that Ron Kurtz demonstrates in many of his videotaped sessions.

Embodying the part. A good way to finish is to have the client find, in their experience of themselves, or in their body, a place for this part to stay, and to invite the part to stay there. It is also good to suggest that we will check in with that part in the next session, to be sure that it is still okay. We can also instruct them on staying in touch with this part during the week by, for instance, finding a picture of themselves at this age, or something they made at school, and placing it on a dresser top, or journaling to or about this part. This is especially important when abandonment is part of the part's issue.

EXAMPLE 2: TRANSCRIPT OF A SEQUENCE FROM AN ACTUAL SESSION

It may be useful to present a second example to further illustrate the application of this technique. The following transcript is rendered from memory, but I believe that it is sufficiently accurate to serve as an example of an actual session. In this scenario, the therapist and client have worked previously for three sessions, and the client is acquainted with parts language, so it is not necessary for the therapist to explain what a part is when the word is introduced. We might imagine that the client has just become aware of some sadness, and has mentioned it to the therapist as the dialogue begins.

Client: Yes, I'm feeling some sadness.

Therapist: Okay. Good. *[Sympathetically]* I see you're feeling sad. Are you okay with that?

Client: Yeah... *[pause, tears]* I'm okay.

Therapist: Okay. So just see if you can stay in connection with that sad part. Let's think of it as a part. A part of yourself, one that's feeling sad. Is that okay?

Pause.

Client: Yeah, okay.

Therapist: Fine. So... how are you feeling right now toward that sad part? What is your feeling or your attitude toward it? *[Evocatively.]*

Client: Well, I'd kind of like it to go away. I don't like to feel sad.

Therapist: Fine. I see. We could say that there's a part around that doesn't like the sad part... doesn't like to feel its sadness. You're noticing that part right now, is that so?

Client: Yeah. Doesn't want to feel sad all day.

Therapist: I wonder if you could let this part know... just quietly, inside... that you're okay now, and you would like it to stand back so you can just be with the sad part and offer it some comfort. Tell it we just want to make the sad part feel better. Is it willing to step back and just watch for a while as we do that?

[This is an IFS move, usually unnecessary in conventional Hakomi, but it is handy and important in this technique. We must be sure that

the client is in Self, and not in some other part, when working with
the subject part.]

Client: Yes. It can do that.

Therapist: Good. Why don't you thank it for doing that… and let's return to the sad part now. Can you reconnect with the sad part now? Is it still there?

Client: Yes. It's here. *[Eyes tear up a bit.] [Nonverbally, the client seems to be accepting the sad part.]*

Therapist: Good. Now, with that other part standing back, and as you connect with this sad part in a compassionate way, from your heart maybe, just go inside… to this sad part… and say to it, "I see how sad you are." *[In saying this acknowledgment, the therapist models a very warm, gentle, and compassionate voice.]*

Pause.

Therapist: What happens to the sad part, when it senses your presence, and hears you saying those words? *[Asks this question in an evocative manner.]*

Client: It's calmer now. Feels better.

Therapist: Fine. You could just say to that part… you could just say, "I see that you are calming down now." *[The tone of voice models talking sympathetically to a child part. Then we ask for a report.]* What happens when you say that, quietly… inside… to that part?

Client: It calms down more, and there is a warm feeling… feels better.

Therapist: Good. It seems like just being present with this part is comforting.

Pause.

Therapist: Fine. Just see if you can stay with the part. It might want to tell us something about its sadness. Or maybe it has other feelings, or a story, maybe even a memory that it would like you to know about.

Client: Father left, and my mother was crying.

Therapist: I think the part is showing you a memory. How old is the part now?

At this point, we are moving into the witnessing phase. The therapist will simply sustain the indirect relationship while the client witnesses the multisensory memory that has been evoked, offering nourishment as needed, and keeping any interfering, critical, judgmental, or worried manager parts at bay, by assuring them that we are not going to empower or provoke the feeling parts, but that we are going to take care of them, so that they will feel better.

DISCUSSION OF EXAMPLE 2

This sequence demonstrates the technique more fully than the first example. It contains all the necessary steps. It also illustrates some points taken from IFS that are important to the method. For example, in Hakomi, we track mindfulness very closely since we realize that bringing mindfulness to unregulated feelings has a soothing and healing effect. We use our heightened awareness of nonverbal signals to do that. Tracking and contact statements also help us to keep the client in present time, with present experience. This is in keeping with the implicit nature of Hakomi work. When we work with clients in the indirect relationship, however, we must be more explicit. We can still use our nonverbal skills to check out what the client says, but it is sometimes a good idea to explicitly ask the client how he or she feels about a subject part.

In IFS, and in this alternative Hakomi method, the initial checking out is done with a direct question: "How do you feel toward that sad part right now?" or, "What is your attitude toward this part right now?" This is preferable to asking, "What do you think…?" since that question invites involvement from intellectual, problem-solving, fixing, and figuring-out parts. If a hostile or a distracting part does emerge, useful moves are (1) being with the intervening part, (2) acknowledging its feelings, giving it reassurance, (3) telling it that it can stand by and watch, (4) assuring it that it can interrupt if it doesn't like what we are doing. If a part won't step back, then it is a good idea to work with it. Just shift the client's attention to the new part, while asking the original subject part to wait. As Ann Weiser Cornell (2005) has so elegantly pointed out, every part is potentially useful to the process. It is good to find out what distracting parts are concerned about, and to have the client listen to and respect their concerns.

If nothing has happened to a part after the client has acknowledged its feelings, if the feelings don't calm down or shift, or if they intensify, it is a good idea to check to see if there is a critical, worried, or hostile part around. Exile parts that carry the bulk of our unresolved feelings are often very sensitive to internal managers, and will not trust the therapist or the client until one or the other, or both, demonstrate their commitment to defend and protect the young, often sensitive part.

We should also be aware of highly sympathetic parts. There is a big difference between compassion and smothering sympathy or self-pity. If a client is feeling sorry for a part, and I suspect that there is a smothering manager around, I usually ask the part that feels sorry to step back. This can be a very effective way to deal with dysfunctional self-pity that keeps clients stuck in feelings and systems of victim-hood. The therapist, however, must be careful not to be insulting or disrespectful to the sympathetic part as we work to tone it down, and to show it that it can take care of the part more effectively by facilitating the connection between the part and the client's Self.

While I have used some IFS language to explain this, the Hakomi therapist does not need to look far to find a good language for discussion. Self can be equated with the client's state of mindfulness or loving presence. A critical part is just a critical voice. Being self-sympathetic is not being mindful, and usually leads to the postures of victimhood (victim, persecutor, rescuer). Victimhood (also called the rescue cycle) is a system, and in Hakomi training we learn how to help a client jump out of it by naming it. IFS therapists usually think of this system as the behavior of a certain kind of manager part, or the result of cooperation between three manager parts, or even three sub-parts of a single part, working together.

RETURNING TO THE DIRECT
OR CONVENTIONAL HAKOMI MODE

It is possible to return from the indirect mode to the direct mode at any time without confusing the client. The important thing is to honor the shift by carefully stepping the client through it each time it happens. If the therapist is not careful and explicit in marking the shift, the client becomes confused, and this interferes with the session and with the future use of the method with this client.

To make the shift from the indirect mode to the conventional Hakomi direct mode, the therapist asks the client whether it would be okay to talk to the client's part directly. If the client consents (and I have never had a client say no to this request), the therapist instructs the client to stand by and observe what happens. It is important that the client observe from a mindful, nonjudgmental space, and the therapist can give whatever coaching is necessary to attain and sustain mindfulness.

Once a client gives the therapist permission to go ahead and talk to a part, she is placing the therapist in the direct mode. The therapist proceeds to do what conventional Hakomi therapists do when they set up mindfulness. When the client is observing mindfully, the therapist says to the client, "Notice what happens when I say (or when I ask this part) 'What do you remember?' or, using an acknowledgment, 'I see how frightened and scared you are,' or, '…I see how disappointed you are.'"

Once in the direct mode, the therapist can reenter the indirect mode, with the same moves we used previously. Just instruct the client to connect with the part, to be with the part's feelings, to acknowledge those feelings, and then to find out what happens.

Conclusions about Hakomi
and Internal Family Systems

After four years of working with this method in private practice, we recommend it, either as an addition to conventional Hakomi, or as a way to combine Hakomi and IFS into a single set of skills that can be joined seamlessly into an integrated approach. In the foregoing examples, we have presented the essential moves, with the expectation that additional elaborations will be forthcoming. The essential elements are very simple, and are set forth below in review:

1. Make the parts language available to a client, and teach the client to label emergent experiences as parts. This should be done before introducing this process. We usually do this in the first session or two.
2. When you are ready to introduce this technique, begin by introducing parts language into the session, to distance the client from an emergent part. This helps the client sustain a mindful (or Self-led) state, while remaining connected with a potentially overwhelming part.
3. Model acknowledgment for the client, and have the client acknowledge the part's feeling, attitude, or situation.
4. Support the client in observing the part after the acknowledgment, and making a report on what happens.
5. Support the client in being a compassionate observer, and support him in self study. Help him to witness the part, its feelings, and its story.
6. Direct the client in effective ways of working with estranged parts to provide attuned presence, connection, emotional nourishment, and affect regulation, along with an opportunity for cognitive

rethinking and restatement of the part's interpretations, decisions, and conclusions.

The use of the indirect method in Hakomi multiplies the repertoire of moves available to therapists who have studied Hakomi and IFS. For example, conventional IFS therapy includes a number of moves that are used to distance the Self from parts that the client perceives as dangerous, terrifying, or otherwise extreme and hard to be with, or hard to separate or unblend from.

Many of the Hakomi methods are adapted to a group situation, where helpers are available to take over the work of parts, voices, or physical behaviors. Ron Kurtz has recommended this, but we find that it is usually not practical in private practice, since many clients cannot afford to pay for more than one therapist, and unpaid assistants and trainees are not always available. One can ask clients to bring in friends, but this comes with complications, for example, issues of trust, confidentiality, and ethical/legal complications. Given these considerations, we have resorted to this indirect method frequently, and it is our preferred method of working. Over time, the indirect method teaches clients how to work with their own parts. This does not happen right away, but after anywhere from six to twelve sessions, clients will often spontaneously recount an experience in which they employed it, without outside support, to handle an upsetting situation. It is an extremely gratifying moment, and one that tells us that we are getting our job done.

While we have taught this method to colleagues, and find that Hakomi therapists can learn it without difficulty, we have not taught it in trainings. It may be better to offer trainings in these skills to therapists who are certified in Hakomi, and want to explore using Hakomi with other methods. Similarly, it can be taught to IFS therapists, who are already familiar with the indirect relationship. They would learn a new set of Hakomi skills, thereby adding very potent refinements to their existing skill set. For those new to both Hakomi and IFS, either entry point is possible. Both forms of training are available throughout the United States, and Hakomi training is also offered in Europe, Japan, Australia, New Zealand, Mexico, Argentinam and Canada.

We have found that Hakomi can be combined not only with IFS and Focusing, but even with cognitive therapy. Hakomi acknowledges the existence of child parts, or aspects of the personality that emerge in therapy as revivified child subpersonalities. These child parts often express themselves with child-like facial expressions, body language, words, verbal inflections, and voices. These expressions are appropriate to memory fragments that emerge simultaneously. As we have already mentioned, Hakomi therapists are trained to interact directly with these child parts: talking to them in age-appropriate vocabularies, and using age-appropriate body language and facial gestures to attune to and engage with them; finding out what happened to them; and sometimes providing missing nourishment or comfort. These child parts display thought patterns appropriate to their age. These almost always include many of the thought distortions described by Burns (generalization, black and white thinking, exaggeration, minimization, personalization, and so forth).

In IFS, working with young parts is a major objective in most sessions. When a client connects with and listens to a young part, we have no doubt that the part is authentic, because the same consistency in voicing and body language can be observed, along with the same "thought distortions." This tells us something very important: that many, if not all, of the thought distortions that cognitive therapists work with can be viewed as the thoughts and verbalizations of young parts with whom the client unconsciously identifies or blends.

When, in a moment of despair, we hear our clients (or ourselves, for that matter) say or think thoughts like, "Nobody loves me," "I never get what I want," or, "She hates me," it is very likely that, in that moment, one is identified with a child part that carries a memory of a similar situation, with associated feelings of despair. The form of a thought is cast with a stamp of the age and developmental period of its thinker. The child part who thinks in generalities, exaggerations, or personalizations, might share the psyche with other, "older" parts who have more mature perspectives, but in the moment of thinking that distorted thought, we are identified with the younger part. Many people are "blended" (unconsciously identified) with one or another young part a good share of the time. Others individuals have developed more dominant adult "manager parts" with whom they are more often identified. Unless one is being mindful or in Self most of the time—and that is a very tall order—we live the ages and agendas of our parts during most of our waking hours.

It is therefore not a large leap from Mindfulness Centered Therapies, as it is presently constituted, to the notion that the distortions of thinking and speaking that cognitive therapists correct and revise (Burns, 1980, 1990) are the thoughts and utterances of young parts. There is therefore no reason to maintain a polemical barrier between these experiential methods and the cognitive approaches. In fact, there are some very good reasons to maintain openness between them, insofar as this openness allows us to share our resources with one another, even as we continue to debate and discuss our theoretical differences.

CHAPTER 7

FOCUSING: A MINDFULNESS BASED APPROACH

Like Hakomi and Internal Family Systems, Focusing is a form of assisted self-study[10] in which mindfulness plays an essential role. Foscusing and felt sense experience were discovered by Eugene T. Gendlin a distinguished American philosopher and psychologist. Gendlin received his Ph.D. in philosophy from the University of Chicago and taught there from 1963 to 1995. His philosophical work is concerned with the relationship between logic and experience, especially a special kind of intricate and implicit experience that he discovered and named "felt sense".

Gendlin has been honored three times by the American Psychological Association for his development of Experiential Psychotherapy. He was a founder and editor for many years of the Association's Clinical Division Journal, Psychotherapy: Theory, Research and Practice. His book Focusing has sold over half a million copies and has appeared in seventeen languages. He has written over three hundred and fifteen books and articles including *Focusing* (1978) *Let Your Body Interpret Your Dreams* (1986) and *Focusing-Oriented Psychotherapy* (1996).

Gendlin's contributions have unfolded on at least four parallel lines of investigation and application; (1) philosophical research and publication; (2) a comprehensive approach to experiential psychotherapy based on a synthesis of Focusing and client-centered experiential psychotherapy; (3) a self help

---

[10] "Self-Study" is a term used by Ron Kurtz to describe Hakomi in Hakomi workshops and in personal communication. I have been unable to find a published citation.

program that includes teaching Focusing to others, and; (4) a relatively new development which synthesizes philosophical and psychological research into a endeavor named "Thinking At the Edge" (TAE).

For purposes of describing Mindfulness Centered Therapy and how we use Focusing we shall confine ourselves to the original Focusing method as it is describe in Gendlin's 1978 book entitled *Focusing*. Another excellent resource is Ann Weiser Cornell's book entitled The *Power of Focusing* (1996). The essence of this process is described in the following section. It is concerned with identifying felt sense experience and facilitating a "shift" by creating or discovering a precise name or "handle". This name is a word, phrase, image or gesture that describes, expresses, or otherwise makes explicit the implicit intricacy and totality of a felt sense experience. However, it is important to keep in mind that there is a much richer, more comprehensive Focusing method that is described in *Focusing-Oriented Psychotherapy*. It would perhaps be more accurate to say "Focusing-Oriented Psychotherapies" since there are many methods and styles that combine Focusing *per se* with different therapeutic approaches. Focusing Oriented Therapies are not therapies that include brief bits of Focusing instruction. Rather they are means for "letting that which arises from the Focusing depths within a person define the therapist's activity, the relationship and process of the client." (Gendlin, 1996 p. 304)

To accomplish that intention by fully integrating it with Hakomi principles and the Internal Family System model of Self and parts, is an ambitious project and beyond the scope of our present effort. Nevertheless, we continue to discover new ways of using Focusing as a part of the approach we call Mindfulness Centered Therapies.

The Focusing Process

As we mentioned above, in his development of Focusing, Eugene Gendlin made two important discoveries, and combined them into a single therapeutic process. One was his discovery of felt sense experience; the other was that the ability of a client to sense and name experience was a primary factor in producing positive outcomes in therapy. While Gendlin and his research colleagues first realized this in clinical research, it has recently been confirmed by UCLA psychologists Matthew Lieberman and David Creswell, using thirty test subjects examined with magnetic resonance imaging brain scan technology while performing an experimental protocol having to do with naming their experience. While a peer-reviewed publication is forthcoming (in *Psychosomatic Medicine*), preliminary releases report that when subjects named their negative present moment experience accurately during MRI observations, the right ventrolateral prefrontal cortex region of the brain (an area associated with thinking in words about emotional experience) became more active, while activity in the amygdala (a brain region involved in emotional processing) subsided, or "was calmed." When the subject was not naming their experience, however, even though they were naming the trigger events and circumstances surrounding that experience accurately, these inversely correlated changes in activity did not occur (Wenner, 2007).

This neuropsychological research confirms what Gendlin and other therapists who use Focusing have known for years, based on the very remarkable shifts that occur in psycho-emotional states when Focusing clients name felt sense experience. There is a very clear example of this in the DVD (see Chapter XIV). To be present in an interaction when such a release occurs for a client is far more than a visual experience for the therapist. It is something a therapist sees and feels viscerally: one knows something important has happened, and one knows it deeply. It alters the quality of the space in the room. It is as if a weight or pressure that one didn't know was there has miraculously lifted.

It is unfortunate that the above-mentioned MRI study—like other studies, and (in our opinion) much of the theory and research addressing felt sense experience that psychologists and psychotherapists, with the exception of Gendlin and trained Focusing therapists, have produced—

fails to sufficiently differentiate felt sense experience from other kinds of experience, and specifically from the categorical experiences described above. The differences between these two types of experiences are substantial, and we therefore feel that it is especially important to exercise rigor when combining Focusing with other methods based on mindfulness.

The categorical experiences that we are most concerned with in Hakomi, IFS, and many other experiential psychotherapies are basically "reactivated." For example, an incident occurs or a situation arises in the present that "triggers" a memory of a past event. That past event may exist as an implicit memory and it may also have some explicit components. A client may or may not remember the wounding incident. However, in the course of our work together new explicit and implicit elements are likely to emerge as present moment experience. This emergent material often includes body sensations, psycho-emotional states, motor reactions, and decisions that were made about the self and or the world.

For example, whenever our client is faced with a public speaking situation, she feels "slightly nauseated, her face burns, and she feels anxiety accompanied by a restricted feeling in her chest." This has happened "for as long as she can remember." When she thinks about or anticipates speaking to an audience, her experience alters almost immediately. The psychosomatic symptoms of this state change intrude upon her previous, more comfortable and "normal" psycho-emotional state. At first, she is conscious of the nausea and flushed cheeks. She does not become conscious of her anxiety or the tightness in her chest until we help her to slow down, and ask her to pay more mindful attention to her body. Nevertheless, these feelings are easy to name, once they are attended to, and they are clearly reactive; having noticed them once, she will be aware of them whenever this memory is triggered.

In considering this kind of experience, we immediately identify its reactive quality as a reactivated or triggered past experience. Fritz Perls would call it "unfinished business"; a psychoanalyst might label her experience as symptoms of trauma or hysteria. The client does not need to sit in silence, sensing inwardly, to have this experience emerge, as one does in the process of Focusing. Indeed, the client has brought it to us because at least some parts of it intrude on her normal state without her deliberate intention, in spite of attempts to manage it away (dismissing, distracting, denying, and so forth).

In addition, when we work with it, using accessing processes from Hakomi (contact, acknowledgment, asking for a memory) or IFS (naming it as a part, placing primary attention on it, creating a connection or relationship with it); we usually discover a memory of an early experience when something similar happened. One possible scenario would be that our client was giving a talk in class and lost her train of thought. She became tongue-tied. The children in her fifth-grade class laughed at her, and the teacher unfairly scolded her for not being prepared. It was an overwhelming experience, a traumatic embarrassment, and no one stepped in to provide the attention and comfort that would have been required to help her learn how to self-comfort or otherwise regulate this overwhelming state.

Presumably, portions of this experience were recorded in one or more neural networks, and these sensory networks are likely to trigger autonomic and motor components in other areas of the brain that control defenses and behaviors having to do with avoiding similar situations. What we see here is reaction combined with association, so that anything that even remotely resembles the initial wounding is likely to become a trigger. This experience is clearly past-based, and reactive; it is not necessarily subtle, and once it is brought into awareness, it is not ineffable. That is, while some clients find it difficult to talk about their inner experience, this kind of experience is not particularly hard to name. The names already exist in common parlance: "nausea," "anxiety," "tight chest," "flushed face," and so on.

In felt sense experience, we see very different properties. First and foremost, in pure felt sense experience, we do not see a reactive quality. This non-reactive aspect of felt sense experience is concretely recognized in the Focusing method. In the original Focusing method, the focuser sits quietly with the subject of the session in mind, and patiently scans the trunk of his or her body for the emergence of a rather indistinct and subtle feeling. Clearly, there is a striking contrast between this kind of experience, which requires a deliberate calling forth, and a reactivated experience, which intrudes spontaneously and intrusively on an existing psycho-emotional state. Secondly, when working with a pure felt sense experience, while we may experience some memories, these are usually fleeting and do not emerge with the force and vividness of a reactivated memory, and they do not usually explain or shift the felt sense.

Felt sense experiences may be related to past events, but they do not seem to be reactivations of past events, and they are not directly caused by "unfinished business" or past traumas. In addition, felt sense experience is far harder to name. In fact, the names that shift the experience are often not conventional names for various kinds of feelings and emotions. They are almost always unconventional metaphors, exclamations, expressions, images, gestures, or combinations of any or all of these. Naming a felt sense experience is an entirely different sort of speech act from recognizing an inner quality of experience, and identifying it with a conventional label chosen from a preexisting lexicon. Naming a felt sense experience is a creative act of symbolization, comparable to producing a poem, sculpture, or painting. Furthermore, in Focusing, the intended tension release, or shift in psycho-emotional state, takes place through the client's achievement of finding an apt name or symbol for the felt sense. This is different from how we usually facilitate change or transformation in the process of working through a reactivated past experience in Mindfulness Centered Therapies.

An example: Using Focusing (*PER SE*) With Felt Sense Experience

In order to illustrate the Focusing process, we will use the following example, taken almost verbatim from DVD Chapter 15. Since the video clip is available and there is further commentary on this DVD chapter in

Part 2, I have not included observations about nonverbal indicators and timing, since this information is very clearly documented in the video clip.

The Focusing process is usually thought of as a series of steps. There are different ways to parse the steps, and I have broken it down here in a way that follows Gendlin's original formulation of the process.

1. **Choosing a subject.** In Mindfulness Centered Therapy this is not always done as deliberately as in the example. The subject often comes up in the course of tracking or just listening to the client.

2. **Focusing attention on the subject,** while mindfully waiting for the felt sense to emerge. Once the subject is selected the therapist helps the client feel the felt sense.

3. **Listening for a handle.** The next step is to find a word or phrase by listening to the felt sense, and letting it speak for itself, as opposed to having the client's mind speak for it. This word or phrase is called a "handle". The handle functions as a name for the felt sense experience. It may be a noun, a verb, a metaphor, an expression, or even a gesture or image.

4. **Checking the word or phrase with the feeling to see if there is a match.** Once a potential "handle" is found, it is checked with the experience. This checking is not an intellectual process. The client is supported in holding the handle up to the feeling, so to speak, and checking to see if a shift in present moment felt sense or in present moment experiential state occurs. A pronounced shift in the felt sense or experience will indicate that there is a match. The therapist supports the checking process by feeding back the "handle" to the client, while the client juxtaposes the handle with the felt sense.

5. **Recognizing a shift.** The shift can be an intensification of the felt sense, a full or partial attenuation, or a change in quality. A complete shift is usually accompanied by a marked sense of relief, sometimes subtle, more often quite profound.

6. **Resonating with the shift.** After a shift, the therapist assists the client in embodying and enjoying the relief, and may also assist in articulating insights that accompany the shift. There is no interpretation or leading by the therapist at this point.

When there is no shift, the therapist helps the client try again by looking for another handle. If the shift is incomplete, or the felt sense transforms but is still there, the therapist asks the client if they would like to try another round.

In the transcript which follows, the therapist is distracted, and does not hear the client's handle correctly when it is first offered. We have not edited this out because it serves to demonstrate the importance of feeding back the handle verbatim. The process is not entirely rational, in this sense: a synonym or approximation will usually not produce a satisfying shift. This is very well documented in the DVD clip, and we have tried to capture it in the following transcript as well.

Transcript of a Focusing Session

Therapist: So let's just take a few moments, and kind of settle in and center… just letting go of all attempts to control. Just notice what are some of the things that are in your life right now that have energy of any kind… things that you're anticipating, concerned about, or looking forward to. If you'd like, you can name them out loud, if that works, or you can name them to yourself.

> **Client: Okay.** A couple things that came to mind are… I'm going next Wednesday to see my mom, you know my dad has Alzheimer's, and I was just talking to her on the way up to your office, and I'm anticipating that visit.
> **Therapist:** Visiting your mother.

Client: Mm-hmm.

Therapist: And there's energy there.

Client: Yeah, there's energy there. In a positive way. But just wanting to be all I can be when I'm there, since I can't be there all the time. And, so, that came up. Work came up for me. I'm doing some transitioning at work, so work came up. Seeing Amy and the kids, my grandkids, some things came up for that. And… what I want to do in my future. I mean, I'm kind of looking at transitioning some different things and… it's a big world. So, those are the things that kind of popped up.

Therapist: Great, so about four major things, that's great. Is there one of those four that you're attracted to, to work with? Or you'd like to work with?

Client: How about if we work with my mom.

Therapist: So, can you go back into your radar screen, and take the other three things and set them aside for the time being? Just for the time being, the next fifteen or twenty minutes.

Client: Okay.

Therapist: Just allow your attention to go to one thing, your visit to your mother. Just allow that to be the center of your attention. And as you do that, see if you can expand your awareness to include the feelings of your body. Notice if your body carries this concern or this subject in some way. It's kind of like watching a Polaroid film develop. It takes a little time. It doesn't have to be distinct, it can be fuzzy.

Client: It feels like there's a strain, it sounds odd, but just kind of a strain going all the way through my neck and all the way down.

Therapist: So you notice a feeling of strain, something that has the word strain in it, it goes down across your body. Would you like to put your attention on that, and give it a little time? Standing back a little from it, observing it, seeing if you can stay friendly to it.

Pause.

Therapist: You might notice if there's an aura of feeling around it or with it.

Pause.

Therapist: What we're going to do now is go to the next step, and I'll help you with that. Is that okay?

Client: Yeah.

Therapist: So we're going to put our attention back on that feeling that comes as you're thinking about visiting your mother. Just see if you can find a word, or a phrase, or a metaphor, or even an image that either describes the quality of this feeling, or expresses this feeling. Just listen to the feeling for a word or a phrase. Taking your time...

Client: The feeling now is more like a choker. And... the word is... "have to be very attentive."

> *[At this point, the therapist makes a mistake. Distracted by the camera equipment, he misses the client's exact phrase, "have to be very attentive," and substitutes, "I have to be really careful." He feeds this inaccurate phrase back, and has the client use it to check against the feeling.]*

Therapist: We'll think of this as a handle for the feeling. Just go in and check it. Compare the word, the phrase, "I have to be really careful," with this feeling at the base of your neck, the top of your chest. Comparing them, sort of the way a carpenter would check a joint, a piece of wood... in a very palpable way. And notice what happens to the feeling when you do that.

Client: It feels... it kind of shifts. It's like, yeah, you got it.

Therapist: Is there some relief with that shift?

Client: Yeah, it feels like... it's doesn't feel like it's as heavy right here.

Therapist: Okay, good. So see if you can just resonate with that shift. See if you can take in the relief. Let yourself have the relief. Take it in with your body.

Pause.

Therapist: It looks like it feels good.

Client: It feels better because I know what it is now.

> *[The nonverbal signs and the client's language, especially the word "because," tips the therapist off to a hunch that this shift is not complete, not totally satisfying. "Because" in this context usually indicates that the client is speculating, or doing something more mental than just sensing and listening. He therefore redirects the client back to the feeling for another round of Focusing. At this point, he does not realize that he made a mistake with the feedback.]*

Therapist: Is there any of the feeling left, has it moved… do you have a sense of it? When you think of the visit to your mother, how does that feel for you now?

Client: I guess I feel a little bit relieved, because it's clearer to me. I couldn't figure out why, because I love going to see her, but there's this tension also. So I couldn't figure that out.

> *[Here the speculation becomes more obvious. Usually, when a felt sense is resolved there is no need for speculation or figuring out, there is just a quality of knowing, what one might call "natural knowing."]*

Therapist: Would you like to work more with this, or does it seem like a stopping point for it?

Client: What comes to me is, it's like a need to pay attention. It's like, okay… that's what all this is about, not to miss anything.

Therapist: You want to try that one, with what's left?

Client: Okay.

Therapist: If you see the other feelings in your body that have to do with this, we could try that as a handle, and see if it responds to the phrase, "You need to pay attention."

Client: Yeah that's it. I got a big shift.

Therapist: Just take that in. That's good, that's great. Just let your body have the relief. Just resonate with it.

Client: It feels clearer, like I have more space. Without the tension.

> *[Notice the lack of speculation or analysis. It's just clear now. There is more space.]*

Therapist: Yeah, I can see it.

Client: I appreciate that, because I'm leaving Wednesday, and I hadn't had time to figure out what was going on with that.

Therapist: So this looks like a stopping point then.

Client: Yeah, I feel relieved.

In concluding, we would like to underscore the fact that, while a pronounced change of state occurred, there was no need to reference any previous psychological history or memory in order to bring about a very satisfying shift into relief, and dissolution of the felt sense. Having worked with this method for many years, we have found this to be generally true of felt sense experience. Sometimes, but not always, in working on our own issues with Focusing, we have noticed a few memories spontaneously flashing by as the shift occurs, and have had clients report a similar memory stream that happens simultaneously, or just following the shift. However, it is emphatically not the case that these memories linger, or need to be worked with or worked through in order to produce the shift.[11]

Reactivated Emotions and Felt Sense Experience

In contrast to Focusing *per se*, other experiential methods bring about

---

[11] This may be because we usually work through reactivated memory based experience first before we move to Focusing. When this not done, and there are many examples in Focusing-oriented psychotherapy transcripts and videos, the quality of the memory material is more sustained and substantial. (Gendlin:1996).

emotional releases and shifts in psycho-emotional states through working with reactivated experiences that occur as a part of a process of exploring memories of an initial wounding. Their methodology is organized by their attention to categorical emotions not felt sense. It is their "working-through processes" that allow for satisfactory resolution and deactivation of emotional pain or discomfort, and the stereotypical or patterned behavioral responses associated with the injury. We may therefore summarize the major differences as in the table that follows:

Reactivated (Categorical) Experience	Felt sense Experience
Reactive and intrusive	Not reactive, not intrusive
Caused and resolved by past experience. The past is central	Not caused by or resolved by past experience; the past is contextual
Conventionally named; effable	Creatively named; ineffable
Shifted by working through	Shifted by naming

Table 1. Comparing reactivated and felt sense experience. This table is summarized and adapted from *Table 6.1* entitled *Emotion VS Felt Sense* in Gendlin (1996, p. 60-61).

In drawing this contrast, we must take care to add that while felt sense experience and reactive experience are markedly different in character, they do not always occur in their pure states. It is not unusual for the totality of our present moment experience to exist as a mixture or blend of categorical and felt sense components. In this case it is often possible to work with the entire blend of feelings using a Focusing approach. Furthermore, doing so often produces a pronounced shift toward relief and other important outcomes including more spaciousness and a new perspective with regard to the immediate circumstantial triggers. With practice, a Hakomi or IFS therapist can learn to shift into a Focusing-oriented psychotherapy mode to facilitate such a process.

In other situations, however, the categorical elements push forward and seem to separate from the totality of the felt sense. One finds oneself interacting with anger, fear, or sadness which obtrudes and obscures the totality of the felt sense. In such a case the movement of the Focusing process often bogs down or becomes stuck. Both therapist and client engage in working hard or "efforting". Gendlin has addressed this situation many times pointing out that when this happens he makes "guiding suggestions" and in his client transcripts and videos there are frequent interventions with empathic paraphrase and reflection that go far beyond the precise feeding back of the client "handles".

This situation has been recognized by Gendlin countless times and is given elegant expression by Mia Leijssen in her important chapter on Focusing in *The Handbook of Experiential Psychotherapy* as she describes interfering or "disturbing ways" of reacting: "The disturbing ways of reacting demand special attention and guidance as they can put the client on a side tract and, when they become dominant lead to an unproductive process" Her prescription is to: "(1) Identify interfering ways of reacting;(2) disidentify from them;(3) visualizing them by giving them a concrete form or putting a "face" to them;(4) exploring what function they had or still have; (5) assigning a new place to them; and (6) returning to the part of the person that was/is in the grips of the interfering character." (in Greenberg, Watson, and Lietaer: 1998:144). Our point is that these disturbing ways of reacting can introduce themselves as a strong categorical emotion or a thought which is experienced as a loud or compelling voice in the mind (a critic or a shaming, judging, warning, threatening, advising, figuring out, fixing, dismissing, or denying thought-voice, to name a few). These interfering elements can also initially take the form of an image, or memory. They are frequently accompanied by strong categorical emotions, for example, anger on the part of a critic, fear associated with a warning voice; or disgust in the case of a judging or self-loathing voice).

In Mindfulness Centered Therapies we also have an exceedingly rich set of resources for turning these interfering categorical elements into important contributions to the process of transformation through self-study. Not only do we have the entire skill set from IFS which works indirectly and includes the exact prescription offered by Mia Leijssen, but we also have Hakomi. Hakomi works with clients directly using contact statements, acknowledgments, little experiments in mindfulness, and taking over. With these skills we can help parts calm down and find comfort, reveal memories in present time, bring to light unconscious decisions that continue to pattern present behavior, and reduce unnecessary suffering and avoid re-traumatization that can arise when clients are encouraged to access all of their feelings simultaneously.

In other words, we find meeting these categorical components (construed or considered to be emotions, parts, or functions of the super-ego) with something other than Focusing *per se* easier and safer for the client than pushing through by asking the client to hold the totality of their experience simultaneously especially when that experience contains overwhelming or chaotic emotions or conflicts which, in IFS work, indicate the presence of polarized parts (parts with opposing emotions, feelings, roles or agendas). Once these categorical elements are resolved we return to the felt sense approach and complete the session with the methods described. The difference between how we do this in Mindfulness Centered Therapies and how it is done in Focusing Oriented Therapies is relatively small; the main difference is in the kind of skills we bring to bear. Most therapists trained by Gendlin and his students use empathic paraphrase and reflection rooted in the tradition Carl Rogers founded. In Mindfulness Centered Therapies we use a blend of Hakomi and Internal Family Systems. Another stylistic difference is that in Mindfulness Centered Therapies we tend to make the transition between the Focusing attitude (working with the totality of the present moment as a felt sense) and working with categorical experience using other skills more often and more opportunistically.

An Example of Working Through a Reactivated Component While Focusing

In order to illustrate how this works in practice, we might imagine a session in which a client complains about the fact that he has been avoiding annual taxes. He is puzzled as to why it is so hard for him to do them before the last minute. In such a case, especially since the client is thinking initially about the future, not the past, we decide to begin the session with Focusing. We therefore evoke mindfulness in the client, helping the client to slow down and turn his attention inward, as he imagines doing his taxes. In the typical Focusing session, the client may begin to sense a vague uneasiness or discomfort in his chest or abdomen. We allow time for this to develop, as we help the client to stand back a little from it to achieve optimal distancing for this kind of work.

In a typical Focusing scenario, the client would become aware of the full-blown felt sense experience corresponding to his anticipation of doing his taxes. Based on past experience, this might be what the therapist expects. When the felt sense is stabilized in awareness, we would then assist him in discovering a way to name or symbolize it. This would lead to a shift, or a series of shifts. Eventually, the experience may disappear entirely. At the outset, therefore, we may anticipate a straightforward Focusing session, and it is very likely that after experiencing these shifts, our client will find it much easier to do his taxes. It may even suddenly occur to him that instead of "dreading" them, he could even be interested or enthused about being thorough and taking advantage of all of the possible deductions, something that is possible when one is not forced to do it in panic and desperation.

While Focusing sessions are often straightforward in this way, any Focusing session can surprise us by taking another turn. If we do not make adjustments for this eventuality, a Focusing process can become bogged down and end in a standstill, or move in frustrating circles with little or no satisfying outcome. For example, as the felt sense experience begins to emerge, it might be replaced and overwhelmed by a far stronger, more reactive categorical experience, such as frustration, anger, fear, or sadness. The frustration and annoyance takes center stage: jaws tighten, eyes narrow, fists tighten. We are now in the presence of a reactive component that hijacks the client's Self and his ability to be a compassionate witness. While we could continue to use Focusing by encouraging our client to hold all that anger in a friendly and accepting manner, we prefer to move to another kind of process that might make it easier to maintain mindfulness and increase distance:

> **Therapist:** I wonder if you would be able to think of this anger as a part. An angry part that wants your attention.
> **Client:** Maybe I can do that.
> **Therapist:** Maybe you could go inside and try it. You might want to put the anger in a room and begin by talking to it through a slot in the door, a door with a real strong window.
> **Client:** Man he's really angry.
> **Therapist:** Maybe you just listen to that part for a few minutes, take some mental notes about what he is saying, as if you were the angry part's lawyer and you are trying to organize his case.

This move is often useful for creating a little distance. It can unblend the Self from an angry part without invoking polarization. In this metaphor therapist and client stay on the anger's side. At the same time it creates some distance. If the client is being a lawyer he cannot be the anger at the same time. Often when anger is really listened to it calms down a bit.

If the client can do this we begin to have him look for what the anger is protecting. It is usually a vulnerable part: frightened, hurt, disappointed, humiliated, treated unfairly, not heard or not seen. Most anger is re-triggered. It rides "atop of" or "in front of" unresolved past circumstances, situations or vulnerable injured parts.

In IFS there are a number of ways to gain the angry part's trust and ask the anger to step back and watch. We can assure the anger that we are here to help. Maybe if we can help this hurt part feel better he won't have to be so angry. The IFS set of skills is rich with ways to work in these situations. In addition, using Hakomi we can work with the anger directly using contact statements, acknowledgments or even helping our client to have a satisfying experience with anger by acting it out in a way that is authentic and doesn't involve forcing.

In such a situation, it is very likely that we will evoke an important and contributory memory. For example, our client might remember a time when his father forced him to do his homework, and restricted him to his room on a Friday night. He remembers the sense of injustice, the outrage that he could not express to his authoritarian and volatile father, and how his girlfriend went out with someone else on that very night, and he lost her. While naming and acknowledging these feelings will be helpful, pure Focusing is not all that we need here. We help him to comfort his feelings of abandonment and betrayal. The mere fact that he can now re-experience this memory, and have someone there for him, someone who is not only present, but who can witness and acknowledge his pain, and help him to comfort these feelings—someone who is in his corner, so to speak—creates what we call a missing experience in Hakomi, and that is what will help him work through this powerful memory.

We work through these experiences until they are resolved. When this work is completed we return to the felt sense component to see if it is still there. Now the Focusing work occupies what would normally be the integration process of a Hakomi or IFS session. We return our client's attention to the tax situation. How does he feel now? It is very likely that a felt sense will arise. Perhaps it will be something close to the felt sense we started with; perhaps something quite different. With or without the existence of a traumatic experience, most adults have a felt sense experience corresponding to filing their income taxes. It is not always negative, since many people look forward to tax refunds, and some see doing their taxes as a satisfying review of their financial performance. Our client is much calmer now. He allows the felt sense to emerge, and we help him symbolize it. When the right word or phrase is found and matched with the felt sense experience, he feels a shift. There is a pronounced sense of relief, and the felt sense, which he described a few moments ago as a "knotted mass of gloom" in his abdomen, dissolves completely.

This is a very typical way that we might combine Hakomi and Focusing, IFS and Focusing, or both, in a single session. Our work is guided by our recognition of the reactive component. We agree with Eugene Gendlin and Mia Leijssen on the importance of this distinction and find that keeping it in mind is helpful as we practice with Mindfulness Centered Therapies. Since this kind of situation is very common, we have mapped it out in the diagram below:

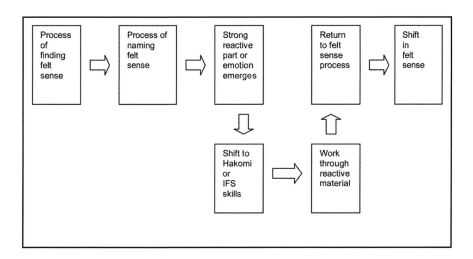

Figure 2. Schematized session in which reactive material replaces felt sense material spontaneously.

While this is one way that we combine Focusing with other mindfulness approaches, there are many other situations, based on different kinds of openings. We have employed Focusing in the integration phases of sessions opened with Hakomi and IFS. We have also coached clients using the indirect coaching method, described earlier, and from that indirect relationship, we have helped them teach Focusing to inner parts.

Re-framing the Past as Anticipated Events

During the years in which we have worked with integrating Focusing into our blend of Hakomi and IFS we have discovered that it is often useful to pay attention to how we frame the content of Focusing sessions with regard to time. While it is true that all felt sense and categorical experience arises in the present moment, one can reframe triggering situations in order to gently shift the initial emphasis away from the reactivated components and toward the felt sense. For example, a client talks about an upsetting encounter with his boss last week. He describes a lingering feeling or mood that has the quality of a felt sense. In such a case it would be natural to invite him to explore this feeling by remembering the past experience. Another option would be to re-frame the remembered experience by having him imagine a future encounter with his boss. We have noticed that this kind of re-framing tends to produce an emphasis on the felt sense component. It is initially less likely to evoke the reactivated component. If and when it does, the reactivated components show up in more vivid contrast to the felt sense. We often continue to work with the totality but if the process gets stuck or the reactivated components escalate, we follow the separation that is already taking place and allow the movement to re-focus on the reactivated component which usually brings up the past in the form of present moment memory material.

In a similar way therapists who use Focusing often check their work by returning their client to the initial situation to see if it brings up the same felt sense. If the same felt sense arises then the Focusing work has not produced a very significant step. When we work through a session without Focusing we often do the same thing to check our work, and often we find that the reactivated components are gone but there lingers a pure felt sense.

Such a situation provides an excellent opportunity to integrate the session with a cycle or two of the Focusing steps. Usually, when the reactivated material has been resolved, the Focusing is effortless and the shifts provide relief, spaciousness, and new and optimistic perspective which invite creative action steps.

Focusing: Summary

In summary, Focusing is a valuable and indispensable addition to Mindfulness Centered Therapies. It allows us to open ourselves to a much broader spectrum of human experience. Without recognition of felt sense experience, therapy (especially an experiential, body-centered therapy) is incomplete and unnecessarily limited. Focusing is also consistent with Hakomi principles and it especially emphasizes and addresses the principles of Mindfulness, Organicity, and Unity. This makes Focusing *per se* an easy and natural addition to the method. Our ability to fully integrate Focusing-oriented psychotherapy is in some ways determined by our starting point in Hakomi and then IFS. Many therapists who use Focusing-oriented psychotherapy are grounded in the tradition of client-centered experiential therapy as it was taught by Carl Rogers and extended by Eugene Gendlin. This tradition relies on empathic paraphrase and reflection and therefore involves having primary attention on verbal content. As we have already mentioned the Hakomi approach requires that the therapist place primary attention on non-verbal communication. This difference as to where the primary attention is placed during the therapeutic process is more than a matter of style since it is difficult and perhaps impossible to do both simultaneously. A complete integration of these methods may therefore require many more years of experimentation and practice. Nevertheless the value of Focusing, the importance of fully addressing the implicit intricacy of felt sense experience, is such that we look forward to the next step in this learning process as our work evolves in Mindfulness Centered Therapies.

CHAPTER 8

THE SELF IN MINDFULNESS CENTERED THERAPIES

The observing self is the transparent center, that which is aware... No matter what takes place, no matter what we experience, nothing is as central as the self that observes. In the face of this phenomenon, Descartes' starting point, "I think; therefore, I am," must yield to the more basic position, I am aware; therefore, I am.

Arthur J. Deikman, *The Observing Self*

IN Mindfulness Centered Therapies, we consider that an increase in our client's ability to access and maintain a stable Self state in the face of life's vicissitudes is one of the most important outcomes of our work. This therapeutic objective motivates us to inquire about what the Self is, what is a stable Self state, and how can we recognize the Self state in ourselves and our clients. In writing about the Self, we use the lower-case "s" to designate self as ego, personality, body, or any combination of these referents. Self, spelled with a capital "S," refers to a far more constant referent, that is, the Self we are when we are identified with our awareness or, one can also say, the Self that we are when we are being mindful.

In order to explain the mindful Self, we turn to the early work of Eugene Gendlin and his co-researchers, who were students and colleagues of Carl Rogers. Eugene Gendlin is primarily known for his discovery and development of Focusing, and many therapists consider him to be the founder of, or a major influence in, the development of experiential psychotherapy. By analyzing thousands of transcripts of therapy sessions, Gendlin and his colleagues identified factors in client behavior that are predictive of positive therapy outcomes. Their studies revealed that clients who frequently observed and symbolized their inner (present moment) experience during therapy sessions had significantly more positive outcomes in therapy. They also discovered that this indicator was the single best predictor of successful outcomes in healing and growth oriented therapy processes (Gendlin. Beebe, Cassens, Kein, and Oberlander, 1968; Hendrick, 1986; Mathieu-Coughlan and Klein, 1984).

Our experience in clinical work has supported this observation. When we meet a client who is able to observe and describe her present moment experience, we are optimistic that our work together will produce satisfactory results. At the same time, we know that this client is not likely to have a serious personality disorder, a disorder classically diagnosed as a disorder that stems from an inadequate development of an authentic core self (Kohut, 1971, 1977). Speaking for myself, I have been mistaken on this matter a few times in my career as a therapist. When I review those errors, I can see that my assessment was incorrect because my judgment was distorted by what I later discovered to be unconscious motivations and misconceptions. In retrospect, mindfulness was not present; it only appeared to be.[12]

Mindfulness Centered Therapies has a practical orientation that values outcomes more than theoretical speculation, and this orientation inspires us to explore what conditions allow one person to observe and describe their inner present moment experience more frequently and consistently than another. In our view, the best trailhead for this exploration lies in the relationship between identity and awareness. It begins with our recognition that a person's ability to observe and describe experience is indirectly proportional to his degree of identification with experiential content. As an individual's identification

---

[12] Richard Schwartz has described a "part" of the personality that is capable of imitating the Self. It seems to have the qualities that we associate with the Self (compassion, curiosity, clarity, and so forth) but is not the Self. He has provided the label "pseudo-self," and has described a way to detect this kind of a part.

with experiential content increases, his observation of experiential content decreases simultaneously (Marlock and Weiss, 2006).

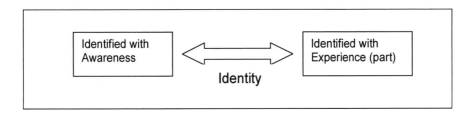

Figure 3. The fluidity of identity: one can be identified with awareness or with one's experience. The degree of identity to either is a gradient.

This observation suggests that identity is fluid, and that we often identify ourselves with our experiential content. This content includes ideas, processes, feelings, parts of ourselves, body sensations, and so forth. The objects and strength of this identification change over time, and vary with circumstances. Another way of saying this is that the referent of the pronoun "I" is not a subjective constant. For example, Stern, who has written extensively about this phenomenon from both experiential and developmental perspectives, writes:

> ...without some continual input from an inter-subjective matrix, human identity dissolves or veers off in odd ways. It does not matter whether this contact is in the form of dyadic mind-sharing, group rituals, or some other form. We are familiar with the idea of multiple selves or distributed selves that shift somewhat, depending on whom one is with or on the prevailing context. This is considered normal. But when does the compass needle [of identity] point to the "true self"?
> (Stern, 2004, p. 107-108).

Questioning the fixity of the Self, or the referent of the "I," challenges common-sense assumptions: namely, that the referent of "I" is: (1) the physical body, a monolithic personality or ego, or a spiritual entity like a soul; (2) fixed or unchangeable, and therefore always the same object or essence; (3) historically prior in the psychological development of the child to the concepts of "me" or "mine."

In truth, people commonly dissociate entirely from their bodies, and often identify with something other than a monolithic personality or ego. Individuals change their sense of identity, depending on circumstances, and in different relationships. In addition, at the age of about two years old, when children begin to use pronouns, the order of their appearance is most frequently "mine," "me," "you," and finally "I" (Gesell, 1940, p. 32). Ames, another professional early childhood observer, writes of preschool children at about 24 months:

> [The] child cannot share. He is still consolidating a sense of self by obtaining and hording possessions. "Mine" is a favorite word." Ames goes on to observe that at about 36 months the Child "no longer seems to need to confirm and embellish self with possessions....At three and a half years of age a sense of self that extends to other children is in evidence
>
> (Ames, 1952, p. 229).

The fluidity of identity is not a distortion of something that is initially and primarily fixed, nor is it an aberration of something that should be fixed. It is present from the very start of life, and persists until the end. It is normal and natural. The premise that identity is fluid is also consistent with an experiential theory of personality that proposes a process model of the self. In the process model, the self is seen as a "dynamic experiential system in a continual process of self-organization. This process model replaces a more static, structural view of a self-concept determining behavior" (Greenberg, et al., p. 452).

In Mindfulness Centered Therapies, we recognize that people identify with a multitude of self states. Most of these states exhibit attributes of a certain persona, and a specific role, function, or agenda. We follow Richard Schwartz and his Internal Family Systems model in calling these states "parts." We also follow Schwartz in recognizing a self-reflexive state, in which the individual is primarily identified with his or her awareness. When so identified, an individual remains more weakly identified or "connected" with experience. Their "experience," in this case, might be construed to be a part (as in IFS), a categorical experience (Hakomi), or a felt sense (Focusing).[13] It may also be an external experience, such as sight, sound, touch, smell, or taste.

When one's primary identification is with awareness, one is able to observe and name experience with a heightened degree of ease and clarity. One is also calmer, more compassionate with self and others, and less reactive. Individuals in this awareness-identified state have more of what Daniel J. Siegel calls "response flexibility" (1999, p. 140-143). In a word, they are more "creative." All of these attributes were long ago identified by Richard Schwartz as characteristics of the Self state, which he also calls a state of Self-leadership. At the same time, they are the attributes of a person who is being mindful, to use the vocabulary of Hakomi. These characteristics also typify what Focusing therapists call a "Focusing attitude." Having practiced all of these methods, we have no doubt that they are each describing one and the same state. Clients who have used these methods also recognize these similarities, and can report with precision their proximity to this awareness-identified state.

Recognition of this state constitutes an answer to Stern's' question: "… when does the compass needle [of identity] point to the 'true self'?" We propose this state as an answer. In other words, the compass points to the "true self" when one is identified with awareness. For this reason, we follow Schwartz in referring to this state as Self, with a capital "S," to distinguished it from other usages where the word "self" is used to refer to the body, a

---

[13] One could easily add Wolinsky's vocabulary of "trance states" (1991) or Watkins' "ego-states" (Watkins and Watkins, 1997; Emmerson, 2003) to this list.

part with which one has become identified, or the sum of all parts which constitute the personality or ego.

Qualities of the Self state

If this vibrational resonance occurs between two human beings a connection is made and their energies expand and begin to fuse. They feel warmth throughout their bodies and their hearts. As their life energy connects they experience vibration, movement; they surpass the boundaries of ordinary reality. A new perception puts them in touch with the divine [the universal].

- John C. Pierrakos *Eros, Love and Sexuality*

To summarize our view of the Self, we offer a set of propositions that articulate a working hypothesis that is, as far as possible, experiential rather than interpretive or theoretical, bearing in mind that these propositions are tentative and incomplete.

1. The Self is experiential insofar as it possesses at least one observable quality. That quality is awareness. While one cannot objectify awareness, and therefore cannot observe it as an object, one can know that one is being aware, and this knowledge is experiential. As with many other aspects of the person, awareness may be but the tip of an iceberg. Much of what the Self is and does—coordination, guidance, knowing, its motivations and properties—may be unconscious or unobservable.

2. At any moment in time, one can be said to be more or less identified with awareness. When one is strongly identified with it, we say that the subject is "Self-led," "mindful," or in a "Focusing [ready] attitude." This state is observable and experiential, insofar as one can know when he or she is in it through direct experience. One can also know when another is in this state, with reasonable

certainty, through observation. When one is in this Self state, one exhibits a high degree of awareness, calm, compassion or empathy, response flexibility or creativity, risk tolerance or courage, groundedness or confidence. It is possible to design test instruments to measure this state, or one's capacity to be in this state.

3. Being in or out of the Self state is a function of identity. Identity is a function of who or what one considers or experiences oneself to be in the present moment. Identity is often in a state of flux. When this flux is between Self-awareness and connection with another, this condition is called a state of "attunement," when the other is present, and "resonance" when the object of attunement is temporarily absent from present moment awareness (Siegel and Hartzell, 2003). When this flux of identity is between a person's awareness and another internal part or external person or being (an animal, for example), it forms the basis for empathy. This is sometimes referred to as the "I-Thou" relationship, originally named by Martin Buber, and adopted by many experiential therapists in the humanistic tradition of Carl Rogers (Greenberg, Watson, and Lietauer, 1998). If identity were fixed or static, it would be impossible to be empathetic, or to have compassion for another. Therefore, while fluidity of identity might be a vulnerability with regard to an individual being, it is probably a necessity for a social being.

4. Because identity is not fixed, it is appropriate to invoke metaphors of distance. We can speak about and know experientially how near or far we are from an internal or external object of experience. This distance metaphor references the degree of attunement or resonance between a person and an internal or external other. Another way of stating this is to say that the metaphor of distance

references the degree to which we are identified with another person, external object, or internal part (Mia Leijssen, 1998, p. 125-135).

5.   When a person is highly identified with an internal experience, whether it is construed as a categorical experience, felt sense, or part, he or she is very likely to "act out" that experience. In extreme cases of dissociation, this acting out can include taking on physical symptoms, while in more ordinary cases, it includes assuming facial expressions, gestures, postures, tone of voice, and other behaviors.

MINDFULNESS CENTERED THERAPIES AND BUDDHISM

While readers may see parallels and influences from Buddhism and Taoism in this model of the Self, it is not our intention to replicate or align this work with either specific Eastern or Western transcendental traditions. The primary Eastern influence lies in the recognition of awareness, and in the idea of dropping attachment, especially the attachment to one's identification with experience. This idea of nonattachment is pervasive in the East, and not unknown in the West, especially with regard to external grasping or greed, but also with regard to holding onto inner drives and feelings considered to be destructive or antisocial: vengeance, excessive ambition, lust, selfishness, as well as other, less obvious forms of attachment, like being right, or self-righteousness, which is often expressed as blaming another.

Since much of what we work with in psychotherapy is related to the personality and personal experience, this shift in identity from object to subject, or experience to awareness, is therapeutically crucial. It allows both therapist and client to distance from the emotionally charged reactions triggered by the vicissitudes of ordinary life. Release from reactivity constitutes a very basic kind of personal freedom. This very personal form of freedom is the same freedom valued in Buddhism. In this regard, Mindfulness Centered Therapies is consistent with Buddhism and Taoism. At the same time, there are also parallels and influences from the Western tradition and Christianity, since the very idea of psychotherapy is basically a Western tradition, and brings with it both the gifts and the baggage of its entire family of origin.

Stephen Wolinsky has pioneered a transcendental psychotherapy that draws deeply on practices, vocabulary, and models from Eastern traditions, and from the field of quantum physics. Citing Werner Heisenberg's theory of quantum physics, he points out that ultimately, "the observer cannot be separated from the thing observed." In Wolinsky's view, "it is important to develop and observe, to realize that you are the looker and not what you are looking at, and that anything you can observe you cannot be." However, quantum psychology shares with many Eastern traditions the view that this is but a way-station on the path to a higher state of realization, in which observer is actually not separate from the observed; that "this observer is actually part of what it is observing and it too has to be gone beyond" (Wolinsky, 1999, p. 40).[14] While we do not disagree with this view, Mindfulness Centered Therapies is specifically concerned with what Wolinsky describes as a secular way-station, in which awareness is experienced as separate. In our view, psychotherapy has its limits, and its contract as an institution is to attend to healing and growth in its secular dimensions. It seems obvious that there is a further step, beyond the realm of psychotherapy, and we applaud those who have the experience and wisdom to lead others forward.

---

[14] In moments of great clarity, I have glimpsed a state of absolute perfection and peace in which this separation is no longer imposed upon experience. Czekzentmihalyi has also attempted to write about this kind of experience as a secular phenomenon, and has used the word "flow" to describe it. I believe that I have experienced this "flow" as well, and in my own limited experience of both states, I sense a significant difference. I am not sure they are the same. The former is far more ineffable, vivid, and in a profound sense, more universal.

CHAPTER 9

ADDITIONAL MINDFULNESS PRACTICES

I lie here with a cover and coffee pot and a pen, Feeling delight in being a child of language—Neither man nor woman exactly, but a young monk
In a skin boat, bobbing among the seals of sound.

Robert Bly, *Morning Poems*

While we are aware that there are many mindfulness based practices used by psychotherapists today, two that are especially important to our work are The Progoff Intensive Journal® method (Progoff, 1975) and the Awareness Wheel and Listening Cycle® (Miller, Wackman, Nunnally, and Miller, 1989). Throughout our many years of teaching and counseling with a wide variety of clients, including couples and young people, these methods have been valuable supplements to the core practices of Mindfulness Centered Therapies.

THE PROGOFF INTENSIVE JOURNAL

"Each person needs then early on to go inside, far enough inside to water the plants, awaken the animals, become friends with the desires and sense what Machado calls 'the living pulse of the spirit.'"

Robert Bly, Morning Poems

The Progoff Intensive Journal process is a unique tool for integration, self-balancing, creativity, and personal growth. It is usually taught in Progoff Intensive Journal Workshops. Within the workshop setting, the facilitator cultivates a spacious and mindful atmosphere that is nonanalytical, nonjudgmental, and self-empowering. The Journal was developed by Dr. Ira Progoff, who was in the vanguard of those who worked toward a dynamic psychology of creative and spiritual experience in the 1960s. He was Director of the Institute for Research in Depth Psychology at Drew University, and a therapist and workshop leader. Following his studies with Carl Jung, he began studying the lives of creative people, with a focus on the common threads, themes, and dynamics of creativity and growth. His own clarity and creativity were imminently apparent in his construction of this integrating tool. He was also a refreshingly humble man, and a compassionate listener. There is a quality of balance, gentle humor, and wholeness immediately apparent in his work.

The Intensive Journal was originally created in 1966, and the book *At A Journal Workshop* was published in 1975 (a revised edition appeared in 1992). For over forty years, the Journal process has helped hundreds of thousands of people explore their own depths and find the inner movement of their lives. In 1978, *Medical Self-Care* magazine hailed Progoff's *At a Journal Workshop* as "the best book on psychological self-care," and in our opinion it continues to be an extremely valuable resource for therapists and clients. The process has more than one set of roots. It borrows from Lao Tzu, Buddha, St. Augustine, St. Francis of Assisi, Dostoevsky, Carl Jung, D.T. Suzuki, and Martin Buber. In this regard, Progoff has said, "I am a synthesizer."

In a workshop setting, the process begins with participants recording personal information about their lives in four dimensions: Life Time, Dialogues, Depth, and Meaning. These include life experiences, persons, works, dreams, images, society, the body, events, and spiritual experiences. Participants receive a three-ring binder with many specific subject dividers to begin the process. One's life experiences, both inner and outer, are recorded in various sections of the journal, in such a way that any experience can be reentered and explored at a future time. The journal process clarifies one's history, and provides a sense of continuity and connection.

While it is possible to learn the journal on one's own, this is no substitute for the journal workshops, due to the quality of the atmosphere that is a hallmark of the method. This atmosphere is created by the presence of the journal consultant, the calmness of voice, the timing, the gentle introduction of the material, the clarity of the structure, the respect for inner process and depth, the quiet that pervades the entire workshop. Like all of the methods included in Mindfulness Centered Therapies, Progoff Intensive Journal Workshops are not conversational; there is a quality of privacy, despite the presence of others. Each person is working in his or her own life, and there is no intrusion by the instructor or other participants.

Optimally, a client begins to learn the Intensive journal process by taking a workshop, so that the structure, principles, and intent are clear. However, clients who are working with a therapist who holds the same principles, and is trained in the method, can be assisted in learning to use parts of the Journal to access depth material and compassion for oneself and others. The workshops are then available to them, as time permits. Although there are infinite ways of introducing parts of the Journal in or after a therapy session, the sections that offer themselves most easily are Inner Process Entries, for writing about the experience and insights of the session, or Daily Log, about daily events (most like a diary), or recording and working with dreams in the dream enlargements, or writing one's personal steppingstones with an eye for the continuity and movement of one's life, or opening a Dialogue.

Just one example from a session would be the following. A client comes in, feeling distressed about a current relationship with their life partner, and as the session progresses, the issues that are arising in the current relationship point directly to an unfinished relationship with a parent who is still living. Or it may be that the parent has died unexpectedly, and the client, after a time of grieving, feels calmer, but finds that there were important things that weren't spoken. Or a dialogue might be opened in order to address the relationship with the life partner directly.

In any case, we begin by introducing the dialogue aspect of the journal, the meaning behind it, and the practice itself. To establish a dialogue within the Intensive Journal structure, it is necessary to have a felt sense of the "other," to walk in their shoes, to sense their continuity and vision. This is true whether one is in dialogue with another person (present, past, or no longer living), one's body, or one's life work. In order to gain a sense of this "other," we use the Steppingstones exercise, in which we honor the important events of a life by listing what we know of its history. It is then possible to converse with the other person, the project (or "work"), or the body, in a fruitful way. The effect of dialogue then is to take a relationship that is in distress, "on pause," or at a stalemate, and lead it forward with compassion.

In a session, we might invite a client to do this as homework, but we might begin by doing a little bit of the work in session to get it started. If there is time in the session, we might begin by helping to describe the current moment in the relationship. For example: "My dad and I seem to be in a difficult place right now. I find I can't talk to him since Mom died, and I see that this is has begun to effect my relationship with my partner".

For homework, we invite our client to complete the above paragraph about the present moment (focusing statement), and then to recall as accurately as possible significant moments (Steppingstones) in the parent's life, beginning with when the parent was born and the circumstances of his birth, then what happened next, and so on, restricting the steppingstones to about a dozen, and bringing his life up to the present moment. All of this is written in the first person—"I was born… I went to grade school at… My first job was…"—as if the client's parent were describing the significant moments in his own life. After these parts of the dialogue process are completed, the client is then invited to read over the paragraph and the steppingstones, steeping herself, so to speak, in the life of the other, and allowing any images to come forward, writing them down as well. Then they begin the dialogue, writing as best they can the truth of their experience, and writing it to the other in this private way. We encourage the client to maintain a mindful, non-judging, and compassionate point of view as she writes.

When her own writing feels complete for the moment, she allows the other to respond and speak *his* truth, allowing the fullness of the response to be written. This proceeds like a script, written freely, knowing it will not be seen. It is an inner process, and is not written with the intent of sharing with the other. It is then read over, and responses are made at the end of the dialogue. This dialogue can then be added to over time with notes and perhaps monologues, important information about the relationship, creating a place for exploring and discovering. It is not written in place of direct communication, but rather is intended to deepen the relationship. This process, of course, could be used with the present moment relationship that our client brought to the session as well, and in any relationship that has a life history, a sense of caring and meaning, and an intention toward the future.

When therapeutic work begins to move deeper, or when themes that are larger than personal emerge regarding the meaning of life, there are specific ways of exploring these areas that respect the inner process and self-discovery. The acceptance inherent in this process enlarges the scope of the question beyond the boundaries of "problem," and instead accesses that which is transpersonal and connected. Instead of paralysis, there is attention, trust, movement, and energy. Just as in Hakomi, IFS, and Focusing, we are working in a quiet, respectful, non-intrusive, private way, encouraging awareness. By its nature, this becomes an experience of depth. In the workshop itself, the silence, privacy, and focused writing of the other participants also create a quality of spaciousness and timelessness.

Once a participant has recorded life data in most of the sections of the journal, there is an opportunity to practice journal feedback; a process of nonanalytical, organic cross-referencing that generates energy and movement. In Journal Feedback, the key questions are: "As I read this that

I have written, what is my response, and to what aspect of my life does this entry call my attention, or where in the journal does this lead me?" Wherever we are drawn—to a memory, a moment of transition, a person we haven't seen in years, an image or a dream—there is a place to put it, and we leave a notation there. Also, as we read, whatever we notice in the present moment is recorded.

All of these notations begin to form threads, and as they overlap, a fabric or braid begins to emerge. In a sense, we see from a different vantage point. We are moved by the process from a viewpoint of fragmentation and separateness toward wholeness, toward seeing the order and strength of the life fabric. As a result of this organic, trusting, gentle process, an emerging pattern is more visible, and the self-led process unfolds. In this space, images and realizations often form within us that we didn't know we knew, and we then record these. There is no forcing in the journal. If there is experience, or if there is a resistance or reaction to something, we do our best not to judge, and we quietly record what is happening. This quality of spaciousness is at the heart of the work; it expresses a quality of love in its most profound sense.

Many people working for the first time in the journal, or thinking about the process beforehand, wonder how often they're supposed to write. In a sense, that's like wondering how often I should use a hammer, or my car. It is truly a tool that is useful when it is useful, but it is not a substitute for life. The Intensive Journal process is about living one's life attentively; oddly enough, it's not about writing, nor is any writing experience necessary.

When the Intensive Journal is used in addition to therapy, and introduced by the therapist, the choice of sections needs to be relevant to the work that is present in the session, and should be offered as an invitation, rather than as required homework. Timing is everything in the healing process. Attending the workshops, and then advanced studies training in the Intensive Journal, would be recommended for therapists who wish to use it with clients in the therapeutic setting.

Although Progoff's work, based on the principles of depth psychology, is infinitely more comprehensive and extensive in scope, it seems worthwhile here to also cite discoveries from the work and research of Dr. James Pennebaker, professor of psychology at the University of Texas at Austin, who conducted early research in the nineteen-eighties that further supports the value of writing as a healing practice. His research has shown that short-term, focused writing on emotional experiences has a beneficial effect on the immune system and the health of the individual. Also, simply writing about secrets that have an emotional content has a positive effect on health.

His instructions to participants are simple. "Write down your deepest feelings about an emotional upheaval in your life for fifteen to twenty minutes a day for four consecutive days." The research gleaned after the writing indicates a strong tendency toward more coherence, more perspective, and more clarity, in addition to the health benefits. He says, "People who engage in expressive writing report feeling happier and less negative than before writing. Similarly reports of depressive symptoms, rumination, and general anxiety tend to drop in the weeks and months after writing about emotional upheavals." His new book is called *Writing to Heal*.

Daniel Siegel writes in *The Developing Mind* about the relationship between parents' capacity for healthy attachment and their ability to narrate clearly and coherently about their own life history. In addition, he speaks of the importance of encouraging children to speak about their daily experiences, and, over time, to be able to track the continuity of their life in a coherent fashion. He sees this as a critical component in the development of the mind. Language is the medium through which we understand experience, and as Progoff says, "Every human being has at least one great creative project, a life."

A person's life story was of great importance to Joseph Campbell, the world's foremost authority on mythology. He said, "The Intensive Journal is one of the greatest inventions of our time." Anais Nin, one of the first people to publish journals of an intimate nature, and also author of twenty novels, said about the Intensive Journal, "One cannot help but be amazed by what emerges from this skillful inner journey. All the elements we attribute to the poet, the artist, become available to everyone at all levels of society." In this exploration we gradually discover that our life has been going somewhere, and that we can understand where it wants to go next.

*At A Journal Work*shop is very extensive, and covers the principles, intent, and practices involved in this work. It is easily available and accessible for those who want to understand the work in more depth. This chapter is just a taste of what is possible in the method. The workshops are offered nationally and internationally. This is an opportunity to sense one's life as process; a seed that is growing itself as a work of art; each individual life as a theme that is trying to express itself, and can be intuited and known. This is the basis of the Intensive Journal process: to discover one's life in its entirety, as an unfolding dance—not a jigsaw puzzle with pieces missing, not an object—but rather, a deep flowing river. To explore the Progoff Intensive Journal process further, we recommend the Progoff Intensive Journal's website: www.intensivejournal.org.[15]

The Awareness Wheel and Listening Cycle

When understood and used correctly, the Awareness Wheel and Listening Cycle (Miller, Wackman, Nunnally, and Miller, 1989) are tools for developing awareness of self and others, for communicating more accurately and clearly, and learning how to listen and acknowledge others. They provide options for building responsible, truthful relationships in the present with friends, family, and associates. The Wheel can be used alone as a self-discovery tool regarding any issue, after one has gained an understanding of each of the sections, and has had practice in using it. The sections of the wheel are visually displayed, like the petals of a flower. The five segments are Sensory Data (inner and outer), Thoughts, Feelings, Wants, and Actions. The Wheel,

---

[15] Website last accessed on 1/21/2008.

fortunately, is available in linen cloth form, large enough to allow a person to stand on each segment comfortably.

When an individual is standing on the wheel and practicing, the statements are made in the form of "I statements," not "you statements," and they reference only the speaker's experience. This is a practice of Self awareness, using language that expresses one's own unarguable truth. *Sensory* data can include what the speaker sees, hears, smells, touches outwardly, and also senses inwardly (holding my breath, tight chest, etc., or inner images). *Thoughts*, like filters of our experience, include: memories, ideas, concepts, inferences, beliefs, convictions, conclusions, assumptions, prejudices, fantasies, etc. *Feelings* are variations of fear, anger, sadness, aroused (excited), happy, and so forth. *Wants* can be wants for oneself, for others, or for the larger family or community. *Actions* are past, current, or in the future.

In therapy and in classrooms, we begin by describing these distinctions and the words that are associated with them. After describing each segment in this way, an instructor or therapist can teach by example:

1. step onto the Wheel, and speak regarding her own experience in the moment, or
2. invite the individual to speak, while the teacher or therapist points to the segment that is being expressed, or writes briefly about his statement under one of the Wheel categories on a white board, or
3. invite the individual to step on the Wheel and begin to speak directly about his experience, while the instructor points to a different segment if the student is unaware of having shifted to another category of experience. The long-term intent will be for the student or client to stand and move around on the wheel, standing on each segment as it corresponds to their language and their experience.

Awareness builds on awareness. Clarity of language creates deeper awareness. Some examples: it is very common for people to use the words,

"I feel that…" as if they are expressing a feeling, when in fact that structure generally indicates that a thought, not a categorical feeling, is being expressed. In this case, when the student is on the Wheel and says "I feel that (she is a liar)," the instructor would merely point to the segment of the wheel labeled Thoughts, and in that way, invite him to stand on Thoughts instead of on Feelings. There will likely be a bit of discussion at first, but nearly everyone gets the distinction, once it is clarified. Another common linguistic form is, "It feels like (nobody likes me)…" which also expresses a thought. Speaking this way is often habitual, and it allows the person to avoid actually speaking and owning a clearly expressed feeling, which might be instead, perhaps, "I feel afraid, or sad."

After learning how to use the Wheel, the individual is invited stand on the Wheel and to speak aloud, and while speaking, to move slowly from segment to segment as the content of the words being spoken shifts from one category to another. The flow of communication is often somewhat slower than normal conversation; this deliberate pace is encouraged, and often appears spontaneously as awareness begins to arise. The listener is not intrusive in any way, except to point to a different segment if the student has not recognized a shift (for example, from Thoughts to Wants, or Feelings to Thoughts, or Thoughts to Sensory data, etc.). Amazingly, that is enough. The Awareness Wheel itself provides a structure for self-discovery. If the listener is able to listen with respect, acknowledge the participant's present moment experience occasionally, stay open to hearing more, and avoid asking questions that might divert the process, the work can reach quite deeply and spontaneously toward insights and forward movement regarding an issue.

In beginning to work with the Wheel, it becomes clear to many people that they are leaving out entire categories of experience in their normal conversation. Others discover that nearly everything they say is a form of thought, rather than evidence - or reality-based observations (sensory data). Many do not have clarity about sensory data, either outer or inner, or at least are not accustomed to using words that express that information in speaking with others. They may find that although they think and feel a lot, they are not expressing wants, and then begin to discover that wants are not allowed in their private universe. This might elicit a memory of a parent saying something like, "Children should be seen and not heard; wants are not allowed in this household." At that point, feelings may emerge, and it might be appropriate for the therapist to offer comfort. New insights may then arise about wants in the present.

We consider the Awareness Wheel to be a mindfulness tool, and a step in the direction of owning one's own experience, naming the present moment experience, learning to recognize the underlying assumptions and convictions that generate emotional upheavals, and discovering cognitive distortions (Burns, 1990). As mentioned earlier in the text, we recognize this naming of the present moment as a valuable ability for experiencing positive results in therapy. The practice of the Awareness Wheel, for some people, may be their first step toward mindfulness. It invites the person to slow down, go inside, and begin to pay attention to their actual experience; to be curious about it, without intrusion from another, in a way that is respectful, without argument. This can begin the process of learning to speak the unarguable truth about the present moment.

After a session, if the instructor or therapist notices that there were no experiences named in the categories of sensory data, wants, or actions, etc., that is valuable information to share with the client. Otherwise, since this is about mindfulness, and is client-led, we offer no advice about the issue, except to suggest that it might be useful for the client to take some notes or journal afterward about what was discovered or noticed. Though it is helpful to have the linen wheel for use in sessions, the Awareness Wheel can also be drawn on a big sheet of paper and taken home for practice.

When we add the Listening Cycle to this process, we find that clients begin to learn about deep listening. The Listening Cycle includes the practice of looking, listening, and tracking; adding simple acknowledgment of the other's present moment experience; making room for a pause or silence, creating space for the speaker to continue speaking; then summarizing what they said. All the while, the listener restrains his impulses to advise, to tell his own story, to change the subject, to ask the kind of questions that lead the speaker away from her present moment experience. Several sessions of this kind provide an experience of the kind of intimacy many people long for in a loving relationship. Contacts for more information and books on the Listening Cycle are posted on www.corecommunication.com.[16]

---

[16] Website Last Accessed on 1/21/2008

CHAPTER 10

CONCLUSION OF PART 1

And Mindfulness, it should also be noted, being about attention, is also of necessity universal. There is nothing particularly Buddhist about it. We are all mindful to one degree or another, moment by moment. It is an inherent human capacity. The contribution of the Buddhist tradition has been in part to emphasize simple and effective ways to cultivate and refine this capacity and bring it to all aspects of life.

- Jon Kabat-Zinn, *Coming to our Senses*

IN the preceding chapters, we have described how three therapies that employ relational mindfulness can be seamlessly combined into a single system of psychotherapy. It is possible to think of the resulting method as a collection of techniques and tools, and that Mindfulness Centered Therapies is simply a bigger mindfulness toolbox, with Hakomi in the deep central compartment, and IFS and Focusing folding out into wings on either side. While this is to some degree a handy metaphor, it would be more useful to see it from a richer and broader perspective about therapy and especially about relational mindfulness.

By and large, the mindfulness practices and traditions that were brought to the West in the Twentieth Century evolved over the past 2,500 years in Asia. The back story of their development, the historical setting, was a succession of feudal kingdoms or regimes organized along the same lines as the fiefdoms and provinces of the European Middle Ages. Feudal systems depend almost solely on agriculture, and therefore require large populations that work the land, either as serfs or slaves. These populations are poor, but productive, providing labor, goods, services, and tax revenues usually paid in crops or livestock. In feudal economies, peasant populations typically farm or sharecrop the plantations of powerful and wealthy lords or barons.

These peasant farmers are largely illiterate. Public education or literacy for the masses does not exist in feudal societies, not even as concepts. Similarly, human rights, equality under the law, capitalism, free markets, taxation with representation, liberalism, and democracy are also nonexistent, and have not been imagined or conceived of in such a society. In feudal regimes, political and economic power lies in the hands of a small and literate elite, who enjoy an elevated standard of living, and wield totalitarian authority over their kingdoms. It was such an elite family and privileged life that the 29-year-old prince Buddha Siddhartha rejected as he set out on his journey of enlightenment, if we are to take literally the stories about his life. According to tradition, Siddhartha left behind three palaces especially built for him by his father King Suddhoadana.

Feudal economies were typical of all of the lands that Buddhism influenced during its first 2400 years of existence. Its diffusion encompassed India, China, Tibet, Southeast Asia, Indonesia, Korea, and Japan. As it spread, it took different forms in different parts of its domain of influence, depending on local traditions and the various kinds of feudal regimes it encountered. In some regions there was more private ownership of the land, and peasants had more freedom to work it as they wished. Their serfdom took the form of taxation and military conscription, rather than direct service. In some regions, Buddhism developed as monasticism, in others as a state-sponsored religion. Buddhism reached many areas inhabited by tribal people who lived on the edges of feudal empires. They often absorbed elements of its esoteric art and practice into their animistic traditions.

This feudal background accounts for how the Buddha narrative survived in the sangha (community of disciples) for over four hundred years without being written down. In the West, this narrative would be somewhat comparable to the story of the fall of Troy, which was recounted in the Iliad as an oral ballad, passed down by bards from the Twelfth to the Eighth Century B.C.E., when it was finally transcribed by Homer. In both cultures, while writing was known, the culture was essentially oral. Writing was for kings and their minions, including priests and members of monastic communities. The literate castes or classes were generally conservative mainstays of the feudal equilibrium. Their role in sustaining conventions would militate against taking interest in a movement as revolutionary as Buddhism. Some things persist, even as political and economic systems evolve, and there will probably always be an elite guard, be it bureaucratic, religious, military, or academic, whose social role is to maintain the conventions that keep power and privilege in place.

With this background in mind, let us consider mindfulness as it now exists in a very different environment. This environment evolved out of Western feudalism, through a period of colonialism and mercantilism, into capitalism. This free-market capitalism is the force that is driving the spread of democratic governments across the globe. This global conversion to democracy is a very recent phenomenon. In 1900 A.D., there was not a single democracy on the planet, if we consider a democracy to be a government created by elections in which every adult citizen votes. A century later, in 2003 A.D., there are one hundred nineteen democracies in existence, representing sixty-two percent of all countries in the world. (Zakaria, 2003). This democratic revolution is not only a revolution in government. It goes far beyond politics. "Hierarchies are breaking down, closed systems are opening up, pressures from the masses are the primary instrument of social change." (Zakaria, 2003) We may see this as progress, or as a breakdown of social order, or as a process of change or even transformation, but is apparently a global process, far too big for one person or even a movement to stop or even slow down. But it is probably safe to say that, given a choice, very few of us would choose to return to feudalism, a condition of existence typified by the Middle Ages, a time when life has been characterized as "solitary, poor, nasty, brutish, and short" (Hobbes, 1651).

Mindfulness had very little to do with the evolution of capitalism, but in the present epoch it is rapidly becoming an unprecedented and potentially transformational new element. As knowledge of mindfulness permeates Western institutions like psychoanalysis, psychotherapy, education, allopathic medicine, physical culture, the environmental movement, and religious traditions, it encounters an unprecedented kind of humanistic and liberal culture. Not only is this culture materialistic and individualistic, perhaps to a fault, it is also far more democratic, decentralized, and egalitarian than any culture the world has ever seen. Authority based on models of top-down control is far more likely to be questioned and challenged. Concepts like human rights, equality under the law, due process, the balance of powers, representative governance, and democratic process have become its inseparable institutions. It is also a culture stitched together by a communication infrastructure the likes of which human beings have never known. This network of speech, image, music, data, and ideas is now also inseparable from capitalism. It goes everywhere, and it usually, though not always, takes capitalism and democratic values with it. And with breathtaking speed, mindfulness and a growing list of Eastern values are being added to that list. These values—non-action, containment, right livelihood, self-compassion, introspection—are basically foreign to the ethos of the West, yet they are being swept into the mainstream of global communications.

Ironically, this new form of culture, with its humanistic, capitalistic, and democratic ideas, has also permeated the East, just as the East has permeated the West with its ideas and practices of mindfulness, and its distinctive being-based values. It is then not surprising that mindfulness and Buddhism might be influenced by these new humanistic ideals and values, and thereby transformed into something more accessible and more effective in liberating us from reactivity and unnecessary suffering.

Today we witness this transformation as new institutions and new applications of mindfulness evolve, including new forms of Buddhism with names like "activist" and "socially engaged" Buddhism, names that sound almost oxymoronic. However, this activist or socially engaged Buddhism is a large and growing international movement, inspired and articulated by leaders like Dr Bhim Rao Ambedkar, author of *Annihilation of Caste*, who orchestrated a mass conversion of an estimated 500,000 Daltis (broken, oppressed people, including untouchables and outcasts) to Buddhism in Nagpur as an act of social liberation from conditions attributed to their feudal and Hindu past. Or Dr. A. T. Ariyaratne, founder of the Sarvodaya Shramadana Movement in Sri Lanka, a program of self-governance based on Buddhist principles that serves the majority of the country's villages. Dr Ariyaratne has been compared to Mahatma Gandhi, Martin Luther King Jr., and His Holiness the Dalai Lama for his lifetime of humanitarian work (Garfinkel, 2006). We could also mention the Reverend Thich Nhat Hahn, expatriate Buddhist monk, teacher, author, and peace activist, who coined the term "Engaged Buddhism" in his book *Vietnam: Lotus in a Sea of Fire* (1967). Rev. Hahn, who prefers to be addressed as Thây (meaning teacher), is a modest and unassuming proponent of "relational Buddhism." When confronted with a journalist's questions: "Aren't there enough relationship gurus? Aren't there more important issues to discuss?" Thây Hahn responded:

Such as war, violence, death, economic problems, terrorism? The conflict in the Middle East, tensions between religious groups—these are about relationships. The Buddha identified ignorance as the second noble truth. We create ignorance through poor communication. Misunderstanding begins in the microcosm, between two people. It creates fear, and fear creates more violence and anger. When you act with violence and anger you create more violence and anger. The majority of the people who come here [speaking of his Plum Village retreat center in France] suffer from relationship, health and work problems. But if your relationship is good, then you are happy, your health improves and you'll be more successful in your enterprise.

(Garfinkel, p. 257)

While Mindfulness Centered Therapies is not a form of Buddhism, we feel a kinship with the spirit of Rev. Hahn's work in promoting a new form of mindfulness that we call relational mindfulness, which is complementary with, not in opposition to, the mindfulness practiced in *Zazen, Vipassana,* and other forms of solitary meditation.

Given this perspective it is possible to hold that Buddhism, both religious and secular, is a foundation and vehicle by which mindfulness has entered and established itself in the West. However, if there is one thing that this new global synthesis—let's drop the "Western"—is not noted for, it is reverence for convention, especially unquestioning obedience to a teacher, whether that teacher is a spiritual guru or the innovator of a form of psychotherapy. The West will tamper with Buddhism and mindfulness; it already has, and it will continue to adapt it to its needs, and align it with its resources. The expectation that the West should mimic the feudal traditions of the East may have some romantic or nostalgic appeal, but it is bound to disappoint, and for this reason, we see the role of mindfulness in Western psychotherapy as being far more than adding meditation or stress reduction to existing methods of cognitive or experiential therapy. As we look toward the immediate future, the next ten to twenty years, we see mindfulness erasing the cognitive versus experiential polemic entirely. By the same token, secular Buddhism and solitary meditation are an excellent starting place, and we are profoundly grateful to have been exposed to them, but we envision much more to come to both East and West as a consequence of this global cross-fertilization process.

There are a few implications of this perspective that we would like to explore in the remaining pages. Primary among these is the question of how therapists are trained in Mindfulness Centered Therapies and other similar mindfulness approaches. The second has to do with the organizations that promote and provide this training.

We find it difficult to envision training in an experiential psychotherapy that does not involve trainees working deeply in the client role with their own unconscious material. In other words, experiential therapists need to do their own work. At the same time, trainees who are learning experiential methods need real clients, with real issues and unconscious material to practice with. This is true of Hakomi, Internal Family Systems, and Focusing. In each of these methods, it is customary to train in a workshop setting with highly-trained facilitators who organize the agenda of exercises in a gentle gradient, introduce conceptual and practical didactic instruction, keep the workshop space psychologically safe, and provide supervision in one-on-one sessions between student therapists and student clients doing real therapy sessions together.

In many Western settings, those who provide trainings in psychotherapies based on mindfulness have adopted top-down, strongly authoritarian organizational models. This was true of the human potential movement, where Scientology and est were major early pioneers, and also in the fields of psychoanalysis and psychotherapy, for example, in the Freudian training regime and in the early Gestalt workshop model. In the field of mindfulness training, this top-down approach might have been inspired or sustained by styles of Eastern teachers and gurus who were, in many cases, the earliest teachers of mindfulness practices like *Zazen, Vipassana*, Transcendental Meditation, and so on.

Whether the training tradition is of Western or Eastern origin, this top-down approach presents a dysfunctional model to students of mindfulness-based therapy. While the content is intended to promote enlightenment, one can hardly say that the organizations and teaching methods are enlightened, if by enlightened we mean reflective of the humanistic values of equality, democratic process, and the right to question authority. The fact that mindfulness practice arose in a feudal context does not mean that it is necessary or optimal to resort to feudal organizational forms as we build on these Eastern foundations. We therefore strongly support honoring humanistic values in workshops and trainings that teach relational mindfulness.

This does not mean that students are at liberty to challenge the curriculum or the method irresponsibly, thereby taxing the time and resources of others.

Nor do we encourage students to disrespect or ignore the wisdom and experience of their trainers. It means that learning a bottom-up approach to therapy should be conducted in a community that respects humanistic values, and does its best to take seriously the responsible feedback of its members. Of primary importance is a leadership that recognizes that mistakes and misalignments inevitably occur between teaching staff and trainees (individually or as a group), and when that occurs, is willing to apologize for the damage done and admit mistakes, thereby modeling, in the most direct way possible, the behavior we encourage in every trainee.

We argue this because we have witnessed the kind of brutality that can occur, unintentionally or through unconsciousness, in top-down organizations. This unintended violence does not advance the training. It makes participants recoil and become inauthentic in order to defend themselves. It is also true that participants feel secure when rules and boundaries are well maintained, and when breaches are acknowledged and corrected. There is nothing that will create insecurity and defensive behavior among trainees more quickly than radical changes to the rules of behavior due to the whims or psychological needs of those in charge.

We are speaking here of humanizing the feudal style that is common to the history of both Eastern and Western cultures, especially with regard to training in psychoanalysis and psychotherapy. We realize that there are many organizations that have already undertaken this kind of transformation. However, rather than attempting to judge, and recommend one or another, based on our own experiences and prejudices, we prefer to offer the reader and prospective trainee some suggested guidelines regarding what to look for in a training environment.

SUGGESTED GUIDELINES FOR
SELECTING TRAINING ORGANIZATIONS

1. The leadership respects democratic process, and the training
    organization reflects a bottom-up approach that is responsive to
    the needs, questions, and concerns of trainees, so that policies
    and decisions regarding the method or the training agenda are not
    set by a single person, but are developed through a process of
    deliberation that includes diverse opinions and points of view.

2. The training program includes instruction and practice in
    communication that empowers trainees to communicate effectively
    to the staff and with each other as the training proceeds.

3. The staff and trainees sign agreements prior to the training that
    provide a container for the training community. These agreements
    address personal responsibility, truth-telling, and logistics
    (punctuality, intentionality, and so forth).

4. Staff and trainees sign a code of ethics that is negotiated before
    the training starts. This code of ethics includes guidelines
    addressing sexual and romantic contact between trainees and
    between trainees and staff members, including assistants.

5. Candidates for the training are carefully screened and known
    personally by the staff before admission.

6. The organization provides sufficient qualified staff and assistants
    to offer coaching and support during one-on-one student therapy
    sessions.

There are many excellent training organizations that provide experiential
workshops in each of the methods discussed here. These are widely available
on the internet. A search with the key words Hakomi, Internal Family
Systems, or Focusing is a good place to start. Fortunately, the academic
environment is beginning to take notice of the enormous resources that

have evolved over the past thirty years. In the best of all possible worlds, we could look forward to an alliance and cross-fertilization, comparable to the cross-fertilization between East and West. A recent book, with the unlikely title *Buddha or Bust*, offers an intriguing and very readable account of the complexity and the enormity of this process with respect to socially engaged Buddhism. If anything can bring about a similar cross-fertilization between the various parallel lines of psychoanalysis and psychotherapy, including psychodynamic, cognitive, experiential, and existential schools of practice, it will be the recognition of a common core of mindfulness and humanistic values that has the potential to unify these diverse approaches to healing and liberation.

Initial steps have already been taken by those who have walked both conventional academic and unconventional spiritual and human potential paths—pioneers like Jon Kabat-Zinn, Daniel Goldman, Chögyam Trungpa, Thich Nhat Hahn, Daniel J. Siegel, Pat Ogden, Donna M. Roy, Thomas Lewis, Daniel Stern, Eugene Gendlin, Richard Schwartz, Marilyn Linehan, Halko Weiss, Greg Johanson, and many others too numerous to mention. There is already Naropa in the United States, an accredited contemplative university inspired by the Oxford-educated Tibetan monk Chögyam Trungpa. Hakomi has been accepted as part of academic training for psychotherapists in Germany, thanks largely to Halko Weiss of the Hakomi Institute, and in New Zealand, thanks to the efforts of other members of the Hakomi Institute. It is therefore possible to imagine that courses in these mindfulness-based methods will become more widely available to the next generation of academically trained psychotherapists. In the meantime, we suggest that students carefully select from among the currently available non-accredited resources, using the guidelines suggested here and their own instincts and intuitions, to supplement conventional academic training.

PART 2

EXPANSION
AND COMMENTARY
ON THE DVD

SUGGESTIONS FOR HOW TO USE THIS SECTION AND THE DVD

PART 2 of this book is a supplement to the Training DVD entitled *Mindfulness Centered Therapies*. It offers an introduction to Mindfulness Centered Therapies, expands the topics covered by narrative chapters in the DVD, and expands and qualifies the video clip demonstrations which are taken from live counseling sessions.

The first chapter of the DVD is a brief didactic introduction summarized some of the material offered in Part 1. Following this introduction seven important skills are described and demonstrated. For each skill there are two DVD chapters. The first contains a brief description of the skill (for example: "Evoking Mindfulness") and then explains when and how the skill is used. The second chapter presents examples of how these mindfulness skills are used in therapy sessions. This chapter presents one to three video clips from real therapy sessions that demonstrate that skill. The menu has been arranged with the narratives and examples in different chapters, so that the viewer may review either the narrative or the example clips. That is, the viewer need not repeat the narrative in order to view the clips a second or third time. In organizing it this way, we anticipated that a student might view the clips for a given skill a number of times in succession, in order to learn the method of delivery, timing, and nuances without having to repeat the narrative.

It goes without saying that learning styles may differ, and readers may use the material in other ways. In any case, it is our sincere hope that students of Mindfulness Centered Therapies will find these resources useful, and will be inspired to follow up with more extensive reading and experiential work, perhaps with trainers like Ron Kurtz, Donna Martin, or The Hakomi

Institute: the Center for Self Leadership for IFS; and the Focusing Institute for the work of Eugene Gendlin.

DVD CHAPTER 1

INTRODUCTION TO MINDFULNESS

As we use mindfulness in Hakomi, it might be called assisted meditation. In therapy, its greatest effect is simply staying with experience longer, before following immediately by emotional reaction, discriminative thought, reflection, purposeful action. It is a matter of staying a little longer, gathering more information and allowing things to happen by themselves. Highly complex, living systems like we humans, organize our perceptions and actions around core images and beliefs. In ordinary consciousness, going about the daily business of life, these core beliefs exert control without our being conscious of their influence. They function in the background, unnoticed. One of the main goals of the therapeutic process is to bring this organizing material into consciousness, to study it and understand it. Mindfulness, as a state of consciousness, is the tool we use.

- Ron Kurtz, *Body-centered Psychotherapy*

WE like to think of mindfulness as a state of compassionate consciousness in which one is aware and attentive to the ever-changing flow of present moment inner experience. This awareness includes thoughts, attitudes, feelings, images, and body sensations as they arise, change, and diminish. We often call this awareness "present moment awareness" because it is focused on experience that is happening in the here and now. Admittedly, any experience that we describe, or even think about, is already in the past as we describe it. If a client says, "I'm frightened," the fear that he is naming is fear that he felt just before naming it. Once having named it, the fear may change. It may even shift, perhaps to anger, sadness, or frustration, or it may disappear. Furthermore, when someone says, "Now the fear is gone, and I feel my jaws getting tight and my fists clenching," even as she speaks, the subject of her speaking is in the past.

We can liken this situation to a savvy gardener on a very fast train, who names the flowers and trees she sees through the window as the train moves through the landscape. Some aspects of our experience are fleeting, like the flowers, while others occupy us for minutes, hours, or even days. Some are like the wheat fields of the vast interior plains, or the Rocky Mountains, that go on for days. These are the kinds of experiences that we often work with in therapy: the persistent or cyclical feelings we feel "stuck" with. So when we say, "I feel anxious," it is true we are talking about the immediate past, but often the same kinds of feelings are still there after we name them, even though, once recognized, named, and shared with another, our experience is usually altered—sometimes mildly, sometimes radically.

In this sense we can think about mindfulness as a state of being aware of experience in the present moment. But there is another aspect of mindful awareness that we have not mentioned. For in our meaning of the word awareness, there is an understanding that we mean "pure" awareness. Another way to say this is "non-judgmental" awareness. Returning to our train analogy, it is not enough for the savvy gardener to be saying or thinking, "There goes a dandelion—what a useless and bothersome flower!" or, "Look at that beautiful Rose!" or, "Horrors! A field of opium poppies—how dangerous they are! They should be poisoned out of existence."

While such a judgmental observer is observing some of her experience (the dandelions, roses, and poppies), she is probably failing to notice others (her judgments, attitudes, opinions, interpretations, and prejudices). Not only does she fail to notice them, but she is unaware that they exist. It is as if they are too close to her for her to see them. We could say that her awareness or her identity is "blended" with her judgments, opinions, interpretations, feelings, and so on. Until her "savvy-ness" expands to include knowledge about her interpretations and attitudes, her observations will be colored by them. She will probably believe in them. She will exist in the state of delusion that most of us occupy most of the time. It is the state in which we say with conviction: "I am so foolish!", "I'm such a loser!", "He's a jerk!", or "This is a terrible headache!"

It usually requires help—a book, a meditation instructor, or a psychotherapist—for one to cultivate nonjudgmental awareness. Without some form of training most of us cannot or do not distinguish the facts of experience from interpretations. We are therefore unable to psychologically step back and unblend our identity from our stories, judgments, interpretations, and so forth. Once the knack for this kind of distancing is grasped, a transformation happens. One might even call it a small enlightenment. In Mindfulness Centered Therapies, this happens over and over again. Eventually clients no longer require their therapists' help to attain and remain in this pure form of awareness for significant intervals. For Hakomi, a significant interval of continuous mindfulness is in the range of thirty seconds to ten minutes. For IFS and Focusing, a somewhat longer interval is desirable, say, ten to thirty minutes. There may be momentary lapses in either case, but there must be sufficient continuity to allow the work to go forward.

AWARENESS AND COMPASSION

One of the most surprising things about this pure awareness of present moment inner experience is that it naturally tends toward friendliness and compassion. I think this is true in the world of outer experience as well. If we suspend our judgments and learn to spend more time in the present moment, our everyday experience takes on freshness. We get out of our heads (where we are constantly blended with our thoughts) and unblend from moods and stereotyped feeling states. Our minds open to new ways of knowing the world. It is like cleaning off life's windshield. It has a miraculous quality—a vital clarity. We feel nourished by it. Naturally we are likely to be more open and receptive to places, situations, and people. In Mindfulness Centered Therapies, we call this nonjudgmental, unblended attitude of awareness "compassion." It shows up when we cultivate mindfulness. As we help our clients cultivate a compassionate attitude toward their inner experience, eventually this compassion is extended to others.

That does not mean that we paint over sorrow with a glossy coat of positive paint, to try to turn it into something it isn't. On the contrary, we help our clients to greet and connect with every kind of experience in an accepting, compassionate way. By modeling this compassion, the therapist teaches clients to stay present and fully witness their feelings. Surprisingly, our clients discover that when they do this, their feelings are comforted. The feelings calm down, and are less painful and less extreme. Furthermore, our clients receive from their compassionate awareness what they did not get from others—especially their parents or caretakers—when early incidents of wounding and trauma took place.

Describing the process of therapy in a language of experience, feelings, awareness, and compassion may suggest that Mindfulness Centered Therapies are based on sympathy, mysticism, soft thinking, or soft science. Many academic training programs intentionally or unintentionally predispose their graduates to eschew these "feeling-based" approaches, and contrast them strongly with methods that have increasingly favored working with cognitive material only, pharmacotherapy, or combinations of both. As one learns more about what initially seems to be an academic consensus, however, one discovers that there is little agreement in the conclusions of research studies. Some of the most solid evidence for the effectiveness of therapy indicates that it is the personhood of the therapist, not the method of treatment that produces the highest rates of successful outcomes (Lambert, M. J. 1989). In addition, it has been found that therapies that encourage clients to recognize and name their inner experience, whether they are cognitive, experiential, or emotionally based, are statistically the most effective (Gendlin, 1975, 1996).

In our own life experience, mindfulness has been the basis for the development of the qualities associated with personhood. It has helped us to calm down, cooperate better, be less volatile, control anger, be patient, be more present, and listen better. We could name a long list of skills like this that are almost impossible without mindfulness. Mindfulness has also given us the ability to recognize and name present moment experience. We are far more able to own and talk about our feelings with others. All of these skills are essential for intimacy. Could it be that cognitive therapies are successful because, without recognizing or naming it, they encourage mindfulness?

In addition, Mindfulness Centered Therapies adopt many of the principles and practices of cognitive approaches, such as the very popular approach described by Dr. Albert Ellis and Aaron Beck in the mid-1950s and early 1960s, all the way to skills taught in the work of David Burns, author of the bestselling books *Feeling Good* (1980) and *The Feeling Good Handbook* (1990). We have used Burns' book often, and occasionally recommend it to clients. In Mindfulness Centered Therapies, we recognize that most cognitive approaches encourage mindfulness with regard to speech and thought. In our work with clients we consider the thought distortions catalogued by Burns to represent the thoughts of young "parts," where "parts" are semiautonomous fragments of the ego or personality. These young parts are often "stuck" in time. When we identify with them, we think the way they do. We generalize, personalize, exaggerate, minimize, and so on. These thought distortions are markers representing early stages in the development of mature cognitive abilities.

When we hear this kind of speaking or infer this kind of interior conversation in a client, we suspect that the client is identified with a young part. It might be a seven-year-old who was overwhelmed by the loss of a parent, a spanking, or some other kind of abuse. Many of our reactive feelings are associated with the unconscious remnants of these kinds of painful and overwhelming life experiences. Helping a client to complete these experiences by working through them with the presence of a compassionate other, and in the presence of their own compassionate awareness, allows clients to unblend from these young parts, and liberates them from reactive thoughts, feelings, and behaviors that move in repetitious orbits around the influence of these significant, yet unconscious, life-altering events.

APPLYING MINDFULNESS IN WORKING WITH OTHERS

I N the DVD we draw from three forms of psychotherapy to provide some examples of how mindfulness can be applied to actual therapy sessions; first and foremost is Hakomi body-centered psychotherapy (Kurtz, 1990) also called "assisted self discovery". This is because Hakomi not only employs mindfulness to explore, name and describe internal experience, it takes this exploration one step further by using precise and gentle experiments done with the client in a temporary state of mindfulness. These "little experiments in mindfulness" evoke emotions, memories, and reactions that reveal the underlying and unconscious beliefs, decisions and convictions that determine the client's habitual patterns of behavior.

In order to employ this method the therapist needs to evoke mindfulness in the client for a very brief period of time (on the order of fifteen to thirty seconds). This is another advantage of Hakomi, since IFS and Focusing require longer periods of continuous mindfulness, sometimes more than a client can sustain when they are new to the method. The techniques for evoking these brief periods of mindfulness is the first subject in the training DVD.

Where Does "Evoking Mindfulness" Fit In the Therapy Session?

Imagine a therapy session that begins in the usual way. A new client is greeted and offered a chair facing the therapist. In this scenario, we will consider the therapist to be female, and the client male, and we will place both therapist and client in a similar swiveling chair, with no desk, no symbol of authority, in the room arrangement. This is done in order to avoid increasing the initial power differential that is likely to exist already while one person is in the role of "therapist" and the other is in the role of "client."

Almost as soon as the client enters the room, our Hakomi therapist is aware that her client is mildly anxious and self-conscious. Once the client is seated, there is that little moment, with the client waiting, and the therapist just being there with the client. After a brief pause, the therapist says, "Maybe a little nervous, eh." It's not exactly a question, but the end of the phrase turns up to indicate that this is a guess, and can be easily corrected if it misses the mark.

In this case, it's a hit, and the client, upon reflection, says "Yeah, I guess I am. I've never done this before."

The therapist offers, "Maybe it would help to go over how it works a little; maybe that would help you to feel more comfortable." The client nods, and the therapist explains a little about the process: "Usually when I work with people, they start by talking about why they are here. I listen and try to understand them—not only what they think, but how they feel. At some point, something might catch my eye, or I might hear or intuit something, and I may call your attention to it. If that happens, we'll see if you would like to explore it. This is about self study. My job is to help you study how your experience is organized, and how that organization effects your actions and behavior. We don't do that intellectually, we do it by observing our experience. If you like what we do in this session, you may wish to make another appointment. We can talk about that later, after the session is over."

The client nods and waits again. The therapist invites him to begin: "You can just talk about anything you like, or we can just sit here. Sooner or later, something will happen that we can look into." The therapist is evoking some kind of behavior; usually that involves talking, but she is trying not to lead or direct. She wants the client to decide what to do.

Now the client talks and the therapist listens. In Hakomi, we call this tracking. Tracking is described in detail in Part I with example transcripts. We call it tracking because the therapist is following the client. She is not asking questions that lead the client toward the therapist's agenda. She is not interrupting the client, or even agreeing or disagreeing with little nods of the head or other judgmental gestures. Ideally, the therapist's face and body posture honestly reflect her authentic state as she listens, one that is receptive, appreciative, friendly, spacious, calm, and open.

It is important to note, however, that something else is going on at the same time. The therapist is not merely listening to the content of what the client is saying. In fact, this verbal content does not have the therapist's primary attention. Rather, the therapist is giving her primary attention to the nonverbal aspects of what the client is saying. This nonverbal content is revealed in body language, gestures, and facial expressions, tone of voice, little habits and tics. Maybe the client is talking very fast. Maybe the client's eye contact is shy or avoidant. Maybe the client's head is tilted, as if he is constantly asking a question, or feeling suspicious. The therapist is not ignoring the client's words. They are being taken in automatically. One might say the therapist is back-grounding the content, and foregrounding the context (everything else). It's the reverse of how we are usually taught to listen. By doing this, the therapist can track the client's changing succession of states: nervous, shy, self-conscious, excited, sad, effortful, exhausted, and so forth.

From time to time, the therapist is also making "contact statement" These are very brief, one- or two-word responses slipped into the flow of the client's speech at points of pause. The therapist might say, "anxious, eh," "some sadness now," or just a single word like, "frustrating." She is just naming or labeling the client's state in a tentative way, leaving room to be wrong, and holding these labels lightly. After making one of these little contact statements, she waits quietly to see what happens next. Sometimes the client will make a correction. More often, he checks out his present moment experience, and his speaking and nonverbal expressions shift to a deeper level.

It takes considerable practice and training to learn how to listen like this, and to make good contact statements, but it is worth the effort. Contact statements are very effective, and when they are made well, they deepen the client's experience of what is happening in the moment, and let him know that the therapist is listening to him, as he has never been listened to before. They also do not lead the client into the therapist's own agenda. They follow the client in the direction that the client is already going. This is another good reason for calling this kind of listening "tracking" (after Ron Kurtz, 1990).

Sometime during tracking, the therapist will get an idea, or see something that is essential. The idea may be something like, "This session is about being safe," or "The client is confused, but does not want to be confused, so the confusion is stuck," or "This is about belonging." There are all kinds of ideas like this, and we use our intuition to sense them. Once we get one, we want to test it. On the one hand, we want to know if we are "on the right track." On the other, we have a hunch that, in testing this idea, we may open up something for the client, something important, something deeper than what is conscious for the client right now.

At this point, we enter the flow of speaking, hopefully with grace, and in the direction that the stream is flowing. We are now leading, in a way, but we are leading the client deeper by helping the client to become aware of his unconscious experience, and by deepening his relationship to feelings and memories that he already has. This kind of leading can be likened to leading a person who cannot see across the street. We see that he wants to cross—he's standing on the corner, probing for the curb with a white cane—and we offer to help him go in the direction he is already going.

We might say, "You know, as you were talking. I noticing something that might be important and I would like to check it out, just to see if I was following you correctly. Would it be okay if we try something out?" There are many ways to do this, and you will see a number of these little interventions in the video clips.

This is the point at which we usually evoke mindfulness. We tell the client what we propose to do. We evoke their curiosity about the clues we've noticed: their rapid speech, their posture, or something about the way they are being. We get their permission. Then we ask them to look inward, and help them to become mindful. While they are being in this quiet, inward-looking state, we do something to test our idea or to deepen something that is already there. We might ask them to notice what happens, or how they respond, when they hear words carefully chosen for our purposes, such as: "You're safe here," or "I'm glad to see you," or "You're a lovable person."

These used to be called probes (following Kurtz, 1990), but some Hakomi therapists think this word is not accurate because it suggests that we are being intrusive. We prefer to call them "nourishing offerings," or just "offerings." It is one of many kinds of experiments that we do in mindfulness. Doing experiments in mindfulness is a method unique to Hakomi. It adds a dimension to mindfulness work that is not found in books about stress relief or teaching meditation to clients. While we can also use offerings to comfort and soothe chaotic or overwhelming feeling states, and thereby help clients to calm themselves down, in the early phases of a session, offerings are usually intended to deepen or study something, or to access unconscious feelings that live in the back-story of the client's present moment experience and behavior.

In forthcoming chapters of the DVD, there are many of examples of these little experiments in mindfulness.

In the foregoing scenario, we have imagined a new client. But the same form is often used with clients who are very familiar with Hakomi after many sessions; the client talks and the therapist tracks. The therapist gets an idea or an intuition about something essential that is happening right now, in the present moment. With the client's permission and cooperation, the therapist sets up a little experiment in mindfulness that tests that intuition, and at the same time may deepen the client's experience and help him access something that, until that moment, was outside of his consciousness. It may be a feeling, a reaction, a body sensation, or a memory. It is almost always something important, something fundamental to what is on the client's plate in present time.

COMMENTS ON DEMONSTRATION CLIPS

IN the video examples of Chapter 3, we have included three examples that demonstrate evoking mindfulness. In each of these examples, the therapist has been very demonstrative. Knowing that this would be used on the DVD, the therapist takes more time than usual to describe to each client exactly what kinds of experience to look for. We did this because we thought that therapists would benefit from seeing the most detailed examples, ones that would work for new clients who find mindfulness difficult. As clients work with Hakomi over time, less and less needs to be said to evoke Mindfulness. Here is a much more typical example taken from Ron Kurtz's textbook on Hakomi:

> "Just notice…you don't have to do anything…you can just be open and…let my words come in and notice anything that goes on in your experience…it could be a thought, a feeling, sensations, and image… it could be a memory…it could be an impulse or a change in muscle tension… and it's all right if nothing happens."
>
> (Kurtz, 1990, p. 86)

Once Hakomi clients have experienced four or five Hakomi sessions, one need merely say, in a soft, slow, evocative voice, "Let's get ready now, and go inside to observe what happens… I'll just wait quietly until you are ready."

The client will know exactly what to do, and the therapist will confirm that mindfulness is present through observations of nonverbal signs, and by the kind and quality of reports clients make about their experience after the experiments have been conducted. Usually when clients have reached a state of mindfulness, their eyes flutter beneath their eyelids. Therapists can observe this fluttering through the very thin skin of the eyelids. This is a good sign to watch for. In fact, you may be able to see this in the demonstration clips. We often forget that clients are learning our method as we work. There is an unavoidable teaching that takes place, even though it is not our intention, and it is usually happening outside of their consciousness.

DVD Chapter 4

MAKING A VERBAL
OFFERING

EMOTIONAL nourishment" is another Ron Kurtz metaphor we use in Hakomi, and like "tracking," it gives us a handle on processes that are vitally important to the work that Hakomi therapists do. It is very easy to understand, yet it is so essential in psychotherapy that it is hard to imagine doing healing work without it. Once again, we are indebted to the genius of Ron Kurtz for his grasp of this idea, and for the development of resources that utilize emotional nourishment to promote therapeutic self-discovery.

We all know what physical nourishment is; basically, it is food, air, and water. We need to consume these at regular intervals in order to survive, thrive, and set our minds free to work, play, and to be productive and creative. When air, food, or water is scarce or lacking, we suffer discomfort. We feel restless and dissatisfied. Eventually craving and compulsiveness develop, as we become frantic to find it. If the deprivation continues, our energy sinks, and we fall into a kind of lethargic stupor as our bodies shut down all activities that are not essential in order to conserve energy. We witness this condition in victims of strangulation or asphyxiation, famine, or drought.

Like physical nourishment, emotional nourishment is something we need in order to grow and thrive and be happy, energetic, and creative. We find it in being inspired by beauty; by feeling connected and belonging with parents, family members, and friends; in being fully seen, understood, and recognized; when we are comforted with sweet words or touch. It lives in the feeling of warmth and safety of a loving relationship, in playing and accomplishing, and when we appreciate others, and see their courage, generosity, and loving kindness.

These are just a few examples of emotional nourishment. You can probably think of many more. The essence of emotional nourishment is that when we receive it, when we take it in, it makes us feel genuinely good. These good feelings range from comfort, security, and relief, to satisfaction, gratitude, joy, and inspiration. Likewise, when we cannot receive it, either because it is not available or because we cannot take it in, we feel miserable, restless, anxious, fearful, insecure, unloved, misunderstood, frustrated, resentful, or dissatisfied. In Hakomi, we know this to be true because we know how quickly someone who has these kinds of feelings responds to the right kind of emotional nourishment. The response is immediate and profound. Finding a way for a client to take in a form of emotional nourishment that is missing is perhaps the most satisfying thing a therapist can do for the client, and it is nourishing and heart-opening for the therapist as well.

The concept of emotional nourishment is extremely simple and obvious once it is pointed out. One might imagine that with this knowledge, psychotherapy becomes a simple matter: just find out what kind of emotional nourishment is missing, and provide it! If ingesting the medicine of emotional nourishment were that simple and straightforward, psychotherapists could be trained to be "emotional dietitians." Unfortunately, it is not that simple. We all know this, but why is this not so?

The reason is that taking in emotional nourishment is often fraught with risk. For example, feeling safe can be a setup for being attacked or abused; feeling loved makes us vulnerable to being deeply hurt; being seen exposes us to criticism and judgment, not to mention rejection, humiliation, and shame. By the same token, accepting comfort from others can quickly become something else that makes us feel smothered, trapped, invaded, or rejected.

It seems that every form of emotional nourishment comes with at least one pitfall. Ideally an adult can handle these pitfalls with equanimity, and can find help and trustworthy comfort when that fails. But the truth is most adults cannot do this with at least one kind of emotional nourishment, and often with many more. Today, for many adults, sexuality offers the only channel through which they hope to experience real connection with another. It is often their only hope for feeling the connection and comfort that comes with touch. Unfortunately, this channel is often fraught with difficulties, and after painful disappointments they may even give up sexuality. In order to understand this, we must consider childhood, and how we learn to shut ourselves off to emotional experience as we negotiate the difficult processes of growing up.

To a child, a betrayal, rejection, abandonment, or disappointment can be a disaster. Because children lack support, power, mobility, social and language skills, understanding, information, and experience, these disasters are all too often suffered alone, without help, understanding, and comfort. When this happens, survival responses take over. The child reacts in order to survive, and in the process, a structure is often put in place that is designed to insure that pain like this—unregulated emotional chaos and hurt, plunges from elation into disappointment, isolation, terror, or shame—will never happen again. Then the entire episode, the circumstances, the reaction, the resulting distortion of one's worldview, even the existence of the memory itself, becomes unconscious. We are left with an automatic and habitual aversion to the kind of nourishment that set us up for the experience.

This aversion deprives us of some kind of essential nourishment, and alters our innocent worldview with regard to something about that experience. For example, where once we perceived the world as a safe place, now that natural trust in life is replaced by a structure (a belief, disposition, or a decision) that the world is dangerous. Or perhaps it is generalized, but not that far, so we decide that people are dangerous or maybe just people that we love. In some way, every intensely painful event, like touching an emotional hot stove, has the potential to teach us lessons that lead to generalizations or overreactions that will shut us down to nourishment in later life.

Injuries suffered in early life are necessarily processed by immature and inexperienced minds. Many refinements in the application of cognitive skills are not yet fully realized. The interpretations, decisions, and lessons derived from these early experiences are therefore subject to all of the thought distortions that we study in cognitive psychology, like the ones Burns has mentioned:

Cognitive Distortions

1. Generalization
2. Exaggeration and minimization
3. Personalization
4. Black and white thinking and so on. (Burns, 1980, 1990)

This is enough to explain most of our inability to recognize and utilize the emotional nourishment that is abundantly provided by our environments, and absolutely essential to our growth. In this respect we, as human beings, live as if we are ironically and needlessly starving, while at the same time we inhabit a cornucopia, a plenitude of the emotional nourishment we so badly crave and require.

How do we know this to be true? We learn this by asking someone to be mindful and, as they pay close attention to their inner responses, offering them a morsel of emotional nourishment. This is what we mean by "making a nourishing offering." Making these offerings is not difficult, because we do not have to offer them the real thing. We can just offer the idea of it—merely the words. That is enough to evoke a response. In other words, we do not have to make a person perfectly safe, we can offer them the idea of safety by saying in a soothing voice something like, "You are safe here," "I'll protect you," "This is a safe place," "No one will harm you here." In doing this, we are not trying to deceive them. We make it clear to them that we are simply offering the words. We can say to them, "Just notice what happens when you hear the words 'It's safe here' (or 'You're a loveable person' or 'You deserve to be loved, ' or 'You are a good person.' ")

When we do this, we find that our clients will exhibit one of three basic responses:

1. The client takes the nourishment in. She reports feelings of relief, or relaxes a little. Perhaps we can see her shoulders drop, and her chest open. Maybe she reports a sensation of inner warmth. We call this "taking the nourishment in." We take it to mean that our client can utilize the kind of nourishment we have offered her.

2. The client notices a reaction. She tightens up; her shoulders rise. Or perhaps we don't see that, but she reports hearing a voice that rebels against or rejects the nourishment we have offered. We offer her, "You're a good person," and she hear a voice in her head saying, "If he only knew!" or "How does he know that?" or "Don't listen to that." Or maybe we just notice that she freezes up, ever so subtly, and her breathing suddenly shifts to a more constricted pattern. Somehow this nourishment—the mere idea of it—sets off a reaction.

3. There is no response to the nourishment. It is psychologically neutral for her at this time, and in this situation. Usually we take this to mean that there is no emotional charge on this kind of nourishment. It is not something the client needs or longs for at the moment, and it is not something she automatically avoids. It is like a bland meal when we are not very hungry.

Let's say we have been listening and watching a client talk, and we get the idea that under the surface conversation, there is a longing for contact with people, but for some reason this contact is difficult. We sense that this session has something to do with his sense of belonging. It might be conveyed by an aversion to eye contact, or by the way he seems to push us away with a loud voice, while he speaks about wanting to be close. We have an idea this is so, but we need to do something to check it out. We are like a space scientist who thinks that there is no air on the moon, and wants to test this theory out. So he designs an experiment.

In psychotherapy, we do the same thing. We ask the client to look inward and become mindful, and then we say something like, "You belong here," or "You're welcome here," or "I'm glad to see you." In each case, the words convey the idea of "belonging," and they are offered as potential nourishment. We wait a few moments, watching for nonverbal reactions, and then we ask for a report.

COMMENTS ON DEMONSTRATION CLIPS

THERE are three video clips illustrating the technique "making a nourishing offering" included in DVD Chapter V. We will review them one at a time to point out a few details that might escape notice. The first clip extracts a part of a session in which the client has been talking about her frustration in completing a school assignment. From key words and nonverbal observations, the therapist has an idea about the essence or undercurrent of this conversation. He silently speculates or intuits that the client is describing a pattern that is organized around a core belief that "there is not enough time," or "there is not enough time for me."

In listening to clients, Hakomi therapists are always looking for signs of these core beliefs or core organizing structures. When we think we have found one, we never believe our intuition blindly. This is one of the very distinctive aspects of Hakomi. In Hakomi, we actually test our hunches instead of offering them as interpretations, and we train ourselves to hold them lightly, without attachment. We are ready to give them up when the evidence does not support them. One way to test an idea is to perform a "little experiment in mindfulness." To do this, the therapist takes the core belief and turns it around into something that is nourishing. In this clip, the therapist takes "There's not enough time for me," a belief that could be associated with panic, freezing, and writer's block, and reverses it into the nourishing statement "There's plenty of time for you, Heather." (The use of the client's name is optional, but sometimes it can personalize the nourishment and make it an even juicier.)

As we see in the video clip, the client clearly rejects this offering by not trusting it. She hears a voice, or thought, that says: "I don't believe it." This is an excellent example of a "thought" reaction to a nourishing offering. It tells us that, even if someone has plenty of time for her, the client operates with a worldview that there is not enough. This is an important piece of evidence for the therapist. It supports the idea that the client's behavioral pattern is related to underlying experiences having to do with time. This is still a theory, but it is a stronger one at this point, and there are number of ways to follow up on it that will help to explore how the client's experience is organized with respect to the subject of time. We will see more of this exploration in DVD Chapter 7.

In the second clip, the therapist tests the idea that the issue underlying the surface behavior and conversation is safety. In other words, he explores the notion that this session is about the unconscious idea that the world is not a safe place, or "Life is essentially dangerous." A worldview such as this can be the result of living through a volatile or brutal environment as a child. It can also be caused by later experiences, such as trauma associated with military service, violent marriages, and so forth. In this case, the client reacts viscerally, with physical sensations, and there are also important nonverbal indicators. For example, look closely at the client's eyes. There is a definite look of hurt and resentment. We can see that the offering has evoked not only a reaction, but at least one experience from the past, a memory of a situation that may have contributed to how he is organized around the issue of safety.

The third clip is especially interesting because it evokes two conflicting reactions that convey the sense that being seen can be a nourishing experience, and it can also be the opposite. This is not uncommon. The human psyche is very capable of this kind of "splitting." In IFS therapy, it is interpreted as a sign of two different parts being present. One part takes delight in being seen, while another is afraid of being seen. We could also interpret that the delighted part is the essential Self, displaying joy at being seen, while there is also a reactive part responding, one that remembers an experience in which being seen led to trouble, or a very overwhelming or disagreeable experience. It is informative to notice how the client's demeanor shifts as she expresses each reaction: "No, it's not," (accompanied by a facial expression that questions and distrusts), and "Oh, I like that," in which the face of a young child seems to shine through with pure and innocent joy.

In the following DVD chapters, we will explore these reactions further, using the technique of "taking over," and we will see how the experiences that unfold in the sessions confirm with concrete memories our hunches and intuitions in these opening experiments. With regard to the second clip, the one involving safety, the session soon brought out memories that involved family members and others, and I felt that it was not appropriate to include this material, even with the client's release and consent. But I can say that the rest of this session clearly confirmed the initial idea that safety was a central concern, and that the feelings of hurt and bitterness were very real, and arose out of painful memories of very violent and dangerous situations.

TAKING OVER REACTIONS

THE roots of Hakomi body-centered psychotherapy tap deeply into Eastern soil, especially the traditions of Buddhism and Taoism. In these traditions, the ethos of yielding or "going with" is fundamental. This principle of supporting or going with what is happening in the present moment is clearly expressed in the following verses from the *Tao Te Ching:*

If you want to shrink something,
You must first allow it to expand.
If you want to get rid of something,
You must first let it flourish,
If you want to take something,
You must first allow it to be given.
This is called the subtle perception
Of the way things are.
(From Johanson and Kurtz, 1991, translated by Mitchell 1988, p.36)

In therapy, Ron Kurtz has translated the Taoist principle of yielding into a way of working with the automatic reactions that manage or suppress emergent unconscious experience. These skills require that the therapist suspend his impulse to react to the client's reaction. When this attitude of "going with" is exercised in therapy, amazing things happen: reactions that are welcomed become sources of valuable information; opposition that is supported finds an ally in the therapist, and ceases the struggle; resistance that is supported yields so completely that we wonder why we called it resistance. In other words, reactivity can be used to carry the process forward.

Taking over a reaction is an example of this kind of therapeutic Aikido, in which the therapist gets on the side of a reaction that opposes a nourishing offering, and not only supports it, but completely takes it over on behalf of the client. One way to think of it is that the client's reaction, whether it is a thought, a physical tightening or pulling back, or an internal compressing or holding the breath, is a way of managing an experience that begins to emerge in response to the permission or invitation conveyed by the nourishing statement offered by a therapist. (Kurtz, 1990)

Another way to think about it is that the client's reaction is a part of the way that the unconscious mind organizes itself (Kurtz, 1990). Just as we can organize our office to minimize or hide an ugly flaw in the architecture—a crack in the wall, an ugly beam, or damaged floor—so we unconsciously organize our inner life so that certain experiences are obviated or hidden from our awareness. By hiding these experiences, we are not troubled by them, and we can attend to the business of living more effectively, at least for the short term. But there are lapses in this mode of organization, and when these experiences begin to intrude, we distract ourselves with a certain thought, or with some action or gesture. When feelings of loneliness begin to trouble us, we unconsciously stroke one hand with the other, take a drink, or eat too much. When anxiety builds, we begin to scratch our right arm, or massage the edge of our sweater.

In "taking over" experiments, our client reports a reaction that he notices when we make a nourishing offering. We can also notice some of these management behaviors by paying very close attention to nonverbal indicators. For example, we offer a nourishing offering, and the client rejects it with the thought, "I don't believe that." If we argue with the client, or try to convince him that the offering is true, we will strengthen the reaction, or drive it underground. If it goes underground, it will take the experience we would like to access along with it. This oppositional approach will also estrange the client, and throw our relationship out of attunement. In other words, this approach leads to stuck or unproductive therapy. If it is repeated a few times, it can result in damage to the process and the therapeutic alliance.

The Hakomi way is to welcome the reaction and to go even further by offering to take it over, to actually do it on behalf of the client. If it is a thought, like "I don't believe it," we suggest a new experiment to the client. We say, "Would it be okay if you become mindful again while I repeat that statement? Then, after I say the statement, I will say, 'I don't believe it.' That way, you won't have to do it or even think it. You can just notice what happens when you don't have to think that thought." If the client agrees, the therapist suggests that he will repeat the offering and the reaction three times, so that the client will have a number of opportunities to observe what happens.

When this kind of taking over is done skillfully, it often evokes an experience that the reactive thought or action has been managing. It might be an emotion, a sensation like tightness in the chest or jaw, or a memory. This experience is sometimes subtle but it can also be quite strong. Whatever it is, we welcome it, and help the client to be with it. Sometimes, when it is subtle, we deepen it, using acknowledgments or deepening questions like "Can you sense what kind of sadness that is?" Questions like this encourage clients to stay with their experience. We would never use a question like, "Why do you feel so sad?" In order to answer questions like these, the client must leave their experience and access their intellectual faculties. Doing so breaks the connection with the experience, and disrupts the flow of the unfolding process (Kurtz, 1990).

Taking over can be applied to a thought, and it can also be applied to a physical reaction, as in a situation where the client actual pulls back physically in her chair upon hearing the offering. In this case, the therapist can actually give the offering again a few times, and gently pull the client back in the chair, taking over the physical response. This kind of taking over may release a thought, or some other experience, and the therapist can help by asking accessing and deepening questions that seek to find the meaning of the physical behavior. For example, "What is your body saying when it pulls back like that?" One likely response would be "No!" We can then do the experiment again, and pull the client back as we say the word "No!" There are many ways to use this taking over behavior, and there are a number of examples in the video clips in DVD Chapter 7.

COMMENTS ON DEMONSTRATION CLIPS

I N the first clip, the therapist takes over a reaction to the offering "It's okay to be seen." The actual reaction includes two voices: "No it's not," and "Oh, I like that." While both of the voices seem to be reactive, and both could have been taken over, it is the thought "No it's not" that seems to have the protective and restraining intention that blocks the client's ability to take in the emotional nourishment. So the therapist goes with that. It's a judgment call.

What happens next is rather surprising. When one does this kind of work, we expect these kinds of surprises. Instead of just unleashing more of the "Oh, I like that" response, something new appears, something that seems rather deeper. It is a feeling of sadness. This is an excellent example of the power of this taking over technique. This sad feeling, and the fullness of its expression in facial expression, including tearing, so clearly spontaneous and authentic, speaks for itself, and perfectly demonstrates the power of this use of "little experiments in mindfulness" when used to access the adaptive unconscious.

(This clip includes an unfortunate piece of camera work that resulted from a miscommunication between the therapist and the photographer. The extreme close up of the client's eyes is unintentional. However, we did not want to edit it out because it is a good demonstration of the taking over process and the spontaneous emergence of a managed experience. The client was gracious enough to allow us to keep it.)

In the second clip, the therapist offers "You can do this." which elicits both a thought and a side-to-side head movement. When this rather rebellious spirit is contacted and welcomed by the therapist, there is a very pronounced shift in the client's energy that is apparent in her complexion and the clarity of her eyes, which the therapist sees and mistakes for tears. While there are no tears, the shift in energy is apparent in the video, and it seems to be accompanied by relief.

In exploring the nonverbal expression of the reaction, the side-to-side head movement, a second meaning is elicited: the "I don't want to." seems to be opposed by the thought "I want to." This opposition seems to be identified with the head movement. Forward motion seems stymied, and the client's intention is thrown into a frustrating side-to-side oscillation between these two impulses or thoughts. The reaction is not simple; it is complex and conflicting. In this example, the therapist has a hunch that perhaps this conflict is what holds the client in a trap of blocked action. He decides to test this idea by offering the probe again and taking over both voices. To this he adds a third technique of gently calling the client forth out of this trapped situation by calling her by name. While this is not the only way this could be handled, the therapist is following a hunch, based on previous experience with similarly blocked clients, and on his observation of this head movement that occurred whenever the client talked about her frustration in getting started with her writing project, the ostensible or surface subject of the session.

This move, the taking over of two voices, is another innovation taught by Ron Kurtz. It is most easily accomplished in a group situation, where there are other people available to take over the various voices while the therapist delivers the offering, and may eventually call the person's name if he detects nonverbal indicators suggesting a frozen or hypnotic state. After the experiment is performed, the client affirms the strength of the "I don't want to" side, when she says, "My head just wanted to go that way." It seems as if she has become clearer about this part of herself that doesn't want to do the project. We are now exploring what began as an unexplainable inability to get on with the assignment. It has become increasingly clear that there is a part of her that doesn't want to do it. This was not apparent in her first discussion about the project. In subsequent clips we will see that underlying this conflict is a memory that seems to be triggered by the writing assignment.

INTERNAL DIALOGUE (WITH A PART OR FEELING)

I N this chapter we review the way of working described in Part I that combines elements of Internal Family Systems therapy with Hakomi body-centered psychotherapy. As you have already seen in the preceding chapters, Hakomi therapists usually work directly with clients' experience—acknowledging emotions, interacting with the client, comforting overwhelming feelings. In this alternative application, the therapist acts indirectly by acting as a Hakomi coach. This coaching relationship allows a therapist to teach and encourage clients to apply Hakomi skills as they nourish, comfort, and relate to their own internal experience.

In this approach the therapist asks the client to place his attention on an emergent experience. The therapist also helps the client to stand back from the feeling, so that he does not get pulled into it. Next, the therapist checks to see that the subject is friendly to the feeling. For example, the therapist might ask, "How do you feel toward that feeling? What is your attitude toward it? Do you find yourself wanting to get rid of it, or can you accept it and just be with it?"

If the client says, "I don't like the feeling," "I want to get rid of it," or "I'm tired of it," the therapist suggests that the client ask the part that doesn't like the feeling to stand back. Sometimes a therapist can determine how a client is relating to an emergent experience by paying attention to the client's tone of voice and body language. When this is the case, it is not necessary to interrupt the process by asking. Either way, it is important that the client be in a state of nonjudgmental and compassionate mindfulness, (also called "Self-leadership") before introducing the next step which is to invite the client to connect with the feeling part.

To make the next step the therapist coaches the client in acknowledging the feeling or feeling part. An acknowledgment is a simple "I statement" that has the form "I see (or sense) how anxious (sad, lonely, scared, or angry) you are." It is important that this acknowledgment come from the subject's heart, so the therapist models this when introducing the suggested acknowledgment. The therapist asks the client to give this message to the feeling or feeling part silently. This acknowledgment does not work as well when it is done aloud. It seems to work best when the therapist models the statement aloud in a warm compassionate voice and then coaches the client in making the acknowledgment silently, or even "as a wordless message sent from the heart".

After the instruction, the client goes inside and makes the acknowledgment. As soon as the therapist senses that this has happened, the therapist asks the client to notice and report what happens to the feeling part when it receives this message. This is extremely important. This question directs the client back to the feeling part, keeping the client connected and noticing the feeling part's response. Usually, the client will say that the part or feeling calms down. Sometimes, the client will report that it intensifies. There is nothing wrong with this. Occasionally the feeling will intensify to the point of erupting in tears. That's fine. The therapist offers comfort and nourishment, without fixing or smothering, and the client will usually calm down. Once the client is calm again, the dialogue can continue. There are many variations on this skill, and we have included many clips illustrating different ways that the dialogue can develop.

If the feeling part does nothing when contact is made, there are a number of possibilities. The client may not be completely mindful or Self-led. The client might be identified with a part that wants to get rid of, or to change the feeling. This will prevent the connection from being made. It is also possible that the feeling part does not trust the Self or the mindful awareness of the client. In this case the client may report that the part we want to work with withdraws, "hides" or does not respond. In this case the therapist coaches the client in winning the suspicious part's trust. The most effective way to do this is give the part time. For example, the client might silently say to the untrusting part: "I see that you do not trust me. That's okay; I know it takes time to trust". This is an extremely effective message to an untrusting part. Once the lack of trust is acknowledged and accepted and the pressure is off, suspicious parts usually make significant moves toward trust and connection. If this fails the client can try to find out what that part might need to restore lost trust. Another approach is to ask the part how long it intends to withhold its trust. This question often can be used to draw a part into communication. Once that happens the connection can be made and the issue of trust is circumvented. There are a number of examples of working with trust in the clips that follow.

COMMENTARY ON CLIPS

W E begin the first clip with the client reporting a feeling of anxiety, including a tight sensation in her chest, accompanied by a sense of restricted breathing. The therapist's first intention is to assist the client in establishing a connection with the anxious part. He checks to see if the client is accepting the anxious apart. This reveals another part that wants the feeling to go away. This is a very common situation: there is a part that has an uncomfortable feeling and wants attention and comfort, but there is another part that wants the discomfort to go away, and does not want the feeling part to be exposed. The client identifies with the protective part that wants the feeling part to go away.

The therapist introduces parts language to help the client to unblend (dis-identify) from the protective part. The parts language is accepted by the client, and he is coached to ask that protective part to step back. If this is done respectfully, the request is often successful, as it is in this instance. Sometimes it requires further work. We have to find out what that dismissing or reluctant part is concerned about, what is it afraid might happen if we allow the Self (as pure awareness) to connect with the part it is protecting. Often the reason is the fear of being overwhelmed, or fear of crying, or just the exposure itself. In this instance, the part was very willing to step back. As soon as the client contacts the anxiety with compassion and acceptance, the anxious part calms down. This calming is very apparent in the client's appearance.

In Hakomi, we try to work with fear and anxiety first. It is considered to be violent to try to access the unconscious otherwise. In IFS, we make sure that we respect protective parts, and only proceed with their permission. In both disciplines, we are doing basically the same thing. We are being respectful, earning trust, and helping the client's "Self" earn the trust of its parts.

Using parts language, the therapist helps the client accept the anxious feeling. There is an immediate shift in how the anxious feeling is experienced; it feels relieved, and the holding in the chest is released. In this case, it would seem that the feeling simply wanted to be seen and acknowledged. This clip was taken from the very beginning of the session. The anxiety was triggered by the situation of being videotaped with the lights, camera, and camera operator present. It is not surprising that such a situation would trigger anxiety. Later, as the session develops, we discover that the session itself is about being seen and not seen.

In the second clip, the client is assisted in working with anger. The therapist helps the client to connect with and begin a dialogue with the angry part. Once the anger is contacted, the client discovers the hurt that lies under the anger. This hurt is very real, and can be seen clearly in the client's eyes once the client makes contact with it. The hurt part then reveals that its way of dealing with the hurt is to give up (resignation). This kind of layering is very common. Notice how quickly this method moves to the crux of the matter: from anger, to hurt, to resignation.

In the third clip, we are working again with anxiety. The therapist assists in setting up a compassionate relationship between the client's awareness, or Self, and the anxious part. Notice that the therapist does not need to use the word part, even though he is using an IFS approach to work with the feeling. When the client acknowledges the feeling, it calms down; then, when the calming down is acknowledged, it calms down further. After the part is calmer, parts language is introduced, and the client is asked to get some further information about the meaning of this anxious feeling. What emerges is that it wants to get things right. The feeling persists, so the therapist shifts into the direct role momentarily, and offers nourishment to the part directly while the client observes, still compassionately mindful and in relationship to the part. The nourishment is, "It's okay to make mistakes." Notice the breath expanding. The client reports some lightening up. The therapist offers more nourishment. This nourishment is taken in. There is a restoration of "flow."

WORKING WITH MEMORIES

IN the Mindfulness Centered Therapy approach, memories are present moment experiences, rich with meaning and healing potential. They are especially useful when they are concrete, and when they arise spontaneously. We do not generally send clients out of present time to look for them with direct questions like, "Do you remember something about that?" A question asked in this manner will take the client out of present time, into a speculative, thinking process. It is not likely that a memory retrieved through such a question will be related to the client's unconscious undercurrents. It will more often cause a distraction, a story to tell, or a frustrating failure that will only delay the natural unfolding of the client's own process.

As you will see from the demonstration clips on the DVD (Chapter 11), in Mindfulness Centered Therapies we prefer to evoke a spontaneous memory while the client's attention is focused on a present-time experience. This present-time experience might be a sadness or an anxiety, revealed by a previous offering, and then deepened with contact and acknowledgment. The therapist first moves from deepening through direct acknowledgment to an indirect role, having the client connect with and relate to the experience as a feeling or part. Then, with the feeling present, and the client in a connected accepting or compassionate state, the therapist might make a suggestion like "It would be nice to have a memory." This remark is not, in itself, designed to access a memory. It is gentle request to the unconscious; it merely lets the unconscious mind know what would be useful in furthering the process. Sometimes a memory will pop up in response to a suggestion, but more often than not, the client will continue staying with the feeling. If the client is eager to please, and begins to look for a memory, we can say, "No need to go looking, one will come up when it is ready." This is another very powerful but indirect appeal to the unconscious.

Finally, when the client is calm, and just being with the evoked experience, perhaps a tight chest, a sense of sadness or hurt, we might make a more direct appeal. We do this by asking the client to become mindful, and to just stay connected with the previously evoked experience. When we see nonverbal signs of mindfulness, or when the client nods to signal they are ready, we say in a gentle, evocative voice, "Just notice what happens when I ask: 'What does that sadness, (tight chest, hurt feeling) remember?'"[17]

When we set this up in mindfulness, we often add statements like, "No need to go looking," and "It's okay if nothing comes up." These remarks help to relieve the client of performance pressure, keep the noise of anxiety down, and allow the unconscious mind to offer up whatever is there.

Working With Remembered Sensory Data

Spontaneous memories that arise naturally or are evoked in this manner reveal two important kinds of unconscious material. First, there is the experience itself, the actual sense data that includes images, voices and other sounds, feelings, moods, and body sensations. These experiential elements of memories are important in themselves. If it is sadness, it is a certain kind of sadness. Something was lost, there was a disappointment, it is a lonely sort of sadness, a hopeless sadness, a kind of despair (sadness combined with resignation).

Memories are often accompanied by strong feelings. When this is the case, the therapist's first job is to stay with the client in a calm and present state, so that she can be useful in helping the client to move through strong

---

[17] I learned this very evocative voicing from Ron Kurtz.

feelings with comfort and support. If the feelings are strong, the client will usually become highly identified with them. His identity will be drawn away from his mindful identification with the Self. In IFS parts language we say "He will blend with the part that has the strong feeling". If that part is a young part, and it often is, the client often embodies that part, speaking and acting nonverbally as if he is that younger part.

We are therefore not surprised to hear what David Burns calls "thought distortions," statements like: "She hates me," "Nobody loves me," or "They are killing me" (1980). This tells us that the client is identified with a younger version of himself, the part that actually experienced the events that are now remembered. This young part thinks with a young mind, a mind that often generalizes, exaggerates, thinks in black and white, and personalizes events by, for example, feeling responsible or guilty for a divorce, or a parent's suffering. We must recognize that this is how this experience lives in the back-story of our client's life. Any decisions, convictions, or actions our client took to manage this situation probably also live on, and are called into play whenever similar situations occur in life. He might also cry that young part's tears, and assume gestures and postures that are associated with the young part in that instant of time.

When we work with remembered sensory data, we do two things. We help the client to regulate or move through any strong feelings, so that he may become re-identified with awareness (Self) as soon as possible. We may do this directly by assuring and comforting the client, using touch, or a soft, touching voice that assures him that he is not alone. If he becomes overwhelmed, we go with his spontaneous experience. If he covers his face with his hands, we can help him to do that by placing our hands over his. If he curls up in a ball, we can physically help him compress by firmly holding him in that ball. These forms of physical support must be undertaken with sensitivity and caution. If we are unsure as to whether we should do it, it is best to use caution and to offer it, either nonverbally or verbally, and look and listen for signs that it is accepted. As we support we check with the client. We ask, "Does this feel good?" or we can observe closely to see whether he is calming down. Any pulling away by the client must be responded to immediately with a gentle backing off. Sometimes just holding a hand can help. If we don't know the client well we can ask, "Would holding a hand feel good?"

If we do not touch him with our hands, we can touch him with our voice: "I'll just stay here while you experience this. I promise not to leave". In saying this, the quality of our voice is extremely important. We want to be steady, assuring, gentle, reliable, and unquestionably present. We must remember that whatever this pain was, what made it so difficult was probably because it had to be endured alone, without comfort or repair, without the presence of another. As it is revivified now, it has an opportunity to be reexperienced with what was missing in that original experience. It is the therapist's job to provide that wholeheartedly, and as completely as the client can accept. The term "missing experience" has been coined by Ron Kurtz to describe this kind of work. It has a very healing effect. If nothing else happens in working with a memory, the therapist's compassion and loving presence will be very helpful to the client, and can result in permanent, positive outcomes.

After overwhelming emotions have been soothed, the therapist's intention shifts to support the client in unblending from parts with strong feelings. At this point the therapist can often introduce parts language and shift to the indirect mode. This gives the client an opportunity to take over the job of acknowledging and soothing the remaining strong but not overwhelming feelings. This is an excellent opportunity to increase trust between an estranged part and the client's awareness, or "Self" as it is called in IFS. Some of this trust comes from having the "Self" stick around and maintain presence. Some comes from trust that the therapist will remain present, and support the Self or the part directly. Additional trust can come when the client defends the vulnerable feeling part from interrupting critical, judgmental, or otherwise hostile or threatened parts. The therapist can support the client in doing this, and can also gain credibility in the eyes of the client's adaptive unconscious through being competent in this support.

WORKING WITH CLIENTS AS THEY APPEAR IN THEIR RECOVERED MEMORIES

With this deeper connection and trust comes an opportunity to explore the memory's meaning. What is the story this part wants us to know? What decisions did it make as a consequence of these events and feelings? What beliefs or anticipatory structures were created to help the client reorganize their worldview into an integrated and constant whole? This opens the door to the second big benefit of working with memories. This benefit arises when we assist the client in creating a relationship between conscious awareness (Self) and the part that has carried the memory up to the present time. To do this, we ask the client to connect with that version of herself which is situated in the memory. In other words, we support the client in relating not just to the memory, but to the child who the client finds in that memory, the child who suffered the circumstances of that situation, and who has been stuck in time, so to speak, ever since.

Once this connection is made, we want to check to make sure that the client is connecting with the part in the memory from "Self," and not from a part that doesn't like this part in the memory, or a part that wants merely to dismiss it or get rid of it (Schwartz, 1995). There are a number of ways to establish this. First, we can observe the client closely as she attempts to connect with the part. Are there difficulty lines between her brows, is she frowning, is her face frozen and unsympathetic, or does she appear to be slightly moved, curious, or compassionate? We can also ask her, "As you connect with this part, standing back just a little, how do you feel towards her, what is your attitude toward that young part in this memory?" If the client is identified with a hostile or unfriendly part, she will usually tell us right out: "I want her to go away." or "I don't really like her."

In this case, we can introduce parts language to name the part that is hostile or unfriendly. We can reassure her that we are not going to give the feeling part more power, that we are going to help it to feel better. And we can ask the threatened parts to step back. Those who are not used to working with parts may find it hard to believe that we can indeed talk to parts like this, and that they generally do step back when they know that we are aware of their concerns, and when we treat them with the same sensitivity and respect that we extend to the part in the memory. Once the protective part steps back, we can continue to work with the part in the memory. We coach the client in acknowledging its feelings, understanding the circumstances of the memory, and helping it to work with any cognitive distortions that were recorded as a part of the memory. Sometimes the part wants to hear nourishment like, "It wasn't your fault." "You're safe now." "There's nothing wrong with you." Sometimes we can have the client take the suffering part out of the terrible circumstances, protect it from an attacker, or just hold the part. Sometimes we need to let the part know that things have changed, that the "Self" is grown up now. Recently I had a client tell a part that he had been sober for four years now. There was an immediate shift in the young part who had grown up with an alcoholic father. We can have our client show pictures of her present life to a young part in order to "update" her (Schwartz, 1995).

Richard Schwartz has developed a complete program of work that can be useful in working with child parts (Schwartz, 1995). His books, cited in the bibliography, are very accessible, and his methods are taught at IFS workshops and trainings in many locations. Similarly, there are a number of excellent books about Hakomi (Kurtz, 1990, the *Hakomi Forum*) and there are workshops and trainings available worldwide through The Hakomi Institute, Ron Kurtz Trainings, and the Hakomi Educational Network. These are excellent resources for learning more about working with memories directly, as in Hakomi, or indirectly, as we do in IFS. In the examples provided in DVD Chapter 11, we demonstrate how these methods can be combined in various ways to explore memories, and provide the following commentary to assist the reader in getting the most from these video clips.

COMMENTARY ON THE VIDEO CLIPS

THE first clip opens with the client accessing memories in a state of mindfulness. The therapist has already helped her to evoke a mindful state. Notice how the therapist uses language, gently and without hurry, and how he waits patiently, allowing the client to receive and sort through her internal experience, a multitude of memory impressions, waiting for her to come to rest on what is important. This is an excellent example of following the client, as opposed to leading or interrupting.

When sadness appears, the therapist notices it nonverbally at the first sign, and verbally contacts it with little more than a word, then waits for the experience to develop. Notice the slow, unhurried pace, and how the therapist slips out of the direct role and into the indirect coaching role, so as to place the client in touch with the remembered part, the little ten-year-old in the memory, while he steps out of the way. From the indirect coaching position, he encourages the client to open a dialogue with the sad little girl part, the subject of the memory.

In this situation, the emotions are not extreme. There is no need to work directly to help the client through overwhelming emotions. There is also little need for the client to unblend from the part. The therapist simply helps the ten-year-old part in coming to trust the client, as the client remains identified with her compassionate witness "Self." Trust is greatly facilitated when it is not demanded, when we help the client to step back and assure the part that she understands her need for time to develop trust. This honoring of her autonomy, and our trust that the young part will come to a good decision if we give her time and space, is a reliable method for building trust with a reluctant part.

In this session, parts language provides all of the separation necessary to maintain the client's "Self" in an unblended state. It is also important to notice that the therapist does not allow the client to simply break off connection with the part once the meaning of the memory is discovered. He takes her back to the part, and helps her to embody the part by finding a place for it. Usually a client will find someplace inside, like in the heart, but here, the client finds a place on her shoulder. This "embodiment" technique is taught by Richard Schwartz, and is very useful after the work with a part is finished. Schwartz also stresses that it is wise to respect the relationships that clients create with parts, and urges his students to honor them in closing the session. Also, it is wise to let them know that we will check in with them next time we are together, and to help the client keep the promises they make for continued contact. Failing to do this can lead to a loss of hard-earned trust.

Most of the second clip is devoted to establishing a relationship between the client's mindful Self and a very young part that shows up in a very brief memory. The method used to evoke the memory is very similar to the one described in the overview. The client has already accessed a "tender feeling" before the clip begins, and the clip starts with the therapist evoking mindfulness, and then evoking a memory, using the words, "What do you remember?" followed by, "What memories do you have?" The therapist also adds, "You need not go looking for one," and "It's okay if one does not come up." There is an immediate response, as if the memory is right there, waiting for attention.

While the memory is fleeting, a part that is identified with the memory, the memory's subject, is contacted, and that contact is sustained over a considerable period of time, even though the contact is not solid and seems to have a peek-a-boo-like quality. When the client is in contact with this part, she experiences mixed feelings. On the one hand, there is a feeling of safety that seems to be associated with the act of hiding. On the other, there is a sadness and tenderness that arises from time to time, especially as the connection with the part deepens. The part appears to be shy and playful at the same time, and we can see this part quite clearly in the client's eyes and other facial expressions as she connects with the child part.

The therapist assists the client in staying in touch with the child part, and the client is helpful as she tell the therapist what she needs to deepen her contact, and to keep from blending with the part. The palpability of the little girl part is very present in this video segment, and if the reader retains doubts about the reality of memory parts, this clip should be useful insofar as it demonstrates how the part animates the client as the client connects with the memory.

This is also a demonstration of the indirect coaching role, and of blending, which the client actually notices herself. There is also a lesson in how the therapist listens and takes the client's advice about how to help her by remaining quiet while she makes contact with the part. This works, and the connection with the part becomes more solid and trusting. We are now in a position to discover more about her life and her mixed feelings. It is very clear that we are still working with the initial issue of being seen, and at least some of the shyness may be the result of being filmed. It should be recalled that the present circumstances are all about being seen and not seen. There is a camera and a cameraman in the room and the subject is in a circumstance of rather unusual scrutiny.

WORKING WITH THE BODY

BECAUSE Mindfulness Centered Therapies is based fundamentally on Hakomi, working with the body is an important component of the work. Here are some of the techniques that use the body in Hakomi body-centered psychotherapy:

Attending to nonverbal communication: Hakomi therapists train their attention to place verbal content in the background, and nonverbal communications in the foreground. The nonverbal aspect of communication is constantly revealing information about current states of being. Even when it is stiff and suppressed, it conveys information about containment, stress, tension states, and sometimes anger, fear, and withdrawal. By observing and contacting the present state through contact statements or acknowledgments, unconscious material is made conscious, trust and relationship are strengthened, and feelings are deepened and made more meaningful.

Identifying nonverbal indicators: By attending to clients' nonverbal behavior, including the nonverbal aspects of their speaking (tone of voice, pace of speaking, verbal tics, and so forth), Hakomi therapists notice "indicators" that are often trailheads to the unconscious. If a client talks for two or three minutes about any important subject, a well-trained Hakomi therapist will notice a number of indicators. It is not necessary to do something with each one. Sooner or later, one will stand out as being significant with regard to the unfolding session, and the therapist usually selects one to work with based on its timing and intensity around a key subject in the session. The therapist is also tracking the storyline. But she is not placing all of her attention there. She has a heightened sensitivity to hearing key words, and within a fairly brief time, it becomes apparent that, for example, every time the client mentions his father, he brings his hand to his mouth and dips his head.

Discovering the meaning of a gesture: When a therapist has noticed an indicator, he gently calls the client's attention to it. If the client is curious and willing to explore its meaning, the therapist asks the client to repeat the gesture very slowly, in a state of mindfulness, noticing what happens or changes during the course of performing the gesture. He may also ask the client questions that help the client to discover the meaning of a gesture. For example, a client who habitually rubs the back of her left hand with the thumb of her right hand, especially when worried or anxious, might be invited to explore this unconscious gesture. The therapist helps the client to evoke mindfulness, and suggests that she perform the gesture very slowly. After the client has exhausted the gesture's meaning using her own resources, the therapist may ask, "If your right hand could talk, what would it be saying to your left hand as it rubs it?" Very often a client will respond with something like "You're okay," or "It's all right," or "I'm here." The therapist can then use these words by offering them to the client as a nourishing offering (see Chapters 6 and 7). Through this kind of exploration one might discover important pieces about missing experiences, longings for support and assurance, conditions in the client's past when parents and others did not provide sufficient nourishment.

Taking over a body gesture or posture: This Hakomi technique has many variations and many uses. Often it is used after a nourishing offering when the client is unable to "take in" what is offered and responds with a gesture or a postural shift like drawing back, lifting the shoulders, cocking the head, or turning or dropping it slightly. In other words, the client exhibits an automatic physical reaction to the nourishing phrase. In Hakomi, reactions like this are interpreted as behaviors that manage emergent experiences. It follows that if we take over these behaviors for the client, and actually enact them without the client's effort, the underlying emergent experience might reveal itself more clearly, or something else might happen, something that opens a door to the unconscious puppet master that is pulling the client's strings.

The application of taking over techniques is not limited to its use with nourishing offerings. It can be employed at any stage of the Hakomi process. Often when a client is just talking about something troubling, or something exciting and joyful, we may see some kind of management behavior that seems to suppress his or her experience or expression. Ron Kurtz developed taking over techniques, and credits Moshe Feldenkrais as his inspiration. Kurtz is a master of using taking over techniques. Here is an explanation he offers from his definitive text book, *Body-Centered Psychotherapy: the Hakomi Method*:

> By taking something over—the weight of the head for instance—we provide an opportunity for the muscles which are holding the head in the forward position to relax. We don't make things happen; we provide opportunities. Letting the head fall forward is usually an unconscious action when it is part of the feeling of sadness. Its function is to help manage the experience of sadness and its expression. The weight of the head, acting on muscles of the chest and back, makes it difficult to breath deeply… the effect of this limit on breathing is a limit to feeling.
>
> (Kurtz, 1990, p. 102)

Some taking over techniques are active. For example, we might ask a client to reach out while we hold his arms back. Here, we are taking over his resistance to reaching out. A passive technique would be for him to be mindful as we draw his arms forward.

Taking over techniques are usually done as little experiments in mindfulness. They are set up in a series of steps:

Steps for Setting up Experiments

1. Therapist notices the behavior
2. Calls clients attention to it
3. Asks the client if he or she is interested in exploring it
4. Describes an experiment
5. Receives the client's consent
6. Evokes mindfulness (See DVD chapters 2 and 3)
7. Enacts the experiment
8. Observes, and has the client describe what happened.

This sequence of steps is practiced so often in Hakomi training and in clinical practice that it becomes completely natural, and there are many little variations and nuances that enrich this simplified sequence so as to address the many different ways that sessions develop. The underlying rules for carrying them out are as follows:

Guidelines for Conducting Experiments in Mindfulness

1. Never bypass fear—work with the fear first
2. Be gentle; don't push for big gains
3. Get the client involved, and make sure you have their curiosity and consent
4. Get the data: find out what happened when the experiment was conducted.
5. If emotions are aroused, provide nourishment and comfort
6. If memories are aroused, help the client remember them
7. Help the client discover what their experience means
8. Provide an experience of presence, acceptance, compassion, and support that was missing when the unconscious experience was acquired

COMMENTARY ON THE VIDEO CLIPS

I N the first clip, we watch the client talking about her struggle with a school project. The therapist contacts her present moment experience as "frustration," and calls attention to a little side-to-side movement that occurs as the client is speaking. This gesture is present throughout her description of the difficulty she has encountered. Viewers who missed this indicator may want to rerun the chapter and examine it again. Once you know what to look for, the gesture becomes very apparent, and it seems to coincide with her sense of frustration. Along with the gesture, we also note the key words "resisting," "making sense of my purpose," "something's not right, where I'm going." All of these indicators and key words suggest some kind of inner conflict: a part that wants to do the assignment, and another part that is pulling in the opposite direction. Also, try playing the clip without sound. Can you see the resistance in the shoulders and head movements, and the tightness of the facial muscles? Also, do you see some sadness there? All of this becomes clearer as the session unfolds, revealing a memory that is recorded in the clip in Chapter 10.

The therapist senses that this may be significant, and sets up a "little experiment in mindfulness." This clip illustrates the procedures listed under the title "Setting up little experiments," described in chapter 12 (above). It is important to notice how the therapist slows the work down as he evokes mindfulness very deliberately; since this is a new client, and then asks the client to enact the gesture in slow motion, as she notices what happens. Working with this gesture patiently by enacting it in mindfulness, and allowing the client to thoroughly examine and name the experiences that it evokes, produces new information about the gesture. The client eventually articulates "feeling trapped," and we notice a finality and a sense of relief that suggest that she has finally arrived at a satisfying verbal expression of the felt sense of this side-to-side gesture. This trapped feeling leads to a memory that is explored in Chapter 10, a memory of being forced to go to church; something that she didn't want to do and that is attended with a sense of sadness or grief.

In the second clip, we explore the meaning of another gesture. This is a tentative peering or peeping gesture that the client repeats a number of times. The gesture has a "young, childlike" aspect. It is as if a shy and guardedly playful young part is there, just under the surface, checking things out, looking to see if it is safe to come out and play. I would guess the age at four to six years old. We can see that there is an emotional charge in this gesture. This becomes apparent as the therapist suggests the experiment and describes it to the client. Her eyes assume a deep watery quality. It is quite subtle, but once it emerges fully, it is easy to see if you replay the clip.

When the experiment is actually enacted, it evokes a very spontaneous sense of sadness and apprehension. This segment illustrates the power of the Hakomi method to access important unconscious feelings and memories almost instantly. It does this through the use of mindfulness in a safe and attuned environment. This little peering gesture could easily be overlooked by a therapist employing a talkative approach, in which most of the attention is held in the grip of the storyline. In Hakomi, the therapist is not occupied with what he is going to say next, since we have already established that neither client nor therapist need follow the rules of conversation by always having something to say. There is no compulsion to keep the conversational ball rolling. It is okay to just sit and listen. It is okay to sustain long pauses.

It is okay to focus on something other than the storyline and the surface meaning of the client's speech.

In addition to noticing how the therapist accesses the unconscious experience, it is useful to note how he handles the feeling when it comes up by immediately attuning to it, letting the client know that he notices, giving it space to be there, and staying present with it without rushing in to fix it. All of these qualities of presence help to make the client feel okay about her feelings, and tell her that it is safe to reveal this young part with all of her memories and her conflicted feelings about being seen.

FOCUSING

L IKE Hakomi and Internal Family Systems, Focusing is a form of assisted self-study in which mindfulness plays an essential role. However, whereas Hakomi places primary attention on the categorical feelings and emotions, Focusing is the art of helping clients to place primary attention on, and name, another kind of inner experience that Gendlin has named *felt sense* experience (1978). Compared to categorical experience, felt sense experience is more subtle and ineffable. It is vague, indistinct, and difficult to name or classify. Quite often it seems to be a blend of body sensations, emotions, and moods.

An example of a felt sense would be a feeling that makes us want to squirm. More subtle examples would include vague feelings of discomfort, feelings related to wanting to withdraw or cringe, or feelings like having a knot in the stomach, or a flutter in the chest. In order to study such an experience, we must deliberately overcome our desire to turn away from it. We must be patient and give the feeling time to develop fully in our awareness. In describing felt sense experience, we sometimes find ourselves rather exasperated as we exhaust the usual nouns and adjectives, and resort to a more creative use of language that includes similes, images, and metaphors. In our attempt to describe felt sense, we must listen and sense patiently to discover what the experience itself wants to say, or how it wants to express or describe itself.

While many therapists do not emphasize the relationship of felt sense experience to time, and use it to explore both remembered and anticipated events indiscriminately, we think of felt sense experience as the way an anticipated or imagined future lives in the present moment experience of our bodies. In my clinical practice, I find Hakomi, or Hakomi combined with IFS, to be far better tools for accessing past traumas and wounds, and for working through remembered categorical emotions and sensations. These therapies are primarily oriented to working with the past, and are seldom used to study responses to the future unless these imagined or anticipated future events trigger memories that client and therapist can then follow back into the past. It is not that they do not contain any tools for working in the future; rather, it is a matter of primary emphasis and orientation.

If we begin a session with Focusing, we are usually helping a client who is avoiding, dreading, or experiencing some uneasiness about a future event. It could be a vague sense of dread that accompanies thoughts about forthcoming income taxes, feelings that pertain to visiting a doctor that are not simple and categorical like fear or anxiety, but are described more metaphorically and have a somatic component. Often our tendencies to ignore or distract ourselves from these uncomfortable felt sense experiences lead us to procrastinate or avoid future events and situations that evoke them. These kinds of situations are perfect for Focusing. However, if we reach a dead end in the Focusing work, especially if the work dead-ends in more specific, effable, categorical experience, we often shift into the Hakomi method, and look for a memory, or work in other ways with categorical experiences or parts.

Focusing is a matter of being mindful of felt sense experience while we search for a way to represent it with a word, phrase, image, metaphor, or gesture. It is easy to learn, and once having learned it, a person can use it without the help of a paid professional. I know this because I have used it myself to move beyond anxieties associated with the anticipation of surgery, the dread of doing income taxes, and a host of people, places and situations that I sought to avoid or procrastinate about.

Working with Felt Sense Experience

When we search for a felt sense experience, we look for sensations that are indistinct, hard to name, not analyzable, not yet recognized. To do this, we develop a number of skills. First we are mindful, just as in Hakomi or IFS; we learn to turn inward with a calm, experience-friendly attitude of compassion or curiosity. We also cultivate patience. We give the felt sense plenty of time to arise. Focusing on a felt sense is a somatic version of watching a Polaroid film develop, or waiting in a darkened room for our eyes to adjust to the low light. As we patiently wait, sensing inwardly, we notice something. We wait. We notice… where is it arising? "There. Oh yes, there in the chest, right in the middle… a vague and indistinct feeling." We silently hold the question: "How does this whole thing live in the experience of my body?" A felt sense usually has a sensation aspect and a feeling tone, and both kinds of experience will be indistinctly blended together. We will not know how to name or describe it at first. We make that okay. Once we have identified a felt sense experience, we move on to the next step.

Experiencing a Shift

In Focusing, the second step is called "finding the handle." The handle is a word, phrase, or sometimes an image or metaphor that describes or expresses the felt sense. We are creating a way to represent the felt sense. In order to do this, we do not go into our heads. We learn to get the handle by consulting the feeling. In Hakomi, the therapist asks, "What does that hand say?" or, "What does your head say, when it tilts like that?" We are going for meaning. We have to ask the felt sense, just like we have to ask the hand or the head, when working with a gesture. This is something that a Hakomi therapist is already trained to do.

We use the felt sense as a reference; we will know that we are close to the right representation if the felt sense stirs, or shifts. It may dissolve with a sense of relief. It may change into another felt sense. It may increase or decrease in intensity. This is like that game of hide-and-seek, where the person who hides the object says, "Warm, warmer... hot, hotter... cold." In this case, it's the felt sense itself that tells us, "You're getting warm... warmer... cold... hot. Oh—you got me!" by how it stirs, and finally shifts, as we hold up our words or phrases against it to see if there is a fit.

WHEN A SHIFT OCCURS

When we get a shift, we take in any relief that arises, and allow time to be in the space of that shift. Sometimes we get an insight. A memory may flit by, sometimes a string of them. After a strong shift, there is a new space around that future event or situation that we were worried about, dreading, or avoiding. There is a space for a new and more creative perspective. We see that we have been cringing and skulking needlessly. We realize that we don't have to do that. We can get help, stand up to it, or reframe it within a more empowering context. After a shift, we are usually more resourceful. The shift can be subtle, or enormous. It is always empowering.

IN CONCLUSION

In conclusion, Focusing is not a complete therapy.[18] It is a tool that can be used with many forms of work. It can be blended with Hakomi or Internal Family Systems, or both, especially in interventions for situational difficulties. Furthermore, Hakomi, with its principles and its ability to create exquisite attunement, provides an ideal context for practicing and teaching Focusing.

---

[18] I do not intend this as a criticism of Focusing or its creator, Eugene Gendlin, but as a comment on how Gendlin himself seems to hold the work, that is, as an open-ended inquiry that invites further discovery and innovation by himself and his students.

COMMENTARY ON THE VIDEO CLIPS

T HE process of Focusing is often described as a series of steps, or stages, which lead from the opening of a Focusing session to its conclusion (Gendlin, 1972, 1996; Friedman, 2000; Cornell, 1996, 2005). The therapist's role is to teach these steps to the client, and provide support as the client uses them to work through ongoing healing and personal growth issues. Eugene Gendlin used six steps to describe the process, and in the video demonstration I have followed his parsing of the process, with minor variations. The 18-minute Focusing session recorded in Chapter 15 is the territory to be explored, and Gendlin's six steps provide the map that will help us to orient ourselves as we work through the demonstration.

In preparing a lesson on Focusing based on a video presentation, we have found that it helps to name the initial moves as "Preparing to Focus." This preparation phase includes three steps or intentions:

Preparing to Focus

1. Evoking mindfulness
2. Finding or confirming the subject of the session
3. Sensing the body, while holding a subject in mind

The Focusing session begins by having the client find a subject for the Focusing process. Often, clients enter the office with a subject already in mind. In this case, a similar process can be used to quiet the mind, begin sensing inwardly, and clarify or confirm the client's initial intentions. The therapist first invites the client to name all of her major concerns and other potential subjects that are presently occupying her thoughts and feelings.

The "radar screen" metaphor used in this session can be useful for clients who have an understanding of the radar screen as a kind of map of their psychological territory. There are many other possible metaphors and approaches to identifying the topic and clearing the space. For example, one can ask the client to clear the clutter in the room of her mind, stacking each item like a piece of furniture, and naming it as she puts it on the stack. Then, when the space is clear, the therapist can ask the client to pull out the one item that has most of her energy or interest right now.

These graphic visual metaphors are useful in invoking mindfulness, creating distance between the mindfully aware Self and experiential contents, and setting up a relationship between the client's awareness and inner life that is optimal for the Focusing process. The relationship that works best in Focusing is the same kind of relationship that is optimal between the Self and a part in IFS, and between awareness and a feeling, body sensation, or "child part" in Hakomi.

There are many other ways to work. Often, we notice a spontaneous body gesture or physical reaction when the client is speaking about something. We see a cringe, or the client touches his chest. It can be subtle, but working in body-centered therapy makes one very observant of fleeting experience and much of this kind of experience has a felt sense quality. A Hakomi therapist will contact these feelings instinctively. She might say, "Something happens, huh," or "Feeling something." It need not be a complete sentence, or a question. It's enough for the client to stop and feel for a moment. It is not necessary to slavishly follow the steps. We contact and evoke mindfulness. Then we move on to sensing and naming. In the

DVD clip, we have tried to follow the steps and illustrate the process as it was originally outlined by Gendlin.

After naming three items, the client identifies her primary interest as her concerns regarding her mother, who suffers from Alzheimer's, and with whom she plans a forthcoming visit. Two other current, but less important, subjects are also noted: (1) transition at work, and (2) grandchildren. These are named, and set aside for the duration of the session. Having selected, confirmed, and clearly stated her chosen subject; she begins sensing how this subject actually lives in her present moment experience as a felt sense. In order to do this, she is encouraged to focus on the trunk of the body.

It is important to support the client at this point and throughout the session in working with the whole subject, in this case "visiting my mom." Any real-life issue can easily be broken up into its component parts. In Focusing, we want to deal with wholes. This is also true of the felt sense. As the felt sense evoked by our subject emerges into consciousness, it is important that the client and therapist avoid breaking it up into component parts, or analyzing it in any way.

In addition, it is important that the client maintain both connection with and distance from the felt sense experience. This means that we do not want the client to be drawn into the experience, as into a vortex of feelings, or the cloudy veil of a mood. We encourage the client to stand back a little—not too far, but far enough to stay on the outside. We also want the client to stay friendly toward the experience. Any sign that the client is just trying to get rid of the experience should be contacted and worked with until the client can be with the experience, accepting it just as it is.

If the client cannot do this, it is unlikely that the experience is a pure felt sense experience. It may very well be a categorical feeling or feeling state arising from a memory of some past event, triggered by the subject or its associations. In Mindfulness Centered Therapies, where we have a number of approaches at our disposal, it may be time to shift gears. We may introduce parts language in order to work indirectly, coaching our client to acknowledge the part, and asking the part to pull its feelings back; or shift to direct mode with Hakomi, to help the client move through the "rapids" of an overwhelming feeling state. When the client has calmed down, and the past experience is resolved, we can return to Focusing, addressing the same subject. Often, after some work with the past, we can return to the subject and its future, in order to resolve remaining felt sense aspects of the experience.

The preference for using the trunk of the body as a sensing area is traditional in Focusing. Even if there is a felt sense experience in a limb or in a subject's head, Gendlin and other writers usually express a preference for finding a correlated felt sense in the body's trunk area. Ann Weiser Cornell has questioned this tradition extensively in her most recent book (*The Radical Acceptance of Everything*, 2005), and it is possible that while the trunk is preferable, the entire body can be accessed for useful felt sense experience and movement.

In the video example, the client is very quick to discover a felt sense experience associated with the selected subject. In the video session a "strain" feeling is reported that extends from the cheek and jaw down through the entire trunk. The therapist helps her to be present with the feeling, and to expand her awareness of it into all of its fullness.

The client in the video has had previous experience in Focusing, and having already recognized the felt sense, moves ahead of the therapist, who is trying to demonstrate all of the steps for purposes of the video. A minor timing problem is acknowledged ("so you've moved on to looking for a handle") and resolved, and they move on together to look for a handle, which is the fourth step in the process.

The map for the next part of the process is included below, under the heading of "finding a handle":

Finding a Handle
4. Naming the felt sense (called "finding a handle")
5. Checking the handle with the felt sense
6. Resonating with the shift

"Finding a handle" refers to a process in which the client listens for a word, phrase, metaphor or image that expresses or describes the felt sense. In the video clip, our client hears the phrase, "I have to be really attentive."

It is very important that the therapist feed back the client's word or words precisely, as he supports the client in working toward an accurate "handle." In this example, as the therapist and client move into the next step, comparing the handle to the felt sense, the therapist (distracted by his agenda pertaining to creating a good video demonstration of the process) inadvertently substitutes the word "careful" for the client's word "attentive," and feeds back the phrase incorrectly as, "I have to be really *careful.*" The client (perhaps wishing to be helpful) accepts the inaccurate phrase, and uses his inaccurate feedback as she matches the handle to the felt sense experience. She checks the phrase "I have to be really careful" instead of her own expression, "I have to be really attentive." In spite of this error, a partial release is achieved, and the client expresses relief. Fortunately, the client recognizes that the optimum relief has not been experienced, and returns to her original handle, using "I have to pay attention." The therapist makes an adjustment, and supports the client in using her own wording without further distraction. The result is a complete release.

In preparing the DVD, the therapist considered discarding this clip, since it demonstrates the breaking of an important rule in Focusing. But upon consideration (and overcoming the narcissistic embarrassment of exposing his mistake), it was decided that it would be instructive to document the mistake and its consequence, in order to stress in a very tangible example what happens when we do not feed back the client's own words.

Once the client's phrase is matched with the felt sense, there is a powerful release, and this is apparent in the video clip. It was also sensed in the room, as these releases often are. There is no question that something important has happened. The client is encouraged to resonate with this shift and the relief that comes with it. Often, this relief comes with a sense of space, and the opportunity for a different perspective. In this case, the sense of strain that was originally evoked by the prospect of the visit was transformed into a sense of relief and resolve.

In a full Focusing session, a therapist might help to draw out the implications of the relief and space for new perspectives, but in this case there seemed to be no need for further work. In a follow-up session, the client reported having experienced a very satisfying visit with her mother, and felt that the Focusing session had allowed her to make full use of the opportunity for connection with her mother and mutual nourishment.

Suggestions for Follow-Up on Focusing

These video demonstrations of Hakomi, Internal Family Systems, and Focusing techniques are intended to be informative and helpful, but in reality they constitute a series of tastes that we hope will stimulate the viewer to undertake further exploration of Mindfulness Centered Therapies approach and its component methods. We therefore strongly recommend that readers and viewers follow up by reading important texts authored by Ron Kurtz, Richard Schwartz, and Eugene Gendlin. While Mindfulness Centered Therapies is an eclectic approach, drawing on a number of modalities, the overall foundation for this work has been the principles of Hakomi, loving presence, and the guidelines for accessing the unconscious that have been brilliantly and delightfully articulated by Ron Kurtz. In all of the methods we have discussed and demonstrated, we have used his guidelines and the training provided in Hakomi for creating and maintaining safe, attuned, and nourishing relationships with our clients.

BIBLIOGRAPHY
FOR PART 1 AND 2

Abrams, D. (1996). *The spell of the sensuous: Perception and language in a more-than-human world*. New York: First Vintage Books.

Ames, L. (1952). The sense of self of nursery school children as manifested by their verbal behavior. *Journal of Genetic Psychology, 81,* 193-232.

Bly, R. (1983). *Times alone: Selected poems of Antonio Machado.* Middletown, CT: Wesleyan University Press.

Bly, R. (1997). *Morning poems.* New York: HarperCollins.

Burns, D. D. (1990a). *The feeling good handbook.* New York: Penguin Putnam.

Burns, D. D. (1990b). *Feeling good: The new mood therapy.* New York: Penguin Putnam.

Caldwell, C. (1996). *Getting our bodies back.* Boston & London: Shambhala.

Caldwell, C. (1997). *Getting in touch.* Wheaton, IL: Quest Books.

Cornell, A. W. (1993), Teaching Focusing with five steps and four skills. In D. Braizer (Ed.), *Beyond Carl Rogers.* London: Constable and Robinsons.

Cornell, A. W. (1996). *The power of Focusing: A practical guide to emotional self-healing.* Oakland: New Harbinger Publications.

Cornell, A. W., & McGavin, B. (2005). *The radical acceptance of everything: Living a Focusing life.* Berkeley: Calluna Press.

Cole, J. David, (2006). Modified Hakomi: Coaching clients with IFS and Hakomi Skills, *Hakomi Forum,* 16-17, 89-98.

Deikman, A. J. (1982). *The observing self: Mysticism and psychotherapy.* Boston: Beacon Press.

Efran, J., Greene, M., & Lukens, M. (2004). Defining psychotherapy. *Psychotherapy Networker, 31*(2), 40-66.

Emmerson, G. (2003). *Ego state therapy,* Carmarthen, UK: Crown House.

Eisman, Jon (2000-2001). *The Hakomi method and re-creation of the Self: Professional*

Training, (Available from the Hakomi Institute of Oregon, 6836 HWY 66, Ashland, OR 97520)

Faucheaux, D., & Weiss, H. (1999). Training psychotherapists in the almost impossible task of just paying attention. *Hakomi Forum, 13,* 1-6.

Fisher, R. (2002). *Experiential psychotherapy with couples.* Phoenix: Zeig, Tucker and Theisen, Inc.

Flores, P. (2003). *Addiction as an attachment disorder.* Northvale, NJ: Jason Aronson.

Friedman, N. (2000). *Focusing: Selected essays 1974-1997.* Philadelphia: Xlibris Corporation.

Gendlin, E. T. (1996). Focusing-oriented psychotherapy: A manual of the experiential method. New York: The Guilford Press.

Gendlin, E. T. (1986). *Let your body interpret your dreams.* Wilmette, IL: Chiron Publications.

Gendlin, E. T. (1978). *Focusing.* New York: Bantam.

Gendlin, E. T. (1962). *Experiencing and the creation of meaning: A philosophical approach to the subjective.* Evanston: Northwestern University Press.

Gendlin, E. T., Beebe, J., Caissens, J., Klein, M., & Oberlander, M. (1968). Focusing ability in psychotherapy, personality and creativity. In J. M. Shlien (Ed.), *Research in psychotherapy, Vol. 3.* (pp. 217-241). Washington DC: American Psychological Association.

Germer, C. K., Siegel, R. D., & Fulton, P. R. (Eds.) (2005). *Mindfulness and psychotherapy.* New York: The Guilford Press.

Gesell, A. (1940). *The first year of life: A guide to the study of the pre-school child.* New York: Harper & Row.

Gindler, Elsa, 1926 ÒGymnastik for busy peopleÓ, Translated from the German, Die *Gymnastic des Berufsmenshen,* originally published in *Gymnastic, the journal of the Deutscher Gymnastic-Bund* (German *Gymnastik* Association) reprinted in The USA body psychotherapy journal, 3:1 from *Elsa Gindler, Volume 1* archives of the Sensory Awareness Foundation.

Goleman, D. (2003). *Destructive emotions and how we can overcome them.* New York: Random House.

Goulding, R., & Schwartz, R. C. (1995). *The mosaic mind: Empowering the tormented selves of child abuse survivors.* New York: W.W. Norton and Company.

Greenberg, L. S., Watson, J. C., & Lietaer, G. (Eds.) (1998). *Handbook of experiential psychotherapy*. New York: The Guilford Press.

GŸnther, Uta, (2006). Hakomi Strengths & Limitations: Indications and Contraindications for the Use of Hakomi with Clients and Significant Clinical Disturbances, Translator: Hugo Schielke. *Hakomi Forum*, 35-45, 89-98.

Hahn, Thich Nhat (1967). *Vietnam: Lotus In a Sea of Fire*. New York: Hill and Wang.

Hertz, P. D. (Trans.) (1971). M. Heidegger, *On the way to language*. San Francisco: Harper & Row.

Hendricks, M. N. (1986). Experiencing level as a therapeutic variable. *Person-Centered Review, 1*, 141-162.

Johanson, G., & Kurtz, R. (1991). *Grace unfolding: Psychotherapy in the spirit of the Tao te Ching*. New York, Belltown Books.

Johanson, G., & Taylor, C. R. (1988). Hakomi therapy with emotionally disturbed adolescents. In C. Schaefer (Ed.), *Innovative interventions in child and adolescent psychotherapy*. New York: Wiley.

Johanson, Greg (2006) A survey of the use of mindfulness in psychotherapy. *The Annals of the American Psychotherapy Association, 9*(2), 15-24.

Jung, C. G. (1948). Forward to D. T. Suzuki, *An introduction to Zen Buddhism*. London: Rider & Company.

Kabat-Zinn, J. (1990). *Full catastrophe living: Using the wisdom of your body and mind to face stress, pain, and illness*. New York: Dell Publishing.

Kabat-Zinn, J. (1994). *Wherever you go, there you are: Mindfulness meditation in everyday life*. New York: Hyperion.

Kabat-Zinn, J. (2005). *Coming to our senses: Healing ourselves and the world through mindfulness*. New York: Hyperion.

Kabat-Zinn, M., & Kabat-Zinn, J. (1998). *Everyday blessings: The inner work of mindful parenting*. New York: Hyperion.

Keleman, S. (2007). A biological vision. *The USA Body Psychotherapy Journal, 6*(1), 11.

Klein, M. H., Mathieu-Coughlan, P., & Kiesler, D. J. (1986). The experience scales. In L. S. Greenberg & W. M. Pinsof (Eds.), *The psychotherapeutic process: A research handbook* (pp. 21-71). New York: The Guilford Press.

Kohut, H. (1971). *The analysis of the self.* Madison, CT: International Universities Press.

Kohut, H. (1977). *The restoration of the self.* Madison, CT: International Universities Press.

Kurtz, R. (1990). *Body-Centered Psychotherapy: The Hakomi method.* Mendocino: Liferhythm.

Kurtz, R. (2007). *Listen to you: Readings on the Hakomi method of mindfulness-based self-study.* (Unpublished manuscript).

Kurtz, R., & Prestera, H. (1984). *The body reveals: What your body says about you.* New York: HarperCollins.

Lambert, M. J. (1989). The individual therapist's contribution to psychotherapy process and outcome. *Clinical Psychology Review, 9,* 469-485.

Leijssen, M. (1998). Focusing microprocesses. In L. S. Greenberg, J. C. Watson, & G. Lietaer, (Eds.), *Handbook of experiential psychotherapy,* New York: The Guildford Press.

Lewis, T., Amani, F., & Lannon, R. (2000). *A general theory of love.* New York: Vintage Random House.

Mahler, M. S., Pine, F., & Bergman, A. (1975). *The psychological birth of the human infant.* New York: Basic Books.

Marciano, F. (1998). *Rules of the wild: A novel of Africa.* New York: Vintage Books.

Marlock, Gustl & Weiss, H. (2006). In Search of the Embodied Self, *Hakomi Forum,* 16-17, 47-55.

Mathieu-Coughlan, P. & Klein, M. H. (1984). Experiencing psychotherapy: Key events in client centered interactions. In L. N. Rice & L.S. Greenberg (Eds.), *Patterns of change: Intensive analysis of psychotherapy process,* (pp. 213-248). New York: The Guilford Press.

Miller, S., Wackman, D., Nunnally, E., & Miller, P. (1989). *Connecting with self and others.* Littleton, CO: Interpersonal Communications Programs.

Mitchell, S. (1988). *Tao Te Ching by Lao Tzu.* New York: Alfred A. Knopf.

Montgomery, S. (1995), *Spell of the tiger: The man-eaters of Sundarbans.* Boston, New York: Houghton Mifflin Company

Neruda, P. (1988). William O'Daly (Trans.), *The sea and the bells.* Port Townsend, WA.: Copper Canyon Press.

Norman, D. M. & Schwartz, R. C. (2003). Maintaining self leadership with ÒborderlineÓ clients. *Journal of Self-Leadership, I*(1), 32-37.

Ogden, P., Minton, K., & Pain, C. (2006). *Trauma and the body: A sensorimotor approach to psychotherapy*. New York: W.W. & Company.

Pennebaker, J. W. (1990). *Opening up: The healing power of confiding in others*. New York: Avon.

Pennebaker, J. W. (2004). *Writing to heal*. Oakland, CA: New Harbinger.

Perls, F. S. (1947, reprinted 1969). *Ego, hunger, and aggression*. New York: Random House.

Pierrakos, J. C. (1977). *Eros, love and sexuality: The forces that unify man and woman*, Mendocino, CA: Liferhythm.

Progoff, I. (1975). *At a journal workshop*, Los Angeles: Tarcher.

Rogers, C. R. (1961). *On becoming a person: A therapist's view of psychotherapy*. New York.: Houghton Mifflin.

Roy, D. M. (1993). Body-Centered Counseling and Psychotherapy. In J. Rowan, *The transpersonal: Spirituality in psychotherapy and counseling*. London: Routledge.

Schwartz, R. C. (1987). Our multiple selves: Applying systems thinking to the inner family. *Family Therapy Networker, 11*(25-31), 80-63.

Schwartz, R. C. (1988). Know thy selves. *Family Therapy Networker, 12*(3), 21-29.

Schwartz, R. C. (1992, March/April). Rescuing the exiles. *Family Therapy Networker, 16*(3), 33-37, 75.

Schwartz, R. C. (1993). Constructionism, sex abuse and the self. *American Family Therapy Academy Newsletter, 50*, 6-10, 24-27.

Schwartz, R. C. (1995). *Internal Family Systems therapy*. New York: The Guilford Press.

Seigel, D. (1999). *The developing mind*. New York: The Guilford Press.

Seigel, D., & Hartzell, M. (2003). *Parenting from the inside out*. New York: Penguin Putnam.

Steinhardt, M. A., Doblier, C. L., Mallon, M. W., & Adams, T. (2003). The development and validation of a scale for measuring self-leadership. *Journal of Self-Leadership, 1*(1) 32-37.

Stern, D. N. (1985). *The interpersonal world of the infant*. New York: Basic Books.

Stern, D. N. (2004). *The present moment in psychotherapy and everyday life*. New York: W.W. Norton & Company.

Suzuki, D. T. (1963). *Outlines of Mahayana Buddhism.* New York: Schocken.

Suzuki, D. T. (1927). *Essays in Zen Buddhism.* New York: Grove Press.

Suzuki, D. T. (1934). *An introduction to Zen Buddhism.* Kyoto: Eastern Buddhist Soc. Republished with Foreword by C.G. Jung, London: Rider & Company, 1948.

Van den Berg, J. H. (1955). *The phenomenological approach to psychiatry.* Springfield, IL: Charles C. Thomas.

Van den Berg, J. H. (1961), *The changing nature of man: Introduction to a historical psychology.* New York: Dell Publishing Co.

Van den Berg, J.H. (1970). *Things: Four metabletic reflections.* Pittsburgh: Duquesne University Press.

Van den Berg, J.H. (1971). Phenomenology and metabletics. *Humanitas, VII*(3), 279-290.

Watkins, J. G., & H. H. (1997) *Ego states: Theory and therapy.* New York: Norton.

Wenner, M. (2007). Brain scans reveal why meditation works. Accessed 1/6/07 at http://www.livescience.com/health/070629_naming_emotions.html.

Werner, M. S. (1998). A client centered approach to therapy work with dissociated and fragile process. In L. S. Greenberg, J. C. Watson, & G. Lietaer, (Eds.), *Handbook of experiential psychotherapy,* (p. 369). New York: The Guilford Press.

Wolinsky, S. (1999). *The way of the human: Quantum psychology: Notebooks, Vol I.* Capitola, CA: Quantum Institute.

Wolinsky, S. (1993). *Quantum consciousness: The guide to experiencing quantum psychology.* Norfolk, CT: Bramble Books.

Wolinsky, S. (1991a). *The Tao of chaos: Quantum consciousness.* Norfolk, CT: Bramble Books.

Wolinsky, S. (1991b). *Trances people live: Healing approaches to quantum psychology.* Norfolk, CT: Bramble Books.

PART 3

SELECTED BIBLIOGRAPHY AND TRAINING RESOURCES

SELECTED BIBLIOGRAPHY OF MINDFULNESS AND THERAPY

GREG JOHANSON, PH.D.
THE HAKOMI INSTITUTE OF BOULDER, COLORADO

THIS is an ongoing project. Special thanks to Christopher Germer, Ph.D. and the Institute for Meditation and Psychotherapy for their many contributions. This bibliography does not try to include all the references to the broader Buddhist/therapy dialogue, which would extend it considerably. Additional references and corrections are welcomed, and may be sent to the author at

2523 West Lunt, Chicago, Illinois 60645-3201, USA
(773) 338-9606 greg@gregjohanson.com

Aaronson, H. (1998). Review of Psychotherapy and Buddhism: Toward an integration, by Jeffrey Rubin. Journal of Buddhist Ethics, 5, 63-73.

Agency for Healthcare Research and Quality, (2007). Meditation practices for health: State of the research. U.S. Department of Health and Human Services, Evidence Report/Technology Assessment, Number 155.

Aiken, G. (2006). The potential effect of mindfulness meditation on the cultivation of empathy in psychotherapy: A qualitative inquiry. (Doctoral dissertation, Saybrook Graduate School and Research Center, 2006).

Alexander, C, Langer, E., Newman, R., Chandler, H., & Davies, J. (1989). Transcendental meditation, mindfulness, and longevity: An experimental study with the elderly. Journal of Personality and Social Psychology, 57(6), 950-964.

Alexander, W. (1997). Cool water: Alcoholism, mindfulness, and ordinary recovery. Boston: Shambhala.

Alfano, C. (2005). Traversing the caesura: Transcendent attunement in Buddhist meditation and psychoanalysis. Contemporary Psychoanalysis, 41(2), 223-247.

Allen, N., Blashki, G., & Gullone, E. (2006). Mindfulness-based psychotherapies: A review of conceptual foundations, empirical evidence and practical considerations. Australian and New Zealand Journal of Psychiatry, 40(4), 285-294.

Alterman, A., Koppenhaver, J., Mulholland, E., Ladden, L., & Baime, M. (2004). Pilot trial of effectiveness of mindfulness meditation for substance abuse patients. Journal of Substance Use, 9(6), 259-268.

Anderson, D. (2005). Empathy, psychotherapy integration, and meditation: A Buddhist contribution to the common factors movement. Journal of Humanistic Psychology, 45(4), 483-502.

Andresen, J. (2000). Meditation meets behavioral medicine. Journal of Consciousness Studies, 7, 17-74.

Antony, M. (2002). Enhancing current treatments for anxiety disorders. Clinical Psychology: Science and Practice, 9(1), 91-94.

Antony, M., & Swinson, R. (2000). Phobic disorders and panic in adults: A guide to assessment and treatment. Washington, DC: American Psychological Association.

Aranow, P. (1998). Some parallels between meditation and psychotherapy. In Psychotherapy and meditation: Cultivating insight and compassion. Symposium conducted by the New England Educational Institute, Eastham MA.

Arch, J., & Craske, M. (2006). Mechanisms of mindfulness: Emotion regulation following a focused breathing induction. Behaviour Research and Therapy, 44(12), 1849-1858.

Arnow, B., & Constantino, M. (2003). Effectiveness of psychotherapy and combination treatment for chronic depression. Journal of Clinical Psychology, 59(8), 893-905.

Arntz, A. (2002). Cognitive therapy versus interoceptive exposure as treatment of panic disorder without agoraphobia. Behaviour Research and Therapy, 40, 325-341.

Astin, J. A. (1997). Stress reduction through mindfulness meditation. Psychotherapy and Psychosomatics, 66, 97-106.

Auerbach, H., & Johnson, M. (1977). Research on the therapist's level of experience. In A. S. Gurman & A. M. Razin (Eds.), Effective psychotherapy: A handbook of research. New York: Pergamon Press.

Austin, J. (2006). Zen-brain reflections. Cambridge, MA: MIT Press.

Austin, J. (1998). Zen and the brain. Cambridge, MA: MIT Press.

Bach, P., & Hayes, S. C. (2002). The use of acceptance and commitment therapy to prevent the rehospitalization of psychotic patients: A randomized controlled trial. Journal of Consulting and Clinical Psychology, 70, 1129-1139.

Baer, R. A. (2003). Mindfulness training as a clinical intervention: A conceptual and empirical review. Clinical Psychology: Science and Practice, 10(2), 125-143.

Baer, R., Fischer, S., & Huss, D. (2005). Mindfulness and acceptance in the treatment of disordered eating. Journal of Rational-Emotive & Cognitive Behavior Therapy, 23(4), 281-300.

Baer, R., Fischer, S., & Huss, D. (2005). Mindfulness-based cognitive therapy applied to binge eating: A case study. Cognitive and Behavioral Practice, 12(3), 351-358.

Baer, R., Smith, G., & Allen, K. (2004). Assessment of mindfulness by self-report: The Kentucky Inventory of Mindfulness Skills. Assessment, 11(3), 191-206.

Baer, R., Smith, G., Hopkins, J., Krietemeyer, J., & Toney, L. (2006). Using self-report assessment methods to explore facets of mindfulness. Assessment, 13(1), 27-45.

Bankart, C. P. (2006). Freeing the angry mind: How men can use mindfulness and reason to save their lives and relationships. Oakland, CA: New Harbinger.

Barlow, D. H. (2002) Anxiety and its disorders: The nature and treatment of anxiety and panic, (2nd Ed.). New York: Guilford Press.

Barman, N. (2005). Transitional outpatient treatment program design for juveniles ages 14-20. (Doctoral dissertation, Carlos Albizu University, 2005).

Barnhofer, T., Duggan, D., Crane, C., Hepburn, S., Fennell, M., & Williams,

J. (2007). Effects of meditation on frontal alpha-asymmetry in previously suicidal individuals. Neuroreport, 18(7), 709-712.

Barnes, S., Brown, K. W., Krusemark, E., Campbell, W. K., & Rogge, R. D. (in press). The role of mindfulness in romantic relationship satisfaction and responses to relationship stress. Journal of Marital and Family Therapy.

Barstow, C. (1985). An overview of the Hakomi method of psychotherapy. Hakomi Forum, 2, 8-18.

Bastis, M. (2000). Peaceful dwelling: Meditations for healing and living. Boston: Tuttle.

Batchelor, S. (1997). Buddhism without Beliefs. New York: Riverhead Books.

Becker, D., & Shapiro, D. (1981). Physiological responses to clicks during Zen, Yoga, and TM meditation. Psychophysiology 18(6), 694-699.

Bedard, M., Felteau, M., Gibbons, C., Klein, R., Mazmanian, D., Fedyk, K., et al. (2005). A mindfulness-based intervention to improve quality of life among individuals who sustained traumatic brain injuries: One-year follow-up. Journal of Cognitive Rehabilitation, 23(1), 8-13.

Bedard, M., Felteau, M., Mazmanian, D., Fedyk, K., Klein, R., Richardson, J., et al. (2003). Pilot evaluation of a mindfulness-based intervention to improve quality of life among individuals who sustained traumatic brain injuries. Disability and Rehabilitation: An International Multidisciplinary Journal, 25(13), 722-731.

Beidel, D. C., & Turner, S. M. (1986). A critique of the theoretical bases of cognitive-behavioral theories and therapy. Clinical Psychology Review, 6, 177-197.

Beitel, M., Ferrer, E., & Cecero, J. J. (2005). Psychological mindedness and awareness of self and others. Journal of Clinical Psychology, 61(6), 739-750.

Benett-Goleman, T. (1988). Mindfulness therapy. The Inquiring Mind, 5, 22.

Benett-Goleman, T. (2001). Emotional alchemy: How the mind can heal the heart. New York: Harmony Books.

Benson, H. (1975). The relaxation response. New York: Morrow.

Benson, H., & Klipper, M. (2000). The relaxation response. New York: Avon.

Benson, H., Beary, J., & Carol, M. (1974). The relaxation response. Psychiatry, 37, 37-46.

Benz-Chartrand, D. (1996). Evoking essence. Hakomi Forum, 12, 23-30.

Benz-Chartrand, D. (1995). Updating the foundation of Hakomi. Hakomi Forum, 11, 53-58

Benz-Chartrand, D. (1987). Yoga and Hakomi: Two friends meet. Hakomi Forum, 5, 38-39.

Benz-Chartrand, D., & Weis, H. (1989). To the core of your experience. Charlottesville, VA: Luminas Press.

Bhikku Bodhi (Ed.). (2000). A comprehensive manual of Abhidhamma. Seattle: BPS Pariyatti Editions.

Bien, T. (2006). Mindful therapy. Boston: Wisdom Publications.

Bien, T., & Bien, B. (2002). Mindful recovery: A spiritual path to healing from addiction. New York: Wiley.

Bishop, S. (2002). What do we really know about mindfulness-based stress reduction? Psychosomatic Medicine, 64, 71-84.

Bishop, S., Lau, M., Shapiro, S., Carlson, L., Anderson, N., Carmody, J., et al. (2004). Mindfulness: A proposed operational definition. Clinical Psychology: Science and Practice, 11(3), 230-241.

Bishop, S., et al (2003). Clarifying the construct of mindfulness in the context of emotion regulation and the process of change in therapy. Clinical Psychology: Science and Practice, 11(3), 255-262.

Bishop, S. (2002). What do we really know about mindfulness-based stress reduction? Psychosomatic Medicine, 64, 71-84.

Bishop, S., Lau, M., Shapiro, S., Carlson, L., Anderson, N., Carmody, J., et al. (2004). Mindfulness: A proposed operational definition. Clinical Psychology: Science and Practice, 11(3), 230-241.

Bobrow, J. (2003). Moments of truth—truths of moment. In J. D. Safran (Ed.), Psychoanalysis and Buddhism: An unfolding dialogue (pp. 199-220). Boston: Wisdom Publications.

Boccio, F. (2004). Mindfulness yoga. Somerville, MA: Wisdom Publications.

Bogels, S., Sijbers, G., & Vonken, M. (2006). Mindfulness and task concentration training for social phobia: A pilot study. Journal of Cognitive Psychotherapy: An International Quarterly, 20(1), 33-44.

Bogart, G. (1991). The use of meditation in psychotherapy: A review of the literature. American Journal of Psychotherapy, 45, 383-413.

Bohus, M., Haaf, B., Stiglmayr, C., Pohl, U., Bohme, R., & Linehan, M. (2000). Evaluation of inpatient dialectical-behavioral therapy for borderline personality disorder: A prospective study. Behaviour Research and Therapy, 38(9), 875-887.

Bohus, M., Haaf, B., Simms, T., Limberger, M., Schmahl, C., Unckel, C., et al. (2004). Effectiveness of inpatient dialectical-behavioral therapy for borderline personality disorder: A controlled trial. Behaviour Research and Therapy, 42(5), 487-499.

Bonadonna, R. (2003). Meditation's impact on chronic illness. Holistic Nurse Practitioner, 17(6), 309-319.

Bondolfi, G. (2005). Mindfulness and anxiety disorders: Possible developments. Constructivism in the Human Sciences, 10(1), 45-52.

Boorstein, S. (2002). Pay attention, for goodness' sake: Practicing the perfections of the heart—the Buddhist path of kindness. New York: Balantine Books.

Boorstein, S. (1994). Insight: Some considerations regarding its potential and limitations. Journal of Transpersonal Psychology, 26(2), 95-105.

Bootzin, R. R., & Stevens, S. J. (2005). Adolescents, substance abuse, and the treatment of insomnia and daytime sleepiness. Clinical Psychology Review, 25(5) 629-644.

Borkovic, T. D. (2002). Life in the future versus life in the present. Clinical Psychology: Science and Practice, 9, 76-80.

Borkovic, T. D., & Sharpless, B. (2004). Generalized anxiety disorder: Bringing cognitive-behavioral therapy into the valued present. In S.C. Hayes, V.M. Follette, & M.M. Linehan (Eds.), Mindfulness and acceptance: Expanding the cognitive-behavioral tradition (pp. 209-242). New York: The Guilford Press.

Borysenko, J., Kutz, I., & Benson, H. (1985). Meditation and psychotherapy: A rationale for the integration of dynamic psychotherapy, the relaxation response, and mindfulness meditation. American Journal of Psychiatry, 142, 1.

Borysenko, J., Kutz, I., Leserman, J., Dorrington, C., Mirrison, C., & Benson, H. (1985). Meditation as an adjunct to psychotherapy: A follow-up study. Psychotherapy and Psychosomatics, 43, 209-218.

Bowen, S., Witkiewitz, K., Dillworth, T., Chawla, N., Simpson, T., Ostafin, B., et al. (2006). Mindfulness meditation and substance use in an incarcerated population. Psychology of Addictive Behaviors, 20(3), 343-347.

Bowen, S., Witkiewitz, K., Dillworth, T. M., & Marlatt, G. A. (2007). The role of thought suppression in the relationship between mindfulness meditation and alcohol use. Annals of Behavioral Medicine, 33(1), 11-21.

Brach, T. (2003). Radical acceptance: Embracing your life with the heart of a Buddha. New York: Bantam/Dell.

Brahm, A. (2006). Mindfulness, bliss, and beyond: A meditator's handbook. Boston: Wisdom Publications.

Brantley, J. (2003). Calming your anxious mind: How mindfulness and compassion can free you from anxiety, fear, and panic. Oakland, CA: New Harbinger.

Brazier, D. (1995). Zen Therapy. New York: Wiley.

Brenner, M., & Homonoff, E. (2004). Zen and clinical social work: A spiritual approach to practice. Families in Society: The Journal of Contemporary Social Services, 85(2), 261-269.

Breslin, F. C., Zack, M., & McMain, S. (2002). An information-processing analysis of mindfulness: Implications for relapse prevention in the treatment of substance abuse. Clinical Psychology: Science and Practice, 9, 275-299.

Brock, T. C., Green, M. C., Reich, C. A., & Evans, L. M. (1996). The Consumer Reports study of psychotherapy: Invalid is invalid. American Psychologist, 51, 1083.

Broderick, P. (2005). Mindfulness and coping with dysphoric mood: Contrasts with rumination and distraction. Cognitive Therapy and Research, 29(5), 501-510.

Brody, L. R., & Park, S. H. (2004). Narratives, mindfulness, and the implicit audience. Clinical Psychology: Science and Practice, 11(2), 147-154.

Brown, D. P. (1986). The stages of meditation in cross-cultural perspective. In K. Wilber, J. Engler, & D. Brown (Eds.), Transformation of Consciousness. Boston: Shambhala.

Brown, D., Forte, M., & Dysart, M. (1984). Visual sensitivity and mindfulness meditation. Perceptual Motor Skill, 85, 775-784.

Brown, K. W., & Ryan, R. M. (2003). The benefits of being present: Mindfulness and its role in psychological well-being. Journal of Personality and Social Psychology, 84(4), 822-848.

Brown, K. W., & Ryan, R. M. (2004). Perils and promise in defining and

measuring mindfulness: Observations from experience. Clinical
Psychology: Science and Practice, 11, 242-248.

Bruce, A., & Davies, B. (2005). Mindfulness in hospice care: Practicing
meditation-in-action. Canadian Journal of Psychiatry, 50(13), 863-9.

Buchheld, N., Grossman, P., & Walach, H. (2001). Measuring mindfulness and
insight meditation (Vipassana) and meditation based psychotherapy: The
development of the Freiburg Mindfulness Inventory (FMI). Journal for
Meditation and Meditation Research, 1, 11-34.

Buck, R., & Morley, S. (2006). A daily process design study of attentional pain
control strategies in the self-management of cancer pain. European Journal
of Pain, 10(5), 385-398.

Burgdorf, J., & Panksepp, J. (2006). The neurobiology of positive emotions.
Neuroscience and Behavioral Reviews, 30, 173-187.

Burpee, L. C., & Langer, E. J. (2005). A study investigating the relationships
among mindfulness, marital satisfaction, and perceived spousal similarity.
Journal of Adult Development, 12(1), 43-51.

Burnard, P. (1987). Meditation: Uses and methods in psychiatric nurse
education. Nurse Education Today, 7, 187-191.

Burpee, L., & Langer, E. (2005). Mindfulness and marital satisfaction. Journal
of Adult Development, 12(1), 43-51.

Cahn, B.R., & Polich, J. (2006). Meditation states and traits: EEG, ERP, and
neuroimaging studies. Psychological Bulletin, 132(2), 180-211.

Cameron, O. G. (2001). Interoception: The inside story—a model for
psychosomatic processes. Psychosomatic Medicine, xx, 697-710.

Campos, P. (2002). Special series: Integrating Buddhist philosophy with
cognitive and behavioral practice. Cognitive and Behavioral Practice, 9,
38-40.

Carlson, L., & Brown, K. (2005). Validation of the Mindful Attention
Awareness Scale in a cancer population. Journal of Psychosomatic
Research, 58(1), 29-33.

Carlson, L., & Garland, S. N. (2005). Impact of mindfulness-based stress
reduction (MBSR) on sleep, mood, stress and fatigue symptoms in cancer
outpatients. International Journal of Behavioral Medicine, 12(4), 278-285.

Carlson, L., Speca, M., Patel, K., & Goodey, E. (2003). Mindfulness-based
stress reduction in relation to quality of life, mood, symptoms of stress,

and immune parameters in breast and prostate cancer outpatients. Psychosomatic Medicine, 65(4), 571-81.

Carlson, L., Speca, M., Patel, K., & Goodey, E. (2004). Mindfulness-based stress reduction in relation to quality of life, mood, symptoms of stress and levels of cortisol, dehydroepiandrosterone sulfate (DHEAS), and melatonin in breast and prostate cancer outpatients. Psychoneuroendocrinology, 29(4), 448-474.

Carlson, L. E., Ursuliak, Z., Goodey, E., Angen, M., & Speca, M. (2001). The effects of a mindfulness meditation-based stress reduction program on mood and symptoms of stress in cancer outpatients: 6-month follow-up. Supportive Care in Cancer, 9, 112-123.

Carson, J. (2006). Loving-kindness meditation findings not related to baseline differences. Journal of Holistic Nursing, 24(1), 5-6.

Carson, J., Carson, K., Gil, K., & Baucom, D. (in press). Self-expansion as a mediator of relationship improvements in a mindfulness intervention. Journal of Marital and Family Therapy.

Carson, J., Carson, K., Gil, K., & Baucom, D. (2004). Mindfulness-based relationship enhancement. Behavior Therapy, 35, 471-494.

Carson, J., Keefe, F., Lynch, T., Carson, K., Goli, V., Fras, A., et al. (2005). Loving-kindness meditation for chronic low back pain. Journal of Holistic Nursing, 23(3), 287-304.

Carson, S., & Langer, E. (2004). Mindful practice for clinicians and patients. In L. Haus (Ed.), Handbook of Primary Care Psychology (pp. 173-186). London: Oxford University Press.

Chadwick, P., Taylor, K., & Abba, N. (2005). Mindfulness groups for people with psychosis. Behavioural and Cognitive Psychotherapy, 33(3), 351-359.

Chambless, D., Baker, M., Baucom, D., Beutler, L., Calhoun, K., Crits-Christoph, P., et al. (1998). Update on empirically validated therapies, II. The Clinical Psychologist, 51(1) 3-16.

Chambless, D. L., & Hollon, S. D. (1998). Defining empirically supported therapies. Journal of Consulting and Clinical Psychology, 66, 7-18.

Chambless, D. L., Sanderson, W. C., Shoham, V., Johnson, S. B., Pope, K. S., et al. (1996). An update on empirically validated therapies. Clinical Psychologist, 49, 5-18.

Chanowitz, B., & Langer, E. (1980). Knowing more (or less) than you can show: Understanding control through the mindlessness/mindfulness distinction. In M. E. P. Seligman & J. Garber (Eds.), Human Helplessness. New York: Academic Press.

Chodron, P. (2001). The wisdom of no escape and the path of loving-kindness. Boston: Shambhala Publications.

Christensen, A., & Jacobson, N. (2000). Reconcilable differences. New York: The Guilford Press.

Christensen, A., Sevier, M., Simpson, L. E., & Gattis, K. S., (2004). Acceptance, mindfulness, and change in couple therapy. In S. C. Hayes, V. M. Follette, & M. M. Linehan (Eds.), Mindfulness and acceptance: Expanding the cognitive-behavioral tradition, (pp. 288-310). New York: The Guilford Press

Christopher, J., Christopher, S., Dunnagan, T., & Schure, M. (2006). Teaching self-care through mindfulness practices: The application of yoga, meditation, and qigong to counselor training. Journal of Humanistic Psychology, 46(4), 494-509.

Chung, C. Y. (1990). Psychotherapist and expansion of awareness. Psychotherapy and Psychosomatics, 53(1-4), 28-32.

Ciarrochi, J., Robb, H., & Godsell, C. (2005). Letting a little nonverbal air into the room: Insights from acceptance and commitment therapy: Part 1: Philosophical and theoretical underpinnings. Journal of Rational-Emotive & Cognitive Behavior Therapy, 23(2), 79-106.

Ciarrochi, J., & Robb, H. (2005). Letting a little nonverbal air into the room: Insights from acceptance and commitment therapy: Part 2: Applications. Journal of Rational-Emotive & Cognitive Behavior Therapy, 23(2), 107-130.

Cicetti, R. (2005). A journey towards awakening. Hakomi Forum, 14-15, 79-84.

Cohen, R. S., & Johanson, G. J. (2003). Editor's introduction to the first edition: Why self leadership? Journal of Self Leadership, 1, 3-8.

Cole, J.D. and Carol Ladas-Gaskin, (2007). Mindfulness Centered Therapies: An integrated approach, Seattle:Silver Birch Press.

Cole, J. D. (2006). Modified Hakomi: Coaching clients with IFS and Hakomi skills. Hakomi Forum, 16-17, 89-98.

Cooper, P. C. (1999). Buddhist meditation and countertransference: A case study. American Journal of Psychoanalysis, 59, 71-85.

Corrigan, F. (2004). Psychotherapy as assisted homeostasis: Activation of emotional processing mediated by the anterior cingulated cortex. Medical Hypotheses, 63(6), 968-973.

Craig, A. D. (2003). Interoception: The sense of the physiological condition of the body. Current Opinions in Neurobiology, 13, 500-505.

Craven, J. (1989). Meditation and psychotherapy. Canadian Journal of Psychiatry, 34, 648-653.

Crook, J., & Fontana, D. (1990). Space in mind: East-West psychology and contemporary Buddhism. Dorset: Element Books.

Curry, S. J., Marlatt, G. A., Gordon, J., & Baer, J. S. (1988). A comparison of alternative theoretical approaches to smoking cessation and relapse. Health Psychology, 7, 545-556.

Dahl, J., Wilson, K., Luciano, C., & Hayes, S. (2005). Acceptance and commitment therapy for chronic pain. Reno, NV: Context Press

Dalai Lama, & Cutler, H. (1998). The art of happiness. New York: Riverhead Books. Dall, M. (1995). Dancing in Neverland: Hakomi therapy from a client's perspective. Hakomi Forum, 11, 37-40.

Davidson, R. (2003). Affective neuroscience and psychophysiology: Toward a synthesis. Psychophysiology, 40(5), 655-665.

Davidson, R. J. (2003). The protean brain. In D. Goleman (Ed.), Destructive emotions and how we can overcome them: A dialogue with the Dalai Lama. London: Bloomsbury.

Davidson, R. J., & Goleman, D. J. (1977). The role of attention in meditation and hypnosis: A psychobiological perspective on transformations of consciousness. The International Journal of Clinical and Experimental Hypnosis, 25(4), 291-308.

Davidson, R., & Harrington, A. (2002). Visions of compassion: Western scientists and Tibetan Buddhists examine human nature. Oxford: Oxford University Press.

Davidson, R., & Kabat-Zinn, J. (2004). Alterations in brain and immune function produced by mindfulness meditation: Three caveats. Comment. Response to letter by J. Smith. Psychosomatic Medicine, 66(1), 149-152.

Davidson, R. J., Kabat-Zinn, J., Schumacher, J., Rosenkranz, M., Muller, D., Santorelli, S., et al. (2003). Alterations in brain and immune function produced by mindfulness meditation. Psychosomatic Medicine, 65(4), 564-570.

Davis, J., Fleming, M., Bonus, K., & Baker, T. (2007). A pilot study on mindfulness based stress reduction for smokers. BMC Complementary and Alternative Medicine, 25(7), 2.

Day, P., & Horton-Deutsch, S. (2004). Using mindfulness-based therapeutic interventions in psychiatric nursing practice: Part I: Description and empirical support for mindfulness-based interventions. Archives of Psychiatric Nursing, 18(5), 164-169.

Day, P., & Horton-Deutsch, S. (2004). Using mindfulness-based therapeutic interventions in psychiatric nursing practice: Part II: Mindfulness-based approaches for all phases of psychotherapy–Clinical case study. Archives of Psychiatric Nursing, 18(5), 170-177.

Deatherage, G. (1975). The clinical use of "mindfulness" meditation techniques in short-term psychotherapy. Journal of Transpersonal Psychology, 7(2), 133-143.

DeBerry, S. (1982). The effects of meditation relaxation on anxiety and depression in a geriatric population. Psychotherapy: Theory, Research, and Practice, 19, 512-521.

Decety, J., & Chaminade, T. (2003). When the self represents the other: A new cognitive neuroscience view on psychological identification. Consciousness and Cognition, 12, 577-596.

deCharms, C. (1998). Two views of mind: Abhidharma and brain science. Ithaca, NY: Snow Lion Publications.

Deepak, K., Manchanda, S., & Maheshwari, M. (1994). Meditation improves clinicoelectroencephalographic measures in drug-resistant epileptics. Biofeedback and Self-Regulation, 19, 25-40.

Deikman, A. (1982). The observing self: Mysticism and psychotherapy. Boston: Beacon Hill Press.

Deikman, A. (1966). Deautomatization and the mystic experience. Psychiatry, 29, 324-38.

Delmonte, M. (1988). Personality correlates of meditation practice: Frequency and dropout in an outpatient population. Journal of Behavioral Medicine, 11(6), 593-597.

Delmonte, M. (1987). Constructivist view of meditation. American Journal of Psychotherapy, XLI(2), 286-298.

Delmonte, M. (1986). Meditation as a clinical intervention strategy: A brief review. International Journal of Psychosomatics, 33(3), 9-12.

Delmonte, M. (1985). Meditation and anxiety reduction: A literature review. Clinical Psychology Review, 5, 91-102.

Delmonte, M. (1984). Electrocortical activity and related phenomenon associated with meditation practice: A literature review. International Journal of Neuroscience, 24, 217-231.

Delmonte, M. (1984). Response to meditation in terms of physiological behavior and self report measures. International Journal of Psychosomatics, 31(2), 3-17.

Delmonte, M., & Kenny, V. (1987). Conceptual models and functions of meditation in psychotherapy. Journal of Contemporary Psychotherapy, 17(1), 38-59.

de Silva, P. (1990). Meditation and beyond: Buddhism and psychotherapy. In M. G. T. Kwee (Ed.), International Conference on Psychotherapy, Meditation, and Health, (pp. 165-182). London: East-West Publications.

Desmond, L. (2004). Baby Buddhas: A guide for teaching meditation to children. Kansas City: Andrews McMeel Publishing.

Dimidjian, S., & Linehan, M. M. (2003). Defining an agenda for future research on the clinical application of mindfulness practice. Clinical Psychology: Science and Practice, 10(2), 166-71.

Ditto, B., Eclache, M., & Goldman, N. (2006). Short-term autonomic and cardiovascular effects of mindfulness body scan meditation. Annals of Behavioral Medicine, 32(3), 227-34.

Doss, B., Thum, Y., Sevier, M., Atkins, D., & Christensen, A. (2005). Improving relationships: Mechanisms of change in couple therapy. Journal of Consulting and Clinical Psychology, 73(4), 624-633.

Dumas, J. (2005). Mindfulness-based parent training: Strategies to lessen the grip of automaticity in families with disruptive children. Journal of Clinical Child and Adolescent Psychology, 34(4), 779-791.

Dunn, B. R., Hartigan, J. A., & Mikulas, W. L. (1999). Concentration and mindfulness meditations: Unique forms of consciousness? Applied Psychophysiology and Bio-feedback, 24, 147-165.

Eifert, G., McKay, M., & Forsyth, J. (2006). ACT on life not on anger. Oakland, CA: New Harbinger Publications.

Eifert, G., & Forsyth, J. (2005). Acceptance and commitment therapy for anxiety disorders. Oakland, CA: New Harbinger Publications.

Ekman, P., Davidson, R., Richard, M., & Wallace, B. (2005). Buddhist and psychological perspectives on emotions and well-being. Current Directions in Psychological Science, 14(2), 59-63.

Emavardhana, T., & Tori, C. D. (1997). Changes in self-concept, ego defense mechanisms, and religiosity following seven-day Vipassana meditation retreats. Journal for the Scientific Study of Religion, 36, 194-206.

Engler, J. (2003). Being somebody and being nobody: A reexamination of the understanding of self in psychoanalysis and Buddhism. In J. D. Safran (Ed.), Psychoanalysis and Buddhism: An unfolding dialogue, (pp. 35-79). Boston: Wisdom Publications.

Engler, J. (1992). Therapeutic aims in psychotherapy and meditation: Developmental stages in the representation of self. Hakomi Forum, 9, 31-50.

Engler, J. (1986). Therapeutic aims in psychotherapy and meditation: Developmental stages in the representation of self. In K. Wilber, J. Engler, & D. Brown, Transformations of consciousness: Conventional and contemplative perspectives on development. Boston: Shambhala.

Engler, J. (1983). Buddhist Satipatthana-Vipassana meditation and an object relations model of developmental-therapeutic change: A clinical case study. (Doctoral dissertation, University of Chicago, 1983).

Engler, J. (1981). Vicissitudes of the self according to psychoanalysis and Buddhism: A spectrum model of object relations development. Psychoanalysis and Contemporary Thought, 6, 29-72.

Engler, J., & Brown, D. (1986). The stages of mindfulness meditation: A validation study, parts I and II. In K. Wilber, J. Engler, & D. Brown, Transformations of consciousness: Conventional and contemplative perspectives on development. Boston: Shambhala.

Epstein, M. (2005). Open to desire. New York: Gotham Books/Penguin.

Epstein, M. (2001) Going on being: Buddhism and the way of change. New York: Broadway Books.

Epstein, M. (1998) Going to pieces without falling apart. New York: Broadway Press.

Epstein, M. (1995). Thoughts without a thinker. New York: Basic Books.

Epstein, M. (1989). Forms of emptiness: Psychodynamic, meditative and clinical perspectives. Journal of Transpersonal Psychology, 2, 61-71.

Epstein, M., & Lieff, J. (1981). Psychiatric complications of meditation practice. Journal of Transpersonal Psychology, 13(2), 137-147.

Epstein, R. M. (2001). Just being. The Western Journal of Medicine, 174(1), 63-65.

Epstein, R. M. (1999). Mindful practice. Journal of the American Medical Association, 282(9), 833-839.

Evans, I. M. (2005). Catching the third wave of behavior therapy: A review of Georg H. Eifert and John P. Forsyth, Acceptance & commitment therapy for anxiety disorders: A practitioner's treatment guide to using mindfulness, acceptance, and values-based behavior change strategies. PsycCRITIQUES, 50(49).

Eyberg, S., & Graham-Pole, J. (2005). Mindfulness and behavioral parent training: Commentary. Journal of Clinical Child and Adolescent Psychology, 34(4), 792-794.

Fargoso, C. M., Grinberg, Z. J., Perez, M. A. G., Ortiz, C. A., & Loyo, J. R. (1999). Effects of meditation on brain electrical activity. Revista Mexicana de Psicologia, 16(1), 101-115.

Faucheaux, D., & Weiss, H. (1999). Training psychotherapists in the almost impossible task of just paying attention. Hakomi Forum, 13, 1-6.

Feinstein, D. (1990). Transference and countertransference in the here-and-now therapies. Hakomi Forum, 8, 7-14.

Feldenkrais, M. (1972). Awareness through movement. New York: Harper & Row.

Fennell, M. (2004). Depression, low self-esteem and mindfulness. Behaviour Research and Therapy, 42, 1053-1067.

Ferrucci, P., & Ferrucci, V. R., (Trans.) (2006). The power of kindness: The unexpected benefits of leading a compassionate life. New York: Penguin Group.

Fields, R. (1992). How the swans came to the lake: The narrative history of Buddhism in America. Boston: Shambala Publications.

Finn, M. (1998). Tibetan Buddhism and comparative psychoanalysis. In A. Molino (Ed.), The Couch and the Tree. New York: North Point Press.

Finn, M. (1992). Transitional space and Tibetan Buddhism: The object relations of meditation. In M. Finn & J. Gartner (Eds.), Object relations and religion. Westport, CN: Praeger.

Finucane, A., & Mercer, S. W. (2006). An exploratory mixed methods study of the acceptability and effectiveness of mindfulness-based cognitive therapy for patients with active depression and anxiety in primary care. BMC Psychiatry, 6, 14.

Fisher, R. (2002). Experiential psychotherapy with couples: A guide for the creative pragmatist. Phoenix, AZ: Zeig, Tucker & Theisen.

Fisher, R. (1996). Using Hakomi in couples psychotherapy. Hakomi Forum, 12, 3-8.

Fishman, B. (2002). Emotional healing through mindfulness meditation. Rochester, VT: Inner Traditions.

Follette, V. M., Palm, K. M., & Rasmussen Hall, M. L. (2004). Acceptance, mindfulness, and trauma. In S. C. Hayes, V. M. Follette, & M. M. Linehan, (Eds.), Mindfulness and acceptance: Expanding the cognitive-behavioral tradition, (pp. 192-208). New York: The Guilford Press.

French, J. (2006). Self within the matrix: Buddhist narrative and a group-analytic paradigm. Group Analysis, 39(2), 243-256.

Fritz, G., & Mierzwa, J. (1983). Meditation: A review of literature relevant to therapist behavior and personality. Psychotherapy in Private Practice, 1(3), 77-87.

Fromm, E., Suzuki, D. T., & DeMartino, R. (1960). Zen Buddhism and psychoanalysis. New York: Harper & Row.

Fruzzetti, A. E., & Iverson, K. M. (2004). Mindfulness, acceptance, validation, and "individual" psychopathology in couples. In S. C. Hayes, V. M. Follette, & M. M. Linehan, (Eds.), Mindfulness and acceptance: Expanding the cognitive-behavioral tradition, (pp. 168-191). New York: The Guilford Press.

Fulton, P. R. (2005). Mindfulness as clinical training. In C. K. Germer, R. D. Siegel, & P. R. Fulton, (Eds.), Mindfulness and psychotherapy, (pp. 55-72). New York: The Guilford Press.

Fulton, P. R., & Siegel, R. D. (2005). Buddhist and Western psychology: Seeking common ground. In C. K. Germer, R. D. Siegel, & P. R. Fulton, (Eds.), Mindfulness and psychotherapy, (pp. 28-54). New York: The Guilford Press.

Galantino, M., Baime, M., Maguire, M., Szapary, P., & Farrer, J. (2005). Association of psychological and physiological measures of stress in health-care professionals during an 8-week mindfulness meditation program: Mindfulness in practice. Stress and Health: Journal of the International Society for the Investigation of Stress, 21(4), 255-261.

Gardner, F., & Moore, Z. (2004). A mindfulness-acceptance-commitment-based approach to athletic performance enhancement: Theoretical considerations. Behavior Therapy, 35(4), 707-723.

Gaudiano, B. A. (2005). Cognitive behavior therapies for psychotic disorders: Current empirical status and future directions. Clinical Psychology: Science and Practice, 12(1), 33-50.

Gaudiano, B., & Herbert, J. (2006a). Acute treatment of inpatients with psychotic symptoms using acceptance and commitment therapy: Pilot results. Behaviour Research and Therapy, 44(3), 415-437.

Gaudiano, B., & Herbert, J. (2006b). Believability of hallucinations as a potential mediator of their frequency and associated distress in psychotic inpatients. Behavioural and Cognitive Psychotherapy, 34(4), 497-502.

Gelkopf, M., & Kreitler, S. (1996). Is humor only fun, an alternative cure, or magic? The cognitive therapeutic potential of humor. Journal of Cognitive Psychotherapy: An International Quarterly, 10, 235-254.

Gendlin, E. T. (1996). Focusing-oriented psychotherapy: A manual of the experiential method. New York: The Guilford Press.

Gendlin, E. T. (1986). Let your body interpret your dreams. Wilmette, IL: Chiron Publications.

Germer, C. (2006). You gotta have heart. Psychotherapy Networker, 30(1), 54-59, 65.

Germer, C. (2006). Getting along: Loving the other without losing yourself. Tricycle, Spring, 25-27.

Germer, C. (2005a). Mindfulness: What is it? What does it matter? In C. K. Germer, R. D. Siegel, & P. R. Fulton (Eds.), Mindfulness and psychotherapy, pp. 3-27. New York: The Guilford Press.

Germer, C. (2005b). Teaching mindfulness in therapy. In C. K. Germer, R.

D. Siegel, & P. R. Fulton (Eds.), Mindfulness and psychotherapy, (pp. 113-129). New York: The Guilford Press.

Germer, C. (2005c). Anxiety disorders: Befriending fear. In C. K. Germer, R. D. Siegel, & P. R. Fulton (Eds.), Mindfulness and psychotherapy, (pp. 152-172). New York: The Guilford Press.

Germer, C., Siegel, R., & Fulton, P. (Eds.) (2005). Mindfulness and psychotherapy. New York: Guilford Press.

Gerza, J. (2005). The integrated mindfulness model (IMM). Transpersonal Psychology Review, 9(1), 68-79.

Gifford, E., Hayes, S., & Strosahl, K. (2004). Examples of ACT components. Retrieved July 23, 2004 from http://www.acceptanceandcommitmenttherapy/resources/components.html.

Gilbert, P. (2005). Compassion: Conceptualizations, research and use in psychotherapy. London: Routledge.

Gilbert, P. (2004). A pilot exploration of the use of compassionate images in a group of self-critical people. Memory, 12(4), 507-516.

Gilligan, S. (1997). The courage to love: Principles and practices of self-relations psychotherapy. New York: W. W. Norton & Co.

Ginter, P. (2003). Brief report: IFS and mindfulness meditation. Journal of Self Leadership, 1, 59-60.

Glaser, A. (2005). A call to compassion: Bringing Buddhist practices of the heart into the soul of psychology. Berwick, ME: Nicolas-Hays.

Goldner, M. (2004). Review of the video Mindfulness and Meditation. Complementary Health Practice Review, 9(3), 213-214.

Goldstein, J. (2002). One dharma: The emerging Western Buddhism. New York: HarperCollins.

Goldstein, J. (1993). Insight meditation: The practice of freedom. Boston: Shambhala Publications.

Goldstein, J. & Kornfield, J. (1987). Seeking the heart of wisdom: The path of insight meditation. Boston: Shambhala.

Goleman, D. (2003). Destructive emotions: How can we overcome them? New York: Bantam Dell.

Goleman, D. (1997). Healing emotions. Boston: Shambhala Publications.

Goleman, D. (1990). The psychology of meditation. In M. G. T. Kwee (Ed.),

Proceedings of the First International Conference on Psychotherapy, Meditation and Health, (pp. 19-35). London: East-West Publications.

Goleman, D. (1988). The meditative mind: The varieties of meditative experience. New York: Tarcher/Putnam Books.

Goleman, D. (1984). The Buddha on meditation and states of consciousness. In D. S. Shapiro & R. N. Walsh (Eds.), Meditation: Classic and contemporary perspectives. New York: Aldine.

Goleman, D. (1977). The varieties of meditative experience. New York: E. P. Dutton.

Goleman, D. (1971). Meditation as meta-therapy. Journal of Transpersonal Psychology, 3, 1-25.

Goleman, D., & Schwartz, G. E. (1984). Meditation as an intervention in stress reactivity. In D. H. Shapiro, Jr., & R. N. Walsh (Eds.), Meditation: Classic and contemporary perspectives, (pp. 77-88). New York: Aldine.

Goleman, D., & Schwartz, G. E. (1976). Meditation as an intervention in stress reactivity. Journal of Consulting and Clinical Psychology, 44, 456-466.

Goodman, T. A. (2005). Working with children: Beginner's mind. In C. K. Germer, R. D. Siegel, & P. R. Fulton (Eds.), Mindfulness and psychotherapy, (pp. 197-219). New York: The Guilford Press.

Grayson, J. (2003). Freedom from obsessive-compulsive disorder: A personalized recovery program for living with uncertainty. New York: Jeremy P. Tarcher/Penguin.

Gregg, J., et al. (2007). Improving diabetes self-management through acceptance, mindfulness, and values: A randomized controlled trial. Journal of Consulting and Clinical Psychology, 75(2), 336-343.

Grepmair, L., Mitterlehner, F., Rother, W., & Nickel, M. (2006). Promotion of mindfulness in psychotherapists in training and treatment results of their patients. Journal of Psychosomatic Research, 60, 649-650.

Gross, C., Kreitzer, M., Russas, V., Treesak, C., Frazier, P., & Hertz, M. (2004). Mindfulness meditation to reduce symptoms after organ transplant: A pilot study. Behaviour Research and Therapy, 42(9), 1053-1069.

Grossman, P. (in press). Mindfulness practice: A unique clinical intervention for the behavioral sciences. In T. Heidenreich & J. Michalak (Eds.), Mindfulness and acceptance in psychotherapy. Tuebingen: DVTG Press.

Grossman, P., Niemann, L., Schmidt, S., & Walach, H. (2004). Mindfulness-based stress reduction and health benefits: A meta-analysis. Journal of Psychosomatic Research, 57, 35-43.

Groves, P., & Farmer, R. (1994). Buddhism and addictions. Addiction Research, 2, 183-194.

Guevara, K. (1996). Creating organizations fit for the human spirit through Hakomi. Hakomi Forum, 12, 9-22.

Gunaratana, B. (2002). Mindfulness in plain English. Somerville, MA: Wisdom Publications.

Hamilton, N., Kitzman, H., & Guyotte, S. (2006). Enhancing health and emotion: Mindfulness as a missing link between cognitive therapy and positive psychology. Journal of Cognitive Psychotherapy, 20(2), 123-134.

Hanh, T. N. (1992). Peace is every step. New York: Bantam Books.

Hanh, T. N. (1976). The miracle of mindfulness. Boston: Beacon Press.

Hart, W. (1987). The art of living: Vipassana meditation as taught by S. N. Goenka. San Francisco: Harper.

Hassed, C. (2004). Bringing holism into mainstream biomedical education. Journal of Alternative and Complementary Medicine, 10(2), 405-407.

Hayes, A. M., & Feldman, G. (2004). Clarifying the construct of mindfulness in the context of emotion regulation and the process of change in therapy. Clinical Psychology: Science and Practice, 11(3), 255-262.

Hayes, S. C. (2004a). Acceptance and commitment therapy, relational frame theory, and the third wave of behavioral and cognitive therapies. Behavior Therapy, 35(4), 639-665.

Hayes, S. C. (2004b). Acceptance and commitment therapy and the new behavior therapies: Mindfulness, acceptance, and relationship. In S. C. Hayes, V. M. Follette, & M. M. Linehan, (Eds.), Mindfulness and acceptance: Expanding the cognitive-behavioral tradition, (pp. 1-29). New York: The Guilford Press.

Hayes, S. C. (2002). Buddhism and acceptance and commitment therapy. Cognitive and Behavioral Practice, 9, 58-66.

Hayes, S. C. (2002). Acceptance, mindfulness, and science. Clinical Psychology: Science and Practice, 9(1), 101-106.

Hayes, S. C., Bissett, R., Korn, Z., Zettle, R., Rosenfarb, I., Cooper, L., et al. (1999). The impact of acceptance versus control rationales on pain tolerance. Psychological Record, 49, 33-47.

Hayes, S., & Feldman, G. (2004). Clarifying the construct of mindfulness in the context of emotion regulation and the process of change in therapy. Clinical Psychology: Science and Practice, 11(3), 255-262.

Hayes, S. C., Follette, V. M., & Linehan, M. M. (Eds.) (2004) Mindfulness and acceptance: Expanding the cognitive-behavioral tradition. New York: The Guilford Press.

Hayes, S. C., Jacobson, N. S., Follette, V. M., & Dougher, M. J. (1994). Acceptance and change: Content and context in psychotherapy. Reno, NV: Context Press.

Hayes, S., & Shenk, C. (2004). Operationalizing mindfulness without unnecessary attachments. Clinical Psychology: Science and Practice, 11(3), 249-254

Hayes, S., & Strosahl, K. (2005). A practical guide to acceptance and commitment therapy. New York: Springer.

Hayes, S., Strosahl, K., & Wilson, K. (1999). Acceptance and commitment therapy: An experimental approach to behavior change. New York: Guilford Press.

Hayes, S. C., & Wilson, K. G. (2003). Mindfulness: Method and process. Clinical psychology: Science and practice, 10(2), 161-165.

Hayes, S., Masuda, A., Bissett, R., Luoma, J., & Guerrero, L. (2004). DBT, FAP, and ACT: How empirically oriented are the new behavior therapy technologies? Behavior Therapy, 35, 35-54.

Hayes, S., Strosahl, K., & Houts, A. (Eds.), (2005). A practical guide to acceptance and commitment therapy. New York: Springer.

Heatherton, T. F., & Baumeister, R. F. (1991). Binge eating as escape from self-awareness. Psychological Bulletin, 110, 86-108.

Hebert, J., Ebbeling, C., Olendzki, B., Hurley, T., Ma, Y., Saal, N., et al. (2001). Change in women's diet and body mass following intensive intervention for early-stage breast cancer. Journal of the American Dietetic Association, 101(4), 421-431.

Hill, G. (1988). Jungian psychotherapy and meditation. Inquiring Mind, 5(1), 21.

Holmes, D. (1984). Meditation and somatic arousal reduction: A review of the experimental evidence. American Psychologist, 39(1), 1-10.

Holroyd, J. (2004). The science of meditation and the state of hypnosis. Behavior Modification, 28(6), 783-811.

Hopkins, J. (2001). Cultivating compassion. New York: Broadway Books.

Hoppes, K. (2006). The application of mindfulness-based cognitive interventions in the treatment of co-occurring addictive and mood disorders. CNS Spectrums, 11(11), 829-851.

Horney, K. (1998). Free associations and the use of the couch. In A. Molino (Ed.), The couch and the tree: Dialogues in psychoanalysis and Buddhism. New York: North Point Press.

Houshmand, Z., Livingston, R., & Wallace, A. (1999). Consciousness at the crosssroads: Conversations with the Dalai Lama on brain science and Buddhism. Ithaca, NY: Snow Lion Publications.

Huss, D., & Baer, R. (2007). Acceptance and change: The integration of mindfulness-based cognitive therapy into ongoing dialectical behavior therapy in a case of borderline personality disorder with depression. Clinical Case Studies, 6(1), 17-33.

Ilardi, S. S., & Craighead, W. E. (1994). The role of nonspecific factors in cognitive-behavior therapy for depression. Clinical Psychology: Science and Practice, 1, 138-156.

Ingram, R. E., & Hollon, S. D. (1986). Cognitive therapy for depression from an information processing perspective. In R. E. Ingram (Ed.), Information processing approaches to clinical psychology, (pp. 261-284). Orlando, FL: Academic Press.

Ito, J. R., Donovan, D. M., & Hall, J. J. (1988). Relapse prevention in alcohol aftercare: Effects on drinking outcome, change process and aftercare. British Journal of Addiction, 83, 171-181.

Jacobson, N. P. (1983). Buddhism and the contemporary world: Change and self-correction. Carbondale, IL: Southern Illinois University Press.

Jacobson, N., Christensen, A., Prince, S., Cordova, J., & Eldridge, K. (2000). Integrative behavioral couple therapy: An acceptance-based, promising new treatment for couple discord. Journal of Consulting and Clinical Psychology, 68, 351-355.

Jain, S., Shapiro, S., Swanick, S., Rowsch, S., Mills, P., Bell, I., et al. (2007). A randomized controlled trial of mindfulness meditation versus relaxation training: Effects on distress, positive states of mind, rumination, and distraction. Annals of Behavioral Medicine, 33(1), 11-21.

Johanson, G. (2006). A survey of the use of mindfulness in psychotherapy. Annals of the American Psychotherapy Association, 9(2), 15-23.

Johanson, G. (1999a). Far beyond psychoanalysis: Freud's repetition compulsion. Hakomi Forum, 13, 27-41.

Johanson, G. (1999b). Making grace specific. (Doctoral dissertation, Drew Graduate School, Madison, NJ, 1999).

Johanson, G. (1996). The birth and death of meaning: Selective implications of linguistics for psychotherapy. Hakomi Forum, 12, 45-53.

Johanson, G. (1994). Editorial: Getting self conscious. Hakomi Forum, 10, 1-2.

Johanson, G. (1992). Editorial: Encouraging communion. Hakomi Forum, 9, 1-6.

Johanson, G. (1988a). Editorial: A wider perspective. Hakomi Forum, 6, 4-7.

Johanson, G. (1988b). A curious form of therapy: Hakomi. Hakomi Forum, 6, 18-31.

Johanson, G. (1986a). Editorial: Taking it home with you. Hakomi Forum, 4, 1-6.

Johanson, G. (1986b). Hakomi in the trenches. Hakomi Forum, 4, 7-17.

Johanson, G. (1985a). The use of biofeedback by Hakomi therapists. Hakomi Forum, 2, 30-34.

Johanson, G. (1985b). A note on Hakomi therapy and psychodrama. Hakomi Forum, 2, 26-29.

Johanson, G. (1984a). Editorial: Watzlawick, Wilbur, and the work. Hakomi Forum, 1, 1-5.

Johanson, G. (1984b). Editor's introduction. In G. J. Johanson (Ed.), Feed my sheep: Sermons on contemporary issues in pastoral care, (pp. 3-10). New York: Paulist Press.

Johanson, G., & Kurtz, R. (1991). Grace unfolding: Psychotherapy in the spirit of the Tao-te Ching. New York: Bell Tower.

Johanson, G., & Taylor, C. (1988). Hakomi therapy with seriously emotionally disturbed adolescents. In C. E. Schaefer (Ed.), Innovative interventions in child and adolescent therapy, (pp. 232-265). New York: John Wiley & Sons.

Jung, C. G. (1992). Psychological commentary on the Tibetan book of great liberation. In D. Meckel & R. Moore (Eds.), Self and liberation: The Jung-Buddhism dialogue. New York: Paulist Press.

Kabat-Zinn, J. (2005). Guided mindfulness meditation. Series 1-3 (Compact disc). Lexington, MA: Stress Reduction CDs and Tapes.

Kabat-Zinn, J. (2003a). Mindfulness-based interventions in context: Past, present, and future. Clinical Psychology: Science and Practice, 10(2), 144-156.

Kabat-Zinn, J. (2003b). Coming to our senses: Healing ourselves and the world through mindfulness. New York: Hyperion.

Kabat-Zinn, J. (2000). Indra's net at work: The mainstreaming of Dharma practice in society. In G. Watson & S. Batchelor (Eds.), The psychology of awakening: Buddhism, science, and our day-to-day lives, (pp. 225-249). North Beach, ME: Weiser.

Kabat-Zinn, J. (1994). Wherever you go, there you are: Mindfulness meditation in everyday life. New York: Hyperion.

Kabat-Zinn, J. (1990). Full catastrophe living: Using the wisdom of your body and mind to face stress, pain, and illness. New York: Dell Publishing.

Kabat-Zinn, J. (1982). An outpatient program in behavioral medicine for chronic pain. General Hospital Psychiatry, 4, 33-47.

Kabat-Zinn, J., & Chapman-Waldrop, A. (1988). Compliance with an outpatient stress reduction program. Journal of Behavioral Medicine, 11, 333-352.

Kabat-Zinn, J., Lipworth, L., & Burney, R. (1985). The clinical use of mindfulness meditation for the self-regulation of chronic pain. Journal of Behavioral Medicine, 8, 163-190.

Kabat-Zinn, J., Lipworth, L., Burney, R. & Sellers, W. (1986). Four-year follow-up of a meditation-based program for the self-regulation of chronic pain: Treatment outcomes and compliance. Clinical Journal of Pain, 2, 159-173.

Kabat-Zinn, J., Kristeller, J., Mahoney, M., DelMonte, M., et al (2003). Special issue on Buddhist psychology, mindfulness, constructivism, and psychotherapy: A tribute to Yukata Haruki. Constructivism in the Human Sciences, 8(2).

Kabat-Zinn, J., Massion, A. O., Kristeller, J., Peterson, L., Fletcher, K. E., Pbert, L., et al. (1992). Effectiveness of a meditation-based stress reduction program in the treatment of anxiety disorders. American Journal of Psychiatry, 149(7), 936-943.

Kabat-Zinn, J., Wheeler, J. E., Light, T., Skillings, Z., Scharf, M. J., Cropley,

T. G., et al. (1998). Influence of a mindfulness meditation-based stress reduction intervention on skin clearing. Psychosomatic Medicine, 60, 625-632.

Kabat-Zinn, M., & Kabat-Zinn, J. (1998). Everyday blessings: The inner work of mindful parenting. New York: Hyperion.

Kakar, S. (1991). The analyst and the mystic: Psychoanalytic reflections on religion and mysticism. Chicago: University of Chicago Press.

Kaplan, A. H. (2006). Listening to the body: Pragmatic case studies in body-centered psychotherapy. (Doctoral dissertation, Rutgers University, 2006.)

Kaplan, A., & Schwartz, L. (2005). Issues of attachment and sexuality: A case study from a clinical research study. Hakomi Forum, 14-15, 19-33.

Kaplan, A., & Schwartz, L. (2005). Issues of attachment and sexuality: Case studies from a clinical research study. In the Proceedings of the 2005 United States Association for Body Psychotherapy (USABP) Conference.

Kaplan, K. H., Goldenberg, D. L., & Galvin, N. M. (1993). The impact of a meditation-based stress reduction program on fibromyalgia. General Hospital Psychiatry, 15, 284-289.

Kapleau, P. (1979). Zen dawn in the West. New York: Anchor Press/ Doubleday.

Karasu, T. B. (1999). Spiritual psychotherapy. American Journal of Psychotherapy, 53, 143-161.

Kavanagh, D., Andrade, J., & May, J. (2004). Beating the urge: implications of research into substance-related desires. Advances in Mind-Body Medicine, 20(2), 20-29.

Kawai, H. (1996). Buddhism and the art of psychotherapy. College Station, TX: A&M University Press.

Keller, R. (2005). Hakomi simplified 2004: A new view of Ron Kurtz's mindfulness-based psychotherapy. Hakomi Forum, 14-15, 518.

Kenny, M., & Williams, J. (2007). Treatment-resistant depressed patients show a good response to mindfulness-based cognitive therapy. Behavior Research and Therapy, 45, 617-625.

Keogh, E., Bond, F., Hanmer, R., & Tilston, J. (2005). Comparing acceptance and control-based coping instructions on the cold-pressor pain experiences of healthy men and women. European Journal of Pain, 9(5), 591-598.

Khong, B. S. L. (2007). The Buddha's influence in the therapy room. Hakomi Forum, 18, 11-18.

Khong, B. S. L. (2006a). Augmenting cognitive-behavior therapy with Buddhist psychology. In M. G. T. Kwee, K. J. Gergen, & F. Koshikawa (Eds.), Horizons in Buddhist psychology: Practice, research, and therapy, (pp. 315-330). Taos, NM: Taos Institute Publications

Khong, B. S. L. (2006b). Personal growth in and beyond therapy. Constructivism in the Human Sciences, 11(1), 7-19.

Khong, B. S. L. (2005). Minding the mind's business (reprint). Hakomi Forum, 14-15, 33-42.

Khong, B. S. L. (2004). Minding the mind's business. The Humanistic Psychologist, 32(3), 257-279.

Khong, B. S. L. (2003a). Buddhism and psychotherapy: Experiencing and releasing dis-ease. Constructivism in The Human Sciences, 8(2), 37-56.

Khong, B. S. L. (2003b). The Buddha teaches an attitude, not an affiliation. In S. R. Segall (Ed.), Encountering Buddhism: Western psychology and Buddhist teachings (pp. 61-74). New York: State University of New York Press.

Khong, B. S. L. (2003c). Buddha, being, and the Black Forest. The Humanistic Psychologist, 31(4), 97-111.

Khong, B. S. L. (2003d). Role of responsibility in Daseinsanalysis and Buddhism. In K. H. Dockett, G. R. Dudley-Grant, & C. P. Bankart (Eds.), Psychology and Buddhism: From individual to global community, (pp. 139-159). New York: Kluwer/Plenum Publishers.

Kingston, J., Chadwick, P., Meron, D., & Skinner, T. (2007). A pilot randomized control trial investigating the effect of mindfulness practice on pain tolerance, psychological well-being, and physiological activity. Journal of Psychosomatic Research, 62(3), 297-300.

KiSchore, C., Verma, S. K., & Dhar, P. L. (1996). Psychological effects of Vipassana on Tihar Jail inmates: Research report. New Delhi: All India Institute of Medical Sciences,.

Kjaer, T. W., Bertelsen, C., Piccini, P., Brooks, D., Alving, J., & Lou, H. C. (2002). Increased dopamine tone during meditation-induced change of consciousness. Cognitive Brain Research, 13, 255-259.

Koerner, K., & Linehan, M. M. (2000). Research on dialectical behavior therapy for patients with borderline personality disorder. Psychiatric Clinics of North America, 23, 151-167.

Kohlenberg, R. J., Hayes, S. C., & Tsai, M. (1993). Radical behavioral psychotherapy: Two contemporary examples. Clinical Psychology Review, 13, 579-592.

Kolodny, R. (2004). Why awareness works—and other insights from spiritual practice. British Gestalt Journal, 13(2), 92-99.

Koons, C. R., Robins, C. R., Tweed, J. L., Lynch, T. R., Gonzalez, A.M., Morse, J. Q., et al. (2001). Efficacy of dialectical behavior therapy in women veterans with borderline personality disorder. Behavior Therapy 32, 371-390.

Kornfield, J. (1993). A path with heart. New York: Bantam Books.

Kornfield, J. (1993). Even the best meditators have old wounds to heal: Combining meditation and psychotherapy. In R. Walsh & F. Vaughan (Eds.), Paths beyond ego. New York: Tarcher/Putnam.

Kornfield, J. (1990). Buddhist meditation and consciousness research. Sausalito, CA: Institute of Noetic Sciences.

Kramer, J. (2004). Buddha mom: A journey through mindful mothering. New York: Jeremy P. Tarcher.

Kreitzer, M. J., Gross, C. R., Ye, X., Russas, V., & Treesak, C. (2005). Longitudinal impact of mindfulness meditation on illness burden in solid-organ transplant recipients. Progress in Transplants, 15(2), 166-72.

Kristeller, J. L., & Hallett, C. B. (1999). An exploratory study of a meditation-based intervention for binge eating disorder. Journal of Health Psychology, 4, 357-363.

Kristeller, J. L., & Hallett, C. B. "Mindfulness Meditation: A Treatment for Binge Eating Disorder." 7th International Conference of the Transnational Network for the Study of Physical Psychological and Spiritual Wellbeing. Wollongong, Australia. July, 2002.

Kumar, S. (2005). Grieving mindfully: A compassionate and spiritual guide to coping with loss. Oakland, CA: New Harbinger.

Kumar, S. (2002). An introduction to Buddhism for the cognitive-behavioral therapist. Cognitive and Behavioral Practice, 9, 40-43.

Kurak, M. (2003). The relevance of the Buddhist theory of dependent co-origination to cognitive science. Brain and Mind, 4, 341-351.

Kurash, C., & Schaul, J. (2006). Integrating mindfulness meditation within a university counseling center setting. Journal of College Student Psychotherapy, 20(3), 53-67.

Kurtz, R. (2007). Three recent essays. Hakomi Forum, 18, 5-10.

Kurtz, R. (2006). Five recent essays. Hakomi Forum, 16-17, 1-8.

Kurtz, R. (2005). Mindfulness-based self study. Hakomi Forum, 14-15, 1-4.

Kurtz, R. (2004). Hakomi method mindfulness-based body psychotherapy. Retrieved Nov. 5, 2005 from www.ronkurtz.com/writing/Readings. Aug.2004.pdf.

Kurtz, R. (1996). Introduction to the process. Hakomi Forum, 12, 6-12.

Kurtz, R. (1995). The origins of the Hakomi method. Hakomi Forum, 11, 3-10.

Kurtz, R. (1990). Body-centered psychotherapy: The Hakomi method. Mendocino, CA: LifeRhythm.

Kurtz, R. (1987). On the uniqueness of Hakomi. Hakomi Forum, 5, 2-8.

Kurtz, R. (1986). Cancer and psychotherapy. Hakomi Forum, 4, 18-32.

Kurtz, R. (1985a). The organization of experience in Hakomi therapy. Hakomi Forum, 3, 3-9.

Kurtz, R. (1985b). Foundations of Hakomi therapy. Hakomi Forum, 2, 3-7.

Kurtz, R., & Minton, K. (1997). Essentials of Hakomi body-centered psychotherapy. In C. Caldwell (Ed.), Getting in touch: The guide to new body-centered therapies, (pp. 45-60). Wheaton, IL: Quest Books.

Kutz, I., Borysenko, J., & Benson, H. (1985). Meditation and psychotherapy: A rationale for the integration of dynamic psychotherapy, the relaxation response, and mindfulness meditation. American Journal of Psychiatry, 142(1), 1-8.

Kutz, I., Leserman, J., Dorrington, C., Morrison, C., Borysenko, J., & Benson, H. (1985). Meditation as an adjunct to psychotherapy. Psychotherapy Psychosomatic, 43, 209-218.

Kwee, M. G. T. (1990). Cognitive and behavioral approaches to Buddhism. In M. G. T. Kwee (Ed.), Proceedings of the 1st international conference on psychotherapy, meditation, and health, (pp. 36-53). London: East-West Publications,.

LaBerge, D. (1995). Attentional processing: The brain's art of mindfulness. Cambridge, MA: Harvard University Press.

Ladas-Gaskin, C. (2005). Patience and letting go: The roots of compassionate healing. Hakomi Forum, 14-15, 75-78.

Ladner, L. (2004). The lost art of compassion: Discovering the practice of happiness in the meeting of Buddhism and psychology. New York: HarperCollins.

Lamagna, J., & Gleiser, K. A. (2004). Building a secure internal attachment: An intra-relational approach to ego strengthening and emotional processing with chronically traumatized clients. Memory, 12(4), 507-16.

Lambert, M. J. (1992). Psychotherapy outcome research: Implications for integrative and eclectic theories. In J. C. Norcross & M. R. Goldfried (Eds.), Handbook of psychotherapy integration. New York: Basic Books.

Langan, R. (2006). Minding what matters: Psychotherapy and the Buddha within. Boston: Wisdom Publications.

Langan, R. (2003). The dissolving of dissolving itself. In J. D. Safran (Ed.), Psychoanalysis and Buddhism: An unfolding dialogue, (pp. 131-145). Boston: Wisdom Publications.

Langer, E. J. (2000). Mindful learning. Current directions in psychological science, 9(6), 220-223.

Langer, E. J. (1989). Mindfulness. Reading, MA: Addison Wesley.

Langer, E. J. (1997). The power of mindful learning. Reading, MA: Addison Wesley.

Langer, E. J., & Moldoveanu, M. (2000). The construct of mindfulness. Journal of Social Issues, 56, 1-9.

Langer, E., Perlumuter, L., Chanowitz, B., & Rubin, R. (1988). Two new applications of mindlessness theory: Alcoholism and aging. Journal of Aging Studies, 2(3), 289-299.

Langer, E., & Piper, A. (1987). The prevention of mindlessness. Journal of Personality and Social Psychology, 53, 280-287.

Lau, M., Bishop, W., Segal, Z., Buis, T., Anderson, N., Carlson, et al. (2006). The Toronto Mindfulness Scale: development and validation. Journal of Clinical Psychology, 62(12), 1445-1467.

Lau, M., & McMain, S. (2006). Integrating mindfulness meditation with cognitive and behavioural therapies: The challenge of combining acceptance- and change-based strategies. Canadian Journal of Psychiatry, 50(13), 863-869.

Lazar, Sara W. (2005). Mindfulness research. In C. K. Germer, R.D. Siegel, & P. R. Fulton (Eds.), Mindfulness and psychotherapy, (pp. 220-240). New York: The Guilford Press,.

Lazar, S., Kerr, C., Wasserman, R., Gray, J., Greve, D., Treadway, M., et al. (2005). Meditation experience is associated with increased cortical thickness. NeuroReport, 16(17), 1893-1897.

Leary, M., Adams, C., & Tate, E. (2006). Hypo-egoic self-regulation: Exercising self-control by diminishing the influence of the self. Journal of Personality, 74(6), 1803-1831.

Leary, M., Tate, E., Adams, C., Allen, A., & Hancock, J. (2007). Self-compassion and reactions to unpleasant self-relevant events: The implications of treating oneself kindly. Journal of Personality and Social Psychology, 92(5), 887-904.

Lehmann, D., Faber, P., Achermann, P., Jeanmonod, D., Gianotti, L., & Pizzagalli, D. (2001). Brain sources of EEG gamma frequency during volitionally meditation-induced, altered states of consciousness, and experience of the self. Psychiatry Research, 108(2), 111-121.

Lehrer, P., Sasaki, Y., & Saito, Y. (1999). Zazen and cardiac variability. Psychosomatic Medicine, 61(6), 812-821.

Leigh, J., Bowen, S., & Marlatt, G. (2005). Spirituality, mindfulness, and substance abuse. Addictive Behaviors, 30(7), 1335-1341.

Lesh, T. (1970). Zen meditation and the development of empathy in counselors. Journal of Humanistic Psychology, 10, 39-74.

Levin, D. M. (1989). Approaches to psychotherapy: Freud, Jung, and Tibetan Buddhism. In R. S. Valle & R. von Eckartsberg (Eds.), Metaphors of consciousness. New York: Plenum Press.

Levine, M. (2000). The positive psychology of Buddhism and yoga: Paths to mature happiness. Mahwah, NJ: Lawrence Erlbaum Associates.

Libet, B. (1999). Do we have free will? In B. Libet, A. Freeman, & K. Sutherland (Eds.), The volitional brain: Towards a neuroscience of free will (pp. 47-55). Thorverton, UK: Imprint Academic.

Linehan, M. M. (1993a). Cognitive-behavioral treatment of borderline personality disorder. New York: Guilford Press.

Linehan, M. M. (1993b). Skills training manual for treating borderline personality disorder. New York: Guilford Press.

Linehan, M. M. (1994). Acceptance and change: The central dialectic in psychotherapy. In S.C. Hayes, N. S. Jacobson, V. M. Follette, & M. J. Dougher (Eds.), Acceptance and change: Content and context in psychotherapy, (pp. 73-86). Reno, NV: Context Press .

Linehan, M. M., Armstrong, H. E., Suarez, A., Allmon, D., & Heard, H.L. (1991). Cognitive-behavioral treatment of chronically suicidal borderline patients. Archives of General Psychiatry, 48, 1060-1064.

Linehan, M. M., Heard, H. L., & Armstrong, H. E. (1993). Naturalistic follow-up of a behavioral treatment for chronically parasuicidal borderline patients. Archives of General Psychiatry, 50, 157-158.

Linehan, M. M., Tutek, D., Heard, H. L., & Armstrong, H. E. (1994). Interpersonal outcome of cognitive-behavioral treatment for chronically suicidal borderline patients. American Journal of Psychiatry, 51, 1771-1776.

Linehan, M., Schmidt, H., Dimeff, L., Craft, J., Katner, J., & Comtois, K. (1999). Dialectical behavior therapy for patients with borderline personality disorder and drug-dependence. American Journal on Addiction, 8, 279-292.

Linehan, M., Dimeff, L., Reynolds, S., Comtois, K., Welch, S., Heagerty, P., et al. (2002). Dialectical behavior therapy versus comprehensive validation therapy plus 12-step for the treatment of opioid dependent women meeting criteria for borderline personality disorder. Drug and Alcohol Dependence, 67, 13-26.

Lok, S., & McMahon, S. (2006). Mothers' thoughts about their children: Links between mind-mindedness and emotional availability., British Journal of Developmental Psychology24(3), 477-488.

Logsdon-Conradsen, S. (2002). Using mindfulness meditation to promote holistic health in individuals with HIV/AIDS. Cognitive and Behavioral Practic, 9, 67-72.

Loizzo, J. (2000). Meditation and psychotherapy. In P. Muskin, (Ed.), Review of psychiatry, volume 19, (pp. 147-197). Washington, DC: American Psychiatric Association Press,

Lopez, F. (2000). Acceptance and commitment therapy (ACT) in panic disorder with agoraphobia: A case study. Psychology in Spain, 4(1), 120-128.

Lou, H., Kjaer, T., Friberg, L., Wildschiodtz, G., Holm, S., & Nowak, M.

(1999). A 150-H2O PET study of meditation and the resting state of normal consciousness. Human Brain Mapping, 7(2), 98-105.

Lundgren, J. D. (2005). A mindfulness-based behavioral treatment for weight loss. (Doctoral dissertation, State University of New York at Albany, 2005).

Lundh, L. (2005). The role of acceptance and mindfulness in the treatment of insomnia. Journal of Cognitive Psychotherapy, 19(1), 29-39.

Lutz, A., Greishar, L., Rawlings, N., Richard, M., & Davidson, R. (2004). Long-term meditators self-induce high-amplitude gamma synchrony during mental practice. Proceedings of the National Academy of Sciences, 101(46), 16369-73.

Lynch, T., Chapman, A., Rosenthal, M., Kuo, J., & Linehan, M. (2006). Mechanisms of change in dialectical behavior therapy: Theoretical and empirical observations. Journal of Clinical Psychology, 62(4), 459-480.

Lynch, T., Morse, J., Mendelson, T., & Robins, C. (2003). Dialectical behavior therapy for depressed adults: A randomized pilot study. American Journal of Geriatric Psychiatry, 11, 33-45.

Lynn, S., Das, L., Hallquist, M., & Williams, J. (2006). Mindfulness, acceptance, and hypnosis: Cognitive and clinical perspectives. International Journal of Clinical and Experimental Hypnosis, 54(2), 143-166.

Ma, S., & Teasdale, J. (2004). Mindfulness-based cognitive therapy for depression: Replication and exploration of differential relapse prevention effects. Journal of Consulting and Clinical Psychology, 72(1), 31-40.

MacLeod, C., & Rutherford, E. (2004). Information-processing approaches: Assessing the selective functioning of attention, interpretation, and memory in GAD patients. In R. G. Heimberg, C.L. Turk, & D. S. Mennin (Eds.), Generalized anxiety disorder: Advances in research and practice, (pp. 109-142). New York: Guilford Press.

Macy, J., & Brown, M. (1998). Coming back to life: Practices to reconnect our lives, our world. Gabriola Island, BC, Canada: New Society.

Magid, B. (2003). Your ordinary mind. In J. D. Safran (Ed.), Psychoanalysis and Buddhism: An unfolding dialogue, (pp. 251-285). Boston: Wisdom Publications.

Magid, B. (2002). Ordinary mind: Exploring the common ground of Zen and psychotherapy. Somerville, MA: Wisdom Publications.

Maharaj, N. (1997). I am that: Talks with Sri Nisargadatta (M. Frydman, Trans.). New York: Aperture.

Majumdar, M., Grossman, P., Dietz-Waschkowski, B., Kersig, S., & Walach H. (2002). Does mindfulness meditation contribute to health? Outcome evaluation of a German sample. Journal of Alternative and Complementary Medicine, 8(6), 719-730.

Mansky, P., & Wallerstedt, D. (2006). Complementary medicine in palliative care and cancer symptom management. Cancer Journal, 12(5), 425-431.

Margolis, J., & Langer, E. (1990). An analysis of addictions from a mindful/mindless perspective. Psychology of Addictive Behaviors, 4, 107-115.

Marlatt, G. A. (2005). Mindfulness for addiction problems. In Carlson, J. (Ed.), Series VI: Spirituality. Compact disc. Washington, D.C.: American Psychological Association

Marlatt, G. A. (1994). Addiction, mindfulness, and acceptance. In S. C. Hayes, N. S. Jacobson, V. M. Follette & M. J. Dougher (Eds.), Acceptance and change: Content and context in psychotherapy, (pp. 175-197). Reno, NV: Context Press.

Marlatt, G. A. (2002). Buddhist philosophy and the treatment of addictive behavior. Cognitive and Behavioral Practice, 9, 44-50.

Marlatt, G. A., & Gordeon, J. R. (1985). Relapse prevention: Maintenance strategy in the treatment of addictive behaviors. New York: Guilford Press.

Marlatt, G. A., & Kristeller, J. L. (1999). Mindfulness and meditation. In W. R. Miller (Ed.), Integrating spirituality into treatment, (pp. 67-84). Washington, DC: American Psychological Association.

Marlatt, G. A., & Marques, J. K. (1977). Meditation, self-control, and alcohol use. In R. Stuart (Ed.), Behavioral self-management: Strategies, techniques, and outcomes. New York: Brunner/Mazel.

Marlatt, G. A., Pagano, R. R., Rose, R. M., & Marques, J. K. (1984). Effects of meditation and relaxation training upon alcohol use in male social drinkers. In D. H. Shapiro & R. N. Walsh (Eds.), Meditation: Classic and contemporary perspectives, (pp. 105-120). New York: Aldine.

Marlatt, G. A., Witkiewitz, K., Dillworth, T. M., Bowen, S. W., Parks, G.A., Macpherson, L. M., et al. (2004). Vipassana meditation as a treatment for alcohol and drug use disorders. In S. C. Hayes, V. M. Follette, & M. M. Linehan. (Eds.), Mindfulness and acceptance: Expanding the cognitive-behavioral tradition, (pp. 261-287). New York: The Guilford Press.

Marlock, G., & Weiss, H. (2006). In search of the embodied self. Hakomi Forum, 16-17, 47-56 (Reprint).

Marra, T. (2005). Dialectical behavior therapy in private practice: A practical and comprehensive guide. Oakland, CA: New Harbinger Publications.

Marra, T. (2004). Depressed and anxious: A dialectical behavior therapy workbook for overcoming depression and anxiety. Oakland, CA: New Harbinger Publications.

Martell, C., Addis, M., & Dimidjian, S. (2004). Finding the action in behavioral activation: The search for empirically supported interventions and mechanisms of change. In S. C. Hayes, V. M. Follette, & M. M. Linehan. (Eds.), Mindfulness and acceptance: Expanding the cognitive-behavioral tradition, (pp. 152-167). New York: The Guilford Press.

Martin, D. (1995). Remembering wholeness: A model for healing and recovery. Hakomi Forum, 11, 47-52.

Martin, J. (2002). The common factor of mindfulness—An expanding discourse: Comment on Horowitz (2002). Journal of Psychotherapy Integration, 12(2), 139-142.

Martin, J. (1997). Mindfulness: A proposed common factor. Journal of Psychotherapy Integration, 7(4), 291-312.

Martin, J. (1999). The Zen path through depression. New York: HarperCollins.

Mason, O., & Hargreaves, I. (2001). A qualitative study of mindfulness-based cognitive therapy for depression. British Journal of Medical Psychology, 74(2), 197-212.

Massion, A. O., Teas, J., Hebert, J. R., Wertheimer, M. D., & Kabat-Zinn, J. (1995). Meditation, melatonin, and breast/prostate cancer: Hypothesis and preliminary data. Medical Hypotheses, 44, 39-46.

Maupin, E. W. (1965). Individual differences in response to a new meditation exercise. Journal of Consulting Psychology, 29, 139-145.

Maupin, E. W. (1962). Zen Buddhism: A psychological review. Journal of Consulting Psychology, 26, 362-378.

May, G. G. (1982). Will and spirit. San Francisco: Harper Collins.

May, M. (2005). The effects of a self-acceptance training emphasizing compassion and mindfulness skills with inner experiences. (Doctoral dissertation, Institute for Transpersonal Psychology, 2005).

Mayland, K. A. (2005). The impact of practicing mindfulness meditation on women's sexual lives. (Doctoral dissertation, Alliant International University, 2005).

McCloy, S. G. O., (2005). A preliminary study of mindfulness in children as a conceptual framework for coping with bullying. (Doctoral dissertation, University of South Carolina, 2005).

McIntosh, W. (1997). East meets West: Parallels between Zen Buddhism and social psychology. The International Journal for the Psychology of Religion, 7(1). 37-52.

McManus, C. A. (2003). Group wellness programs for chronic pain and disease management. St. Louis: Butterworth-Heinemann.

McQuaid, J., & Carmona, P. (2004). Peaceful mind: Using mindfulness and cognitive behavioral psychology to overcome depression. Oakland, CA: New Harbinger Publications.

McQuillan, A., Nicastro, R., Guenot, F., Girard, M., Lissner, C., & Ferrero, F. (2005). Intensive dialectical behavior therapy for outpatients with borderline personality disorder who are in crisis. Psychiatric Services, 56(2), 193-197.

Meditation in psychotherapy (2005). Harvard Mental Health Newsletter, 21(10), 1-4

Meili, T. & Kabat-Zinn, J. (2004). The power of the human heart: A story of trauma and recovery and its implications for rehabilitation and healing. Advances in Mind/Body Medicine, 20, 6-16.

Mennin, D., Heimberg, R., Turk, C., & Fresco, D. (2002). Applying an emotion regulation framework to integrative approaches to generalized anxiety disorder. Clinical Psychology: Science and Practice, 9, 85-90.

Mikalus, W. (1990). Mindfulness, self-control, and personal growth. In M. G. T. Kwee (Ed.), Proceedings of the First International Conference on Psychotherapy, Meditation, and Health, (pp. 51-164). London: East-West Publications.

Miller, J. (1993). The unveiling of traumatic memories and emotions through mindfulness and concentration meditation: Clinical implications and three case reports. The Journal of Transpersonal Psychology, 25(2), 169-176.

Miller, J, Fletcher, K., & Kabat-Zinn, J. (1995). Three-year follow-up and clinical implications of a mindfulness meditation-based stress reduction intervention in the treatment of anxiety disorders. General Hospital Psychiatry, 17, 192-200.

Miller, W. R. (1998). Researching the spiritual dimensions of alcohol and other drug problems. Addictions, 93(7), 979-990.

Molino, A. (Ed.) (1998). The couch and the tree. New York: North Point Press.

Monda, L. (2005) Bringing mindfulness to despair. Hakomi Forum, 14-15, 59-62.

Monda, L. (2000). The practice of wholeness: Spiritual transformation in everyday life. Placitas, NM: Golden Flower Publications.

Monti, D., Peterson, C., Kunkel, E., Hauck, W., Pequignot, E., Rhodes, L., et al. (2006). A randomized, controlled trial of mindfulness-based art therapy (MBAT) for women with cancer. Psycho-Oncology, 15, 363-373. Retrieved May 25, 2006, from http://www3.interscience.wiley.com/cgi bin/abstract/112137081/ABSTRACT

Morgan, S. P. (2005). Depression: Turning toward life. In C. K. Germer, R. D. Siegel, and P.R. Fulton (Eds.), Mindfulness and psychotherapy, (pp. 130-151). New York: The Guilford Press.

Morgan, W. D. & Morgan, S. T. (2005). Cultivating attention and empathy. In C. K. Germer, R. D. Siegel, & P. R. Fulton (Eds.), Mindfulness and psychotherapy, (pp. 73-90). New York: The Guilford Press.

Moustgaard, A. K. (2005). Mindfulness-based cognitive therapy (MBCT) for stroke survivors: An application of a novel intervention. (Doctoral dissertation, Lakehead University, Canada, 2005).

Moyer, L. (1986). The context for Hakomi in the treatment of eating disorders. Hakomi Forum, 4, 33-41.

Mruk, C. & Hartzell, J. (2003). Zen and psychotherapy: Integrating traditional and nontraditional approaches. New York: Springer Publishing Co.

Murphy, M., Donovan, S., & Taylor, E. (1997). The physical and psychological effects of meditation: A review of contemporary research with a comprehensive bibliography, 1931-1996. 2nd ed. Sausalito, CA: The Institute of Noetic Sciences

Myllerup, I. M. (2000). From mind body fragmentation to bodymind wholeness. (Doctoral dissertation, Institute of Psychology, University of Aarhus, Denmark, 2000).

Napoli, M. (2004). Mindfulness training for teachers: A pilot program. Complementary Health Practice Review, 9(1), 31-42.

Napoli, M., Krech, P., & Holley, L. (2005). Mindfulness training for elementary school students: The Attention Academy. Journal of Applied School Psychology, 21(1), 99-125.

Napthali, S. (2003) Buddhism for mothers: A calm approach to caring for yourself and your children. Crows Nest, Australia: Allen & Unwin Pty.

Nauriyal, D., Drummond, M., & Lai, Y. (2006). Buddhist thought and applied psychological research: Ttranscending the boundaries. New York: Routledge.

Neff, K. (2004). Self-compassion and psychological well-being. Constructivism in the Human Sciences, 9(2), 27-37.

Neff, K. (2003a). The development and validation of a scale to measure self-compassion. Self and Identity, 2, 223-250.

Neff, K. (2003b). Self-compassion: An alternative conceptualization of a healthy attitude toward oneself. Self and Identity, 2, 85-101.

Neff, K., Hsieh, Y., & Dejitterat, K. (2005). Self-compassion, achievement goals, and coping with academic failure. Self and Identity, 4, 263-287.

Neff, K. D., Kirkpatrick, K. & Rude, S. S. (2007). Self-compassion and its link to adaptive psychological functioning. Journal of Research in Personality, 41, 139-154.

Neff, K. D., Rude, S. S., & Kirkpatrick, K. (in press). An examination of self-compassion in relation to positive psychological functioning and personality traits. Journal of Research in Personality.

Newberg, A., Alavi, M., Baime, M., Pourdehnad, J., Santanna, J., & d'Aquili, E. (2001). The measurement of regional cerebral blood flow during the complex cognitive task of meditation: A preliminary SPECT study. Psychiatry Research, 106, 113-122.

Newman, J. (1994). Affective empathy training with senior citizens using Zazen (Zen) meditation. Dissertation Abstracts International, 55(5-A).

Nhat Hanh, T. (1991). Peace is every step: The path of mindfulness in everyday life. New York: Bantam Books.

Nhat Hanh, T. (1975). The miracle of mindfulness. Boston: Beacon Press.

Nhat Hanh, T. (1998). The heart of the Buddha's teaching: Transforming suffering into peace, joy, and liberation. Berkeley, CA: Parallax Press,.

Nielsen, L., & Kaszniak, A. W. (2006). Awareness of subtle emotional feelings: A comparison of long-term meditators and nonmeditators. Emotion, 6(3), 392-405.

Norcross, J. (Ed.) (2001). Empirically supported therapy relationships: Summary report of the Division 29 Task Force. Psychotherapy, 38(4), 345-356.

Norris, G. (1991). Being home: A book of meditations. New York: Bell Tower.

Norris, G. (1992). Sharing silence: Meditation practice and mindful living. New York: Bell Tower,.

Norris, G. (2004). Inviting silence: Universal principles of meditation. New York: BlueBridge.

Nyanaponika, T. (1972). The power of mindfulness. San Francisco: Unity Press.

Nyanaponika, T. (1965). The heart of Buddhist meditation. York Beach, ME: Red Wheel/Weiser.

Nyanaponika, T. (1949/1998). Abhidhamma studies. Boston: Wisdom Publications.

Odajnyk, V. W. (1993). Gathering the light: A psychology of meditation. Boston: Shambahala.

O'Donoghue, M. (2002). A Buddhist Middle Way in therapy. Australian and New Zealand Journal of Family Therapy, 23(4), 196-201.

O'Donohue, J., & Siegel, D. J. (2006). Awakening the mind. Mindsight Institute Audio Recordings, October. Los Angeles: Mindsight Institute.

Ogden, P. (1997). Hakomi integrated somatics: Hands-on psychotherapy. In C. Caldwell (Ed.), Getting in touch: The guide to new body-centered therapies, (pp. 153-178). Wheaton, IL: Quest Books.

Ogden, P. (1996). Hands-on psychotherapy. Hakomi Forum, 12, 31-44.

Ogden, P., & Minton, K. (2000). Sensorimotor psychotherapy: One method for processing trauma. Traumatology, 1(6), 149-173.

Ogden, P., Minton, K., & Pain, C. (2006). Trauma and the body: A sensorimotor approach to psychotherapy. New York: W. W. Norton.

Ogden, P., & Peters, A. (1990). Translating the body's language. Hakomi Forum, 8, 31-34.

Olendzki, A. (2005). The roots of mindfulness. In C. K. Germer, R. D. Siegel, & P. R. Fulton (Eds.), Mindfulness and psychotherapy, (pp. 241-261). New York: The Guilford Press.

Oman, D., Shapiro, S., Thoresen, C., Plante, T., & Flanders, T. (in press).

Meditation lowers stress and supports forgiveness among college students: A randomized controlled trial. Journal of American College Health.

Orsillo, S., & Roemer, L. (Eds.) (2005). Acceptance and mindfulness-based approaches to anxiety: Conceptualization and treatment. New York: Springer.

Orsillo, S., & Batten, S. (2005). Acceptance and commitment therapy in the treatment of posttraumatic stress disorder. Behavior Modification, 29(1), 95-129.

Orsillo, S. M., Roemer, L., & Barlow, D. H. (2003). Integrating acceptance and mindfulness into existing cognitive-behavioral treatment for GAD: A case study. Cognitive and Behavioral Practice, 10, 223-230.

Orsillo, S. M., Roemer, L., Lerner, J. B., & Tull, M. T. (2004). Acceptance, mindfulness, and cognitive-behavioral therapy: Comparisons, contrasts, and application to anxiety. In S. C. Hayes, V. M. Follette, & M. M. Linehan (Eds.), Mindfulness and acceptance: Expanding the cognitive-behavioral tradition, (pp. 66-95). New York: The Guilford Press.

Ostafin, B., Chawla, H., Bowen, S., Dillworth, T., Witkiewitz, K., & Marlatt, G. (2006). Intensive mindfulness training and the reduction of psychological distress: A preliminary study. Cognitive and Behavioral Practice, 13, 191-197.

Otani, A. (2000). Eastern meditative techniques and hypnosis: A new synthesis. American Journal of Clinical Hypnosis, 46(2), 97-108.

Ott, M., Norris, R., & Bauer-Wu, S. (2006). Mindfulness meditation for oncology patients: A discussion and critical review. Integrative Cancer Therapies, 52, 98-108.

Palm, K. M. (2005). An examination of mindfulness: Assessment and relationship to PTSD. (Doctoral dissertation, University of Nevada at Reno, 2005).

Parks, G. A., Anderson, B. K., & Marlatt, G. A. (2001). Relapse prevention therapy. In N. Heather, T. J. Peters, & T. Stackwell (Eds.), Interpersonal handbook of alcohol dependence and problems, (pp. 575-592). New York: John Wiley.

Pauzano-Slamm, N. M. (2005). Mindfulness meditation for chronic fatigue syndrome: A controlled trial. (Doctoral dissertation, Hofstra University, 2005).

Pearl, J., & Carlozzi, A. (1994). Effect of meditation on empathy and anxiety. Perceptual and Motor Skills, 78, 297-298.

Pelletier, K. R., & Garfield, C. (1976). Consciousness East and West. New York: Harper & Row.

Peng, C., Mietus, J., Liu, Y., Khalsa, G., Douglas, P., Benson, H., et al. (1999). Exaggerated heart rate oscillations during two meditation techniques. International Journal of Cardiology, 70, 101-107.

Pesso, A. (1973). Experience in action. New York: New York University Press.

Pesso, A. (1969). Movement in psychotherapy. New York: New York University Press.

Pope, T. (2005). Vehicle of life. Hakomi Forum, 14-15, 57-58.

Quale, K. (2007). Nourish the body, ease the mind, and brighten the spirit. Hakomi Forum, 18, 41-46.

Quartana, P., Laubmeier, K., & Zakowski, S. (2006). Psychological adjustment following diagnosis and treatment of cancer: An examination of the moderating role of positive and negative emotional expressivity. Journal of Behavioral Medicine, 29(5), 487-498.

Plews-Ogan, M., Owens, J., Goodman, M., Wolfe, P., & Schorling, J. (2005). A pilot study evaluating mindfulness-based stress reduction and massage for the management of chronic pain. Journal of General Internal Medicine, 20(12), 1136-1138.

Rabten, G., & Batchelor, S. (1983). Echoes of voidness. Somerville, MA: Wisdom Publications.

Ramel, W., Goldin, P., Carmna, P., & McQuaid. (2004). The effects of mindfulness meditation on cognitive processes and affect in patients with past depression. Cognitive Therapy and Research, 28(4), 433-455.

Randolph, P. D., Caldera, Y. M., Tacone, A. M., & Greak, M. L. (1999). The long-term combined effects of medical treatment and a mindfulness-based behavioral program for the multidisciplinary management of chronic pain in West Texas. Pain Digest, 9, 103-112.

Rapee, R. M. (1998). Overcoming shyness and social phobia. Killara, Australia: Lifestyle Press.

Records, D. (1984). The Hakomi method and couples. Hakomi Forum, 1, 29-38.

Reibel, D., Greeson, J., Brainard, G., & Rosenzweig, S. (2001). Mindfulness-based stress reduction and health-related quality of life in a heterogeneous patient population. General Hospital Psychiatry, 23(4), 183-192.

Reiman, J. (1985). The impact of meditative attentional training on measures of select attentional parameters and on measures of client perceived counselor empathy. Dissertation Abstracts International, 46(6-A), 1569.

Reynolds, D. K. (2003). Mindful parenting: A group approach to enhancing reflective capacity in parents and infants. Journal of Child Psychotherapy, 29(3), 357-374.

Reynolds, D. K. (1988). The quiet therapies: Japanese pathways to personal growth. Honolulu: University of Hawaii Press.

Riedesel, B. (1983). Meditation and empathic behavior: A study of clinically standardized meditation and affective sensitivity. Dissertation Abstracts International, 43(10-A), 3274.

Ritchart, R., & Perkins, D. (2000). Life in the mindful classroom: Nurturing the disposition of mindfulness. Journal of Social Issues, 56(1), 27-47.

Robins, C. (2002). Zen principles and mindfulness practice in dialectical behavior therapy. Cognitive & Behavioral Practice, 9(9), 50-57.

Robins, C., & Chapman, A. (2003). Dialectical behavior therapy: Current status, recent developments, and future directions. Journal of Personality Disorders, 18(1), 73-89.

Robins, C. J., Schmidt, H., & Linehan, M. M. (2004). Dialectical behavior therapy: Synthesizing radical acceptance with skillful means. In S. C. Hayes, V. M. Follette, & M. M. Linehan (Eds.), Mindfulness and acceptance: Expanding the cognitive-behavioral tradition, (pp. 30-44). New York: The Guilford Press.

Robinson, F., Mathews, H., & Witek-Janusek, L. (2003). Psycho-endocrine-immune response to mindfulness-based stress reduction in individuals infected with the human immunodeficiency virus: A quasiexperimental study. Journal of Alternative and Complementary Medicine, 9(5), 683-694.

Roemer, L., & Orsillo, S. (2007). An open trial of an acceptance-based behavior therapy for generalized anxiety disorder. Behavior Therapy, 38, 72-85.

Roemer, L., & Orsillo, S. (2003). Mindfulness: A promising intervention strategy in need of further study. Clinical Psychology: Science and Practice, 10(2), 172-178.

Roemer, L., & Orsillo, S. (2002). Expanding our conceptualization of and

treatment for Generalized Anxiety Disorder: Integrating mindfulness/
acceptance-based approaches with existing cognitive-behavioral models.
Clinical Psychology: Science and Practice, 9(1), 54-68.

Rosen, E. G. (1983). Contemporary theory and methodology in three body-
centered, experiential psychotherapies. (Masters thesis, University of West
Georgia, 1983.)

Rosenbaum, R. (2003). Reflections on mirroring. In S. R. Segall (Ed.),
Encountering Buddhism: Western psychology and Buddhist teachings, (pp.
143-163). Albany: State University of New York Press.

Rosenbaum, R. (1999). Zen and the heart of psychotherapy. New York:
Plenum Press.

Rosenberg, L. (1998). Breath by breath: The liberating practice of insight
meditation. Boston: Shambhala Publications.

Rosenzweig, S., Reibel, D., Greeson, J., Brainard, G., & Hojat, M. (2003).
Mindfulness-based stress reduction lowers psychological distress in medical
students. Teaching and Learning in Medicine, 15(2), 88-92.

Rossy, L. (2005). Mindfulness: More than just a new technique: A review
of C. K. Germer, R. D. Siegel, & P. R. Fulton (Eds.), Mindfulness and
psychotherapy. PsycCRITIQUES, 50(46).

Roth, B., & Creasor, T. (1997). Mindfulness meditation-based stress reduction:
Experience with a bilingual inner-city program. Nurse Practitioner, 22,
150-176.

Roth, B., & Robbins, D. (2004). Mindfulness-based stress reduction and
health-related quality of life: Findings from a bilingual inner-city patient
population. Psychosomatic Medicine, 66, 113-123.

Roth, B., & Stanley, T. (2002). Mindfulness-based stress reduction and
healthcare utilization in the inner city: Preliminary findings. Alternative
Therapy Health Medicine, 8(1), 60-62, 64-66.

Roy, D. M. (2003). Body-centered counseling and psychotherapy. In D.
Capuzzi & D. Gross (Eds.), Counseling and psychotherapy: Theories and
interventions, 4th edition, (pp. 387-414). Upper Saddle River, NJ: Merrill
Prentice Hall.

Rubin, J. B. (2003). A well-lived life: psychoanalytic and Buddhist contributions.
In J. D. Safran (Ed.), Psychoanalysis and Buddhism: An unfolding dialogue,
(pp. 387-409). Boston: Wisdom Publications.

Rubin, J. B. (1997). Psychoanalysis is self-centered. In C. Spezzano & G. Spessano (Eds.), Soul on the couch: Spirituality, religion, and morality in contemporary psychoanalysis. Hillsdale, NJ: Analytic Press.

Rubin, J. B. (1996). Psychotherapy and Buddhism. New York: Plenum Press.

Russell, S., & Browne, J. (2005). Staying well with bipolar disorder. Australian and New Zealand Journal of Psychiatry, 39(3), 187-193.

Ryback, D. (2006). Self-determination and the neurology of mindfulness. Journal of Humanistic Psychology,46(4), 474-493.

Sadlier, M., Stevens, S., & Kennedy, V. (2007). Tinnitus rehabilitation: A mindfulness meditation cognitive behavioural therapy approach. Journal Laryngol Otol, 116, 1-7.

Safer, D., Telch, C., & Agras, W. (2001). Dialectical behavior therapy for bulimia nervosa. American Journal of Psychiatry, 158, 632-634.

Safran, J. (Ed.) (2003a). Psychoanalysis and Buddhism. Boston: Wisdom Publications.

Safran, J. (2003b). Introduction: Psychoanalysis and Buddhism as cultural institutions. In J. D. Safran (Ed.), Psychoanalysis and Buddhism: An unfolding dialogue, (pp. 1-34). Boston: Wisdom Publications.

Sagula, D., & Rice, K. G. (2004). The effectiveness of mindfulness training on the grieving process and emotional well-being of chronic pain patients. Journal of Clinical Psychology in Medical Settings, 11(4), 333-342.

Salmon, P. G., Santorelli, S. F., & Kabat-Zinn, J. (1998). Intervention elements promoting adherence to mindfulness-based stress reduction programs in the clinical behavioral medicine setting. In S. A. Shumaker, E. B. Schron, J. K. Ockene, & W. L. Bee (Eds.), Handbook of health behavior change, 2nd ed. (pp. 239-268). New York: Springer,:

Salmon, P., Sephton, S., Weissbecker, I., Hoover, K., Ulmer, C., & Studts, J. (2004). Mindfulness meditation in clinical practice. Cognitive and Behavioral Practice, 11, 434-446.

Salomon, G., & Globerson, T. (1987). Skill may not be enough: The role of mindfulness in learning and transfer. International Journal of Education Research, 11, 623-627.

Salzberg, S. (1995). Lovingkindness: The revolutionary art of happiness. Boston: Shambhala Publications.

Santorelli, S. Heal thyself: Lessons on mindfulness in medicine. New York: Bell Tower, 1999.

Saxe, G., Hebert, J., Carmody, J., Kabat-Zinn, J., Rosenzweig, P., Jarzobski, D., et al. (2001). Can diet in conjunction with stress reduction affect the rate of increase in prostate specific antigen after biochemical recurrence of prostate cancer? Journal of Urology, 166(6), 2202-2207.

Sayadaw, M. (1971). Practical insight meditation: Basic and progressive stages. Kandy, Sri Lanka: The Forest Hermitage.

Schanzer, L. (1990). Does meditation-relaxation potentiate psychotherapy? (Doctoral dissertation, Massachusetts School of Professional Psychology, 1990.)

Schanzer, L. (1988) Non-invasive methodologies of studying neurological correlates of human mental states, in particular those during psychotherapy: A review of recent literature. Hakomi Forum, 6, 32-46.

Scheel, K. (2000). The empirical basis of dialectical behavior therapy: Summary, critique, and implications. Clinical psychology: Science and practice, 7(1), 68-86.

Schmidt, A., & Miller, J. (2004). Healing trauma with meditation. Tricycle, 14(1), 40-43.

Schraw, G. (1998). Promoting general metacognitive awareness. Instructional Science, 26, 113-125.

Schulmeister, M. (1992). Grace in therapy: What a therapist must trust in. Hakomi Forum, 9, 51-55.

Schulmeister, M. (1988). The Hakomi method in therapy groups. Hakomi Forum, 6, 47-56.

Schwartz, J. (1996). Brain lock. New York: Regan Books.

Schwartz, J., & Begley, S. (2002). The mind and the brain: Neuroplasticity and the power of mental force. New York: HarperCollins Publishers.

Schwartz, J. M., Gulliford, E. Z., Stier, J., & Thienemann, M. (2005). Mindful awareness and self-directed neuroplasticity: Integrating psychospiritual and biological approaches to mental health with a focus on obsessive-compulsive disorder. In S. G. Mijares & G. S. Khalsa (Eds.), The psychospiritual clinician's handbook: Alternative methods for understanding and treating mental disorders. New York: Haworth Press, Inc.

Schwartz, J., Stapp, H., & Beauregard, M. (2005). Quantum physics in neuroscience and psychology: A neurophysical model of mind-brain interaction. Philosophical Transactions of The Royal Society, 360(1458), 1309-1327.

Schwartz, R. (1995). Internal Family Systems therapy. New York: The Guilford Press.

Seeman, T., Dubin, L., & Seeman, M. (2003). Religiosity/spirituality and health: A critical review of the evidence for biological pathways. American Psychologist, 58(1), 53-63.

Segal, S. (2003). Encountering Buddhism: Western psychology and Buddhist teachings. Albany, NY: State University of New York Press.

Segal, W. (1995). Interviewed in T. Cochran & J. Zaleski, Transformations: Awakening to the sacred in ourselves. New York: Bell Tower.

Segal, Z. (2005). Mindfulness-based cognitive therapy for depression. In Carlson, J. (Ed.) Series VI: Spirituality. Compact disc. Washington, D.C.: American Psychological Association

Segal, Z. V., Teasdale, J. D., & Williams, J. M. G. (2004). Mindfulness-based cognitive therapy: Theoretical rationale and empirical status. In S. C. Hayes, V. M. Follette, & M. M. Linehan (Eds.), Mindfulness and acceptance: Expanding the cognitive-behavioral tradition, (pp. 45-65). New York: The Guilford Press.

Segal, Z., Williams, J., & Teasdale, J. (2002). Mindfulness-based cognitive therapy for depression: A new approach to preventing relapse. New York: The Guilford Press.

Semple, R., Reid, E., & Miller, L. (2005). Treating anxiety with mindfulness: An open trial of mindfulness training for anxious children. Journal of Cognitive Psychotherapy, 19(4), 379-392.

Semple, R. (2004). Review of Z. Segal, J. Williams, & J. Teasdale, Mindfulness-based cognitive therapy for depression: A new approach to preventing relapse. Journal of Cognitive Psychotherapy, 18(4), 370-371.

Sephton, S., Salmon, P., Weissbecker, I., Ulmer, C., Floyd, A., Hoover, K., et al. (2007). Mindfulness meditation alleviates depressive symptoms in women with fibromyalgia: results of a randomized clinical trial. Arthritis Rheumatology, 57(1), 77-85.

Shannahoff-Khalsa, D. (2005). Patient perspectives: Kundalini yoga meditation techniques for psycho-oncology and as potential therapies for cancer. Integrative Cancer Therapy, 4(1), 87-100.

Shannahoff-Khalsa, D. (2003). The complications of meditation trials and research: Issues raised by the Robinson, Mathews, and Witek-Janusek paper "Psycho-endocrine-immune response to mindfulness-based stress reduction in individuals infected with the human immunodeficiency virus: A quasiexperimental study." Journal of Alternative and Complementary Medicine, 9(5), 603-605.

Shapiro, D. H. (1982). Overview: Clinical and physiological comparisons of meditation with other self-control strategies. American Journal of Psychiatry, 139, 267-274.

Shapiro, D. H. (1992). Adverse effects of meditation: A preliminary investigation of long-term meditators. International Journal of Psychosomatics, 39, 62-66.

Shapiro, D. H., & Walsh, R.N. (1984). Meditation: Classic and contemporary perspectives. New York: Aldine.

Shapiro, S., Astin, J., Bishop, S., & Cordove, M. (2005). Mindfulness-based stress reduction for health care professionals: Results from a randomized trial. International Journal of Stress management, 12(2), 164-176.

Shapiro, S., Bootzin, R., Figueredo, A., Lopez, A., & Schwartz, G. (2003). The efficacy of mindfulness-based stress reduction in the treatment of sleep disturbance in women with breast cancer: An exploratory study. Journal of Psychosomatic Research, 54, 85-91.

Shapiro, S., Carlson, L., Astin, J., & Freedman, B. (2006). Mechanisms of mindfulness. Journal of Clinical Psychology, 62(3), 373-386.

Shapiro, S., Schwartz, G., & Bonner, G. (1998) Effects of mindfulness-based stress reduction on medical and premedical students. Journal of Behavioral Medicine, 21(6), 581-599.

Shapiro, S. L., & Walsh, R. (2003). An analysis of recent meditation research and suggestions for future directions. The Humanistic Psychologist, 31(2-3), 86-114.

Sharples, B. (2006). Meditation and relaxation in plain English. Boston: Wisdom Publications.

Siegel, D. J. (in press). Mindsight: Our seventh sense. New York: Bantam.

Siegel, D. J. (2007). The mindful brain: Reflection and attunement in the cultivation of well-being. New York: W. W. Norton.

Siegel, D. J. (2001). Toward an interpersonal neurobiology of the developing mind: Attachment, "mindsight," and neural integration. Infant Mental Health Journal, 22, 67-94.

Siegel, R. D. (2005). Psychophysiological disorders: Embracing pain. In C. K. Germer, R. D. Siegel, & P. R. Fulton (Eds.), Mindfulness and psychotherapy, (pp. 173-196). New York: The Guilford Press.

Siegel, R. D., Urdang, M., & Johnson, D. (2001). Back sense: A revolutionary approach to halting the cycle of back pain. New York: Broadway Books.

Silananda, U. (2002). The four foundations of mindfulness. Somerville, MA: Wisdom Publications.

Singh, N. N., Lancioni, G. E., Winton, A. S., Adkins, A. D., Wahler, R. G., Sabaawi, M., et al. (2007). Individuals with mental illness can control their aggressive behavior through mindfulness training. Behavior Modification, 31(3), 313-328.

Singh, N., Lancioni, G., Winton, A., Curtis, W., Wahler, R., Sabaawi, M., et al. (2006). Mindful staff increase learning and reduce aggression in adults with developmental disabilities. Research in Developmental Disabilities, 27(5), 545-548.

Singh, N. N., Wahler, R. G., Winton, A. S. W., & Adkins, A. D. (2004). A mindfulness-based treatment of obsessive-compulsive disorder. Clinical Case Studies, 3(4), 275-287.

Singh, N., Singh, S., Sabaawi, M., Myers, R., & Wahler, R. (2006). Enhancing treatment team process through mindfulness-based mentoring in an inpatient psychiatric hospital. Behavior Modification, 30(4), 423-441.

Singh, N., Wahler, R., Adkins, A., & Myers, R. (2003). Soles of the feet: A mindfulness-based self-control intervention for aggression by an individual with mild mental retardation and mental illness. Research in Developmental Disabilities, 24(3), 158-169.

Singh, N., Wahler, R., Sabaawi, M., Goza, A., Singh, S., Molina, E., et al (2002). Mentoring treatment teams to integrate behavioral and psychopharmacological treatments in developmental disabilities. Research in Developmental Disabilities, 23(6), 379-89.

Smith A. (2004). Clinical uses of mindfulness training for older people. Behavioral and Cognitive Psychotherapy, 32(4), 385-388.

Smith, J. (2005). Relaxation, meditation, and mindfulness. New York: Springer Publishing Co.

Smith, J. (Ed.) (1998). Breath sweeps mind: A first guide to meditation practice. New York: Riverhead Books.

Smith, J. C. (2004). Alterations in brain and immune function produced by mindfulness meditation: Three caveats. Psychosomatic Medicine, 66, 148-152.

Smith, J. C. (1975). Meditation as psychotherapy: A review of the literature. Psychological Bulletin, 82(4), 558-564.

Smith, J. E., Richardson, J., Hoffman, C., & Pilkington, K. (2005). Mindfulness-based stress reduction as supportive therapy in cancer care: Systematic review. Journal of Advanced Nursing, 52(3), 315-27.

Smith, W. R. (1996). The Hakomi psychotherapy system: Facilitating human change. (Thesis, University of Waterloo, Canada, 1996.)

Snyder, C. R., & Lopez, S. J. (2007). Positive psychology: The scientific and practical explorations of human strengths. Thousand Oaks, CA: Sage.

Snyder, M. (1984). When belief creates reality. Advances in Experimental Social Psychology, 18, 247-305.

Sorajjakool, S. (2001). Wu Wei, negativity, and depression: The principle of non-trying in the practice of pastoral care. New York: The Haworth Pastoral Press.

Sowattanangoon, N., Katchabhakdi, N., Chitvanish, S., Plengvidhaya, N., & Petrie, K. (2006). Buddhism values are associated with better control of diabetes in Thai patients. International Journal of Behavioral Medicine, 299.

Speca, M., Carlson, L. E., Goodey, E. (2000). A randomized, wait-list controlled clinical trial: The effect of a mindfulness meditation-based stress reduction program on mood and symptoms of stress in cancer outpatients. Psychosomatic Medicine, 62, 613-622.

Stanley, S., Reitzel, L., Wingate, L., Cukrowics, K., Lima, E., & Joiner, T. (2006). Mindfulness: A primrose path for therapists using manualized treatments? Journal of Cognitive Psychotherapy, 20(3), 327-335.

Stern, D. (2003). The present moment. Psychology Networker, 27, 52-57.

Stern, D. (2004). The present moment in psychotherapy and everyday life. New York: Norton.

Sternberg, R. (2000). Images of mindfulness. Journal of Social Issues, 56(1), 11-26.

Stewart, T. (2004). Light on body image: Acceptance through mindfulness. Behavior Modification, 28(6), 783-811.

Stile, J., Lerner, J., Plumb, L., & Orsillo, S. (2003). Mindfulness as an underlying mechanism of empathic concern. (Poster session presented at the annual meeting of the Association for Advancement of Behavior Therapy, Boston, MA.)

Stoller, R. J. (1985). Observing the erotic imagination. New Haven: Yale University Press.

Styron, C. W. (2005). Positive psychology: Awakening to the fullness of life. In C. K. Germer, R. D. Siegel, & P. R. Fulton (Eds.), Mindfulness and psychotherapy, (pp. 262-284). New York: The Guilford Press.

Suler, J. (1993). Contemporary psychoanalysis and Eastern thought. Albany, NY: State University of New York Press.

Sun, T. F., Wu, C. K., & Chiu, N. M. (2004). Mindfulness meditation training combined with eye movement desensitization and reprocessing in psychotherapy of an elderly patient. Behaviour Research & Therapy, 42(9), 1053-67.

Surrey, J. L. (2005). Relational psychotherapy, relational mindfulness. In C. K. Germer, R. D. Siegel, & P. R. Fulton (Eds.), Mindfulness and psychotherapy, (pp. 91-112). New York: The Guilford Press.

Sun, T. F., Wu, C. K., & Chiu, N. M. (2004). Mindfulness meditation training combined with eye movement desensitization and reprocessing in psychotherapy of an elderly patient. Chang Gung Medical Journal, 27(6), 464-9.

Suzuki, S. (1971). Zen Mind, Beginner's Mind. New York: Weatherhill.

Sweeney, N. M. (2005). New tool in the treatment of addictions: A review of American Psychological Association Mindfulness for Addiction Problems, APA Psychotherapy Videotape Series VI. PsycCRITIQUES, 50(28).

Sweet, M., & Johnson, C. (1990) Enhancing empathy: The interperssonal implications of a Buddhist meditation technique. Psychotherapy: Theory, Research, Practice, Training, 27(1), 19-29.

Tacon, A., McComb, J., Caldera, Y., & Randolph, P. (2003). Mindfulness meditation, anxiety reduction, and heart disease: A pilot study. Family and Community Health, 26, 25-33.

Takahashi, T., Murata, T., Hamada, T, Omori, M., Kosaka, H., Kikuchi, M., et al. (2005). Changes in EEG and autonomic nervous activity during meditation and their association with personality traits. International Journal of Psychophysiology, 55(2) 199-207.

Taylor, C. R. (1985). Use of elements of Hakomi therapy with seriously emotionally disturbed adolescents. Hakomi Forum, 2, 35-36.

Teasdale, J. D. (1999a). Metacognition, mindfulness, and the modification of mood disorders. Clinical Psychology and Psychotherapy, 6, 146-155.

Teasdale, J. D. (1999b). Emotional processing: Three modes of mind and the prevention of relapse in depression. Behaviour Research and Therapy, 37, S53-S78.

Teasdale, J. D. (1997). The relationship between cognition and emotion: The mind-in-place in mood disorders. In D. M. Clark & C. G. Fairburn (Eds.), Science and practice of cognitive behaviour therapy. (pp. 67-93). Oxford, UK: Oxford University Press.

Teasdale, J. D., Moore, R. G., Hayhurst, H., Pope, M., Williams, S., & Segal, Z. V. (2002). Metacognitive awareness and prevention of relapse in depression: Empirical evidence. Journal of Consulting and Clinical Psychology, 70, 275-287.

Teasdale, J., Segal, Z., & Williams, J. (2003). Mindfulness training and problem formulation. Clinical Psychology: Science and Practice, 10(2), 157-160.

Teasdale, J., Segal, Z., & Williams, J. (1995). How does cognitive therapy prevent depressive relapse and why should attentional control (mindfulness training) help? Behavior Research and Therapy, 33, 25-39.

Teasdale, J., Segal, Z., Williams, J., Ridgeway, V., Soulsby, J., & Lau, M.A. (2000). Prevention of relapse/recurrence in major depression by mindfulness-based cognitive therapy. Journal of Consulting and Clinical Psychology, 68(4), 615-623.

Telch, C., Agras, W., & Linehan, M. (2001). Dialectical behavior therapy for binge eating disorder. Journal of Consulting and Clinical Psychology, 69(6), 1061-1065.

Thomas, D. (2006). Domain and development of cultural intelligence: The importance of mindfulness. Group & Organization Management, 31(1), 78-99.

Thompson, E. (2001). Empathy and consciousness. In Thompson, E. (Ed.), Between ourselves: Second-person issues in the study of consciousness, (pp. 1-32). Thorverton, England: Imprint Academic.

Thomson, R. (2000). Zazen and psychotherapeutic presence. American Journal of Psychotherapy, 54(4), 531-548.

Tloczynski, J., & Tantnells, M. (1998). A comparison of the effects of Zen breath meditation or relaxation on college adjustment. Psychologia, 41, 32-43.

Toneatto, T. (1999). A metacognitive analysis of craving: Implications for treatment. Journal of Clinical Psychology, 55, 527-537.

Toneatto, T. (2002). A metacognitive therapy for anxiety disorders: Buddhist psychology applied. Cognitive & Behavioral Practice, 9(1), 72-78.

Tremlow, S. (2001). Training psychotherapists in attributes of mind from Zen and psychoanalytic perspectives, Part II: Attention, here and now, nonattachment, and compassion. American Journal of Psychotherapy, 55(1): 22-39.

Trungpa, C. (2005a). Training the mind and cultivating loving-kindness. Boston: Shambhala Publications

Trungpa, C. (2005b). The sanity we are born with: A Buddhist approach to psychology. Boston: Shambhala.

Trungpa, C. (1973). Cutting through spiritual materialism. Berkeley: Shambala.

Tulku Thondup (1996). The healing power of mind. Boston: Shambhala.

Twohig, M., Hayes, S., & Masuda, A. (2006). Increasing willingness to experience obsessions: Acceptance and commitment therapy as a treatment for obsessive-compulsive disorder. Behavior Therapy, 37(1), 3-13.

Unno, M. (Ed.) (2006). Buddhism and psychotherapy across cultures. Boston: Wisdom Publications.

Urbanowski, F., & Miller, J. (1996). Trauma, psychotherapy, and meditation. The Journal of Transpersonal Psychology, 28(1), 31-47.

Vacarr, B. (2001). Moving beyond polite correctness: practicing mindfulness in the diverse classroom. Harvard Educational Review, 71(2), 285-294.

Valentine, E., & Sweet, P. (1999). Meditation and attention: A comparison of the effects of concentrative and mindfulness meditation on sustained attention. Mental Health, Religion & Culture, 2(1), 59-70.

VanderKooi, L. (1997). Buddhist teachers' experience with extreme mental states in Western meditators. The Journal of Transpersonal Psychology, 29(1), 31-46.

Van Dusen, W. (1958). Wu Wei, no-mind, and the fertile Void in psychotherapy. Psychologia: An International Journal of Psychology in the Orient, 1, 253-256.

Van Dusen, W. (1957). Zen Buddhism and Western psychotherapy. Psychologia: An International Journal of Psychology in the Orient, 1, 229-230.

Varela, F., Thompson, E., & Rosch, E. (1991). The embodied mind: Cognitive science and human experience. Cambridge, MA: MIT Press.

Verplanken, B., Friborg, O., Wang, C., Trafimow, D., & Woolf, K. (2007). Mental habits: Metacognitive reflection on negative self-thinking. Journal of Personality and Social Psychology, 92(3), 526-541.

Walach, H., Buchheld, N., Buttenmüller, V., Kleinknecht, N., & Schmidt, S. (2006). Measuring mindfulness: The Freiburg Mindfulness Inventory (FMI). Personality and Individual Differences, 40(8), 1543-1555.

Wall, R. (2005). Tai Chi and mindfulness-based stress reduction in a Boston public middle school. Journal of Pediatric Health Care, 19(4), 230-237.

Wallace, A. (2006). The attention revolution: Unlocking the power of the focused mind. Boston: Wisdom Publications.

Wallace, B.A. (2006). Genuine happiness: Meditation as the path to fulfillment. Hoboken, NJ: John Wiley.

Wallace, B. A., & Shapiro, S. L. (2006). Mental balance and well-being: Building bridges between Buddhism and Western psychology. American Psychologist, 61(7), 690-701.

Wallace, R. K., Benson, H., & Wilson, A. F. (1984). A wakeful hypometabolic physiologic state. In D. H. Shapiro, Jr., & R. N. Walsh (Eds.), Meditation: Classic and contemporary perspectives. New York: Aldine.

Wallace, R. K., Benson, H., & Wilson, A. F. (1971). A wakeful hypometabolic physiological state. American Journal of Physiology, 221(3), 795-799.

Waller, B., Carlson, J., & Englar-Carlson, M. (2006). Treatment and relapse prevention of depression using mindfulness-based cognitive therapy and Adlerian concepts. Journal of Individual Psychology, 62(4), 443-454.

Walsh, R. N., & Vaughan, F. (Eds.) (1980). Beyond ego: Transpersonal dimensions in psychology. Los Angeles: J. P. Tarcher.

Walsh, R., & Shapiro, S. (2006a). The meeting of meditative disciplines and Western psychology: A mutually enriching dialogue. American Psychologist, 61(3), 227-239.

Walsh, R., & Shapiro, S. (2006b). Mental balance and well-being: Building bridges between Buddhism and Western psychology. American Psychologist, 61(7), 690-701.

Watts, A. (1963). Psychotherapy: East and West. New York: New American Library.

Weber, S. L. (2003). An analyst's surrender. In J. D. Safran (Ed.), Psychoanalysis and Buddhism: An unfolding dialogue, (pp. 169-188). Boston: Wisdom Publications.

Weiss, A. (2004). Beginning mindfulness: Learning the way of awareness. Novato, CA: New World Library.

Weiss, H. (in press). The use of mindfulness in psychodynamic and body oriented psychotherapy.

Weiss, M., Nordlie, J., & Siegel, E. (2005). Mindfulness-based stress reduction as an adjunct to outpatient psychotherapy. Psychotherapy & Psychosomatics, 74(2), 108-112.

Wells, A. (2005). Detached mindfulness in cognitive therapy: A metacognitive analysis and ten techniques. Journal of Rational-Emotive & Cognitive Behavior Therapy, 23(4), 337-355.

Wells, A. (2002). GAD, metacognition, and mindfulness: An information processing analysis. Clinical Psychology: Science and Practice, 9(9), 95-100.

Wells, A. (2000). Emotional disorders and metacognition: Innovative cognitive therapy. New York: John Wiley & Sons.

Wells, A., & King, P. (2006). Metacognitive therapy for generalized anxiety disorder: An open trial. Journal of Behavior Therapy and Experimental Psychiatry, 37(3), 206-212.

Welwood, J. (2000). Toward a psychology of awakening. Boston: Shambhala Publications.

Westen, D. (1999). Psychology: Mind, brain and culture, 2nd ed. New York: Wiley.

Westen, D. (2000a). Commentary: Implicit and emotional processes in cognitive-behavioral therapy. Clinical Psychology: Science and Practice, 7(4), 386-390.

Westen, D. (2000). The efficacy of dialectical behavior therapy for borderline personality disorder. Clinical Psychology: Science and Practice, 7(1), 92-94.

Whitehead, T. (1992). Hakomi in jail: A programmatic application with groups of psychotic, disruptive jail inmates. Hakomi Forum, 9, 7-14.

Wilber, K. (2004). The simple feeling of being: Embracing your true nature. Boston: Shambhala.

Wilber, K. (2000a). Integral psychology: Consciousness, spirit, psychology, therapy. Boston: Shambhala.

Wilber, K. (2000b). The eye of spirit: An integral vision for a world gone slightly mad. Vol. 7, The collected works of Ken Wilber. Boston: Shambhala.

Wilber, K. (1995). Sex, ecology and spirituality. Boston/London: Shambhala.

Wilber, K. (1979). No boundary: Eastern and Western approaches to personal growth. Los Angeles: Center Publications, Whole Mind Series.

Wilber, K., Engler, J., & Brown, D. (1986). Transformations of consciousness: Conventional and contemplative perspectives on development. Boston: Shambhala.

Williams, J., Duggan, D., Crane, C., & Fennell, M. (2006). Mindfulness-based cognitive therapy for prevention of recurrence of suicidal behavior. Journal of Clinical Psychology, 62(2), 201-210.

Williams, J. & Swales, M. (2004). The use of mindfulness-based approaches for suicidal patients. Archives of Suicide Research, 8(4), 315-329.

Williams, J., Teasdale, J., Segal, Z., & Soulsby, J. (2000). Mindfulness-based cognitive therapy reduces overgeneral autobiographical memory in formerly depressed patients. Journal of Abnormal Psychology, 109(1), 150-155.

Williams, J. M. G., Teasdale, J. D., Segal, Z. V., & Kabat-Zinn, J. (2005). Mindfulness and the transformation of emotion. New York: Guildford.

Williams, K., Kolar, M., Reger, B., & Pearson, J. (2001). Evaluation of a wellness-based mindfulness stress reduction intervention: A controlled trial. American Journal of Health Promotion, 15(6), 422-432.

Wilson, K. G., & Murrell, A. R. (2004). Values work in acceptance and commitment therapy: Setting a course for behavioral treatment. In S. C. Hayes, V. M. Follette, & M. M. Linehan (Eds.), Mindfulness and acceptance: Expanding the cognitive-behavioral tradition, (pp. 120-151). New York: The Guilford Press.

Wilson, G. T. (2004). Acceptance and change in the treatment of eating disorders: The evolution of manual-based cognitive-behavioral therapy. In S. C. Hayes, V. M. Follette, & M. M. Linehan (Eds.), Mindfulness and acceptance: Expanding the cognitive-behavioral tradition, (pp. 243-260). New York: The Guilford Press.

Wiser, S., & Telch, C. F. (1999). Dialectical behavior therapy for binge-eating disorder. Journal of Clinical Psychology, 55, 755-768.

Witkiewitz, K., & Marlatt, G.A. (2004). Relapse prevention for alcohol and drug problems: That was Zen, this is Tao. American Psychologist, 59(4), 224-235.

Witkiewitz, K., Marlatt, G., & Walker, D. (2005). Mindfulness-based relapse prevention for alcohol and substance use disorders. Journal of Cognitive Psychotherapy, 19(3), 211-228.

Witooonchart, C., & Bartlet, L. (2002). The use of a meditation programme for institutionalized juvenile delinquents. Journal of the Medical Association of Thailand, 85, 790-793.

Wolanin, A. T. (2005). Mindfulness-Acceptance-Commitment (MAC) based performance enhancement for Division I collegiate athletes: A preliminary investigation. (Doctoral dissertation, La Salle University, 2005).

Wolinsky, S. (1996). Hearts on fire: The Tao of meditation. San Diego: Blue Dove Press.

Wolinsky, S. (1994). Aspects of quantum psychology. Hakomi Forum, 10, 33-42.

Wolinsky, S. (1991). Trances people live: Healing approaches in quantum psychology. Falls Village, CT: The Bramble Company.

Yeshe, L. (1999). Becoming your own therapist. Boston: Lama Yeshe Wisdom Archive.Young-Eisendrath, P., & Muramoto, S. (2002). Awakening and insight: Zen Buddhism and psychotherapy. New York: Taylor & Francis.

Young, L., Bruce, A., Turner, L., & Linden, W. (2001). Evaluation of mindfulness-based stress reduction intervention. Canadian Nurse, 97(6), 23-26.

Young, S. (1994). Purpose and method of Vipassana meditation. The Humanistic Psychologist, 22, 53-61.

Zajonc. A. (2006). Love and knowledge: Recovering the heart through contemplation. Teachers College Record, 108(9), 1742-1759.

Zvolensky, M., Solomon, S., McLeish, A., Cassidy, D., Bernstein, A., Bowman. C., et al. (2006). Incremental validity of mindfulness-based attention in relation to the concurrent prediction of anxiety and depressive symptomatology and perceptions of health. Cognitive and Behavioral Therapy, 35(3), 148-58.

TRAINING AND EDUCATIONAL RESOURCES

Ron Kurtz Trainings

Ron teaches workshops and trainings in several formats, in both the U.S. and abroad. Introductory workshops on Loving Presence, Nonverbal Awareness, Mindfulness (called: Quieting the Mind), Emotional Nourishment, Supporting Emotional Healing and Therapy Intensives for Individuals and Couples are available.

There are also complete trainings in the Method, taught by Ron and by a number of associated Trainers. For people already acquainted with Hakomi, Ron teaches Advanced Practice groups in which demonstrations and coaching sessions are done by Ron, with participants having sessions and practitioners being coached. Ron also gives talks and does one-day introductory workshops at various conferences. Contact Ron Kurtz at rktinc@ronkurtz.com and **mention Hakomi in subject line.**

Hakomi Institite

The Hakomi Institute was founded in 1981 in Boulder, Colorado by Ron Kurtz and a core group of faculty. Since then, the Institute has developed training centers worldwide. Our Central Office in Boulder, Colorado networks these organizations and serves as a resource for people seeking information about Hakomi. Our website provides an international Directory of Practitioners, a schedule of workshops and trainings, issues of our professional journal.

Contact the Hakomi Institute at P.O. Box 1873, Boulder, CO 80306, 303-499-6699 (1-888-421-6699 toll-free in the U.S.), email HakomiHQ@aol.com, or visit our website at HakomiInstitute.com.

Seattle Hakomi Educational Network (SHEN)

The Seattle Hakomi Educational Network provides trainings and workshops for professionals and nonprofessionals by Certified Hakomi Trainers. SHEN Level I workshops are approved for CEUs for MSWs, LMHCs, MFTs, and LMPs. Referrals are also available to Certified Hakomi Therapists in the Seattle area. Contact Carol Ladas-Gaskin, Dave Cole, Lynn Morrison, Dennis Gaither at 206-533-9601, or email to hakomi@speakeasy. net, or visit our website at www.seattlehakomi.net.

The Focusing Institute

The Focusing Institute was founded in 1986 as a not-for-profit organization whose purpose is to help make focusing and the philosophy available to the public and to the international scholarly community through teaching, research and written materials. At www.focusing.org : learn the first level of Focusing on the phone; find a Workshop near you; find a Focusing teacher or therapist; find a Focusing partner (you take turns and divide the time); visit our on-line store for books, audio and video tapes; become a member to get our newsletter; browse in the Gendlin Online Library; find articles on Focusing-Oriented Psychotherapy, Focusing and medicine, Focusing and children and many other application areas.

The Focusing Institute, 34 East Lane, Spring Valley NY 10977, Tel: 845-362-5222,Fax: 845-678-2276. http://www.focusing.org. info@focusing. org.

The Center For Self-Leadershp

The Center for Self Leadership (CSL) is dedicated to the healing transformation of lives and cultures through educating therapists, health care professionals and the public in the Internal Family Systems model of therapy.

CSL supports professional development for therapists utilizing IFS by hosting trainings, workshops, seminars and retreats; arranging speaking engagements; and publishing educational materials, including books, articles, audio and video resources.

Many trainings and workshops meet national certification requirements for continuing education. Information about the Model, training schedules and speaking engagements is available at: www.selfleadership.com.

INDEX